We invite you to enjoy the many other international
best-selling books from the Ignite series

———————

Ignite Your Life for Women

Ignite Your Female Leadership

Ignite Your Parenting

Ignite Your Life for Men

Ignite Your Life for Conscious Leaders

Ignite Your Health and Wellness

Ignite Your Adventurous Spirit

Ignite Female Change Makers

Ignite the Modern Goddess

Ignite Happiness

Ignite Love

Ignite Your Inner Spirit

Ignite the Entrepreneur

Ignite Possibilities

Ignite the Hunger in You

Ignite Your Wisdom

Ignite Forgiveness

IGN TE™ Your Faith

INSPIRING STORIES THAT WILL UPLIFT
YOUR HEART AND ENRICH YOUR SOUL

INTRODUCTION BY

JB Owen
Founder and CEO of Ignite Publishing™
and JBO Global Inc.™

PROJECT MANAGER

Steph Elliott
Life Purpose Life Coach and Author.

PROJECT LEADERS

Jameece Pinckney
President & CEO of HyQuest,
Speaker, Author, and Entrepreneur.

Ash Bhadani
Certified Empowerment Life
Coachinternational and Author.

ADDITIONAL FEATURED AUTHORS

AVA V. MANUEL • BOBBIE KOWALSKI • BECCA RAE EAGLE
CANDICE CPOETICSTEW • CAROLINE OETTLIN • CHERYL VICZKO
CHRISTINE EBELTOFT-BANCALARI • DAN GILMAN • JACKI SEMERAU TAIT
JAMMIE MATHESON • JEANNE BUNDY • DR. JO DEE BAER • JOANNE LATIMER
JUDY 'J' WINSLOW • KAREN ROSSER • KAREN RUDOLF • KATHY STRAUSS
LEA BARBER • MAKENZIE ELLIOTT • MIMI SAFIYAH • NATASHA RAE
NICOLE FREEMAN • NOLAN PILLAY • BECCA RAE EAGLE
SCAN THE GODDESS • VANESSA SARACINO • XILA C. HOPE

Published by Ignite Publishing™

Dedication

This book is dedicated to all the amazing people who are here to read it and all the loving souls who are not with us but were a part of its creation in their own special way. So many have come together to make this book special and touch your heart. Numerous caring family members have watched overhead as these stories were written and shared. We dedicate this book to all of them.

DR. JO DEE BAER

Dania Zafar was uniquely gifted with soulful and intelligent insight and radiated through her ingenious design skills. nia is embodied in the famous lyrics of the song 'Candle in the Wind' by Elton John.

Dania lived her faith and shared the light of her candle throughout her life in all ways. The artistry found in her original Ignite graphic masterpieces will live on as part of her legacy.

ASH BHADANI
To my dear Dadu,

Even though you are no longer with us, your memory and legacy live on in the love and lessons you left behind. You were a shining star in my life, and your unwavering love and support inspire me daily. I will always treasure our shared memories, from listening to your life stories and experiences to savoring our delicious food. Your wisdom and guidance have shaped me into the person I am today, and I am forever grateful for everything you did for me.

I dedicate my faith chapter to you, in honor of all that you accomplished in your life and all the lives you touched with your kindness, generosity, and unfailing optimism. Your legacy lives on in the countless people who were fortunate enough to have known you, and I am blessed to have you as my grandpa. I love you more than words can express, and I am grateful every day for the blessings you brought into my life.

With love and admiration,
Ash Bhadani

Bobbie Kowalski

In memory of Dania, may this book land in the hands of those whose hearts may be in pain or whose ears need to hear the gift of Love and Faith. May your spirit sing in the peace you now have so that it may be held for those who are now needing it. You may be gone from our sight—but you will always live on in our hearts. May the energy held in this book always contain a piece of your loving heart.

With Great Love, Bobbie.

Becca Rae Eagle

I dedicate this story to the precious fathers in my life, those present among us in person (Michael, Kenneth, Russell, Scott), and those fallen, yet remaining with us in Spirit (Raymond, Reynolds, Boris, Melvin).

Caroline Oettlin

For my parents, who supported me with patience, unconditional love, and understanding while I was rewriting this challenging chapter of my life. I honor and love both of you. For my son, with whom I'm not only connected through my love but also through our blood and family lineage. You gave me the strength to ride this rollercoaster of life. I love you. For my ex-husband, who pushed me into the deepest transformation of my soul. Thank you for the good times, for the hard times, for the laughter and the tears. I'm grateful for all the experiences and the moments we shared in love and for being the father of our child. For all my friends, which boosted me, took care of me, and held me in a safe space of love and compassion during these months.

Cheryl Viczko

I wouldn't be in this space and time without the love and guidance of my family. I dedicate this story to my parents, Pauline and Tony Viczko, and my brother Jim Viczko; it is their stories that I share in mine.

CANDICE CPOETICSTEW

I would like to dedicate Ignite Faith to readers whose situation looks hopeless and who need a miracle. Keep the faith. Also, I would like to thank my mother, JoAnne Aldridge-Cathey, for the gift of life. To my sister Shante Aldridge—never stop dreaming. The Ignite Faith Staff for countless hours to make this project a success. Thank You.

CHRISTINE EBELTOFT-BANCALARI

Dedicated to my Proverbs 31 role model, Elna Kristine Grindahl: Thank you for showing me how to pray without ceasing, serve others with complete abandon, and love Jesus.

JAMEECE PINCKNEY

I would like to dedicate my story to All cancer survivors... let the joy of the Lord be your strength.

JOANNE LATIMER

I dedicate my story to Mr. Les Brown and his son John-Leslie Brown.

JUDY 'J' WINSLOW

I would like to dedicate this chapter to my parents: Anita and Manny, my fellow travelers for this story, and so many others that make up my life's journey. Although you are no longer with us on earth, I thank you both for being adventurous souls, while treating me to some of the finer things in life!

JAMMIE MATHESON

My family, I love you and thank our savior for all of you, every single day.

We so often lose people in our lives unexpectedly. The empty space this leaves us may never be filled. I would like to also dedicate my chapter, The Whisper, to Dania, from our Ignite family, and to those around her who are now suffering from an unexpected loss.

I also dedicate this chapter to young families that have a parent struggling with cancer that are not able to get the treatment they need for this terrible disease due to lack of health insurance or insurance refusing to pay, not allowing the most appropriate treatment at the most opportune time because of finances.

LEA BARBER

With heartfelt thanks for loving me, I dedicate my chapter in Ignite Your Faith to my mom and my beautiful children, who made me a mom.

JEANNE BUNDY

I am dedicating my story to my oldest granddaughter: Ellie; her strength and bravery is an inspiration to be admired!

KAREN ROSSER

I dedicate my story of Faith to my favorite girl, my forever Valentine, my first love, my mother, Mrs. Joan Gooch-White. Fond memories of you make my heart smile. I'm thankful for the fifty-six years of unconditional love you gave me. When I look in the mirror each day, the reflection I see is YOU! Forever in love with you, my dear Mother!

KATHY STRAUSS

For my dear husband, GC Schow, who, no matter what health challenges he faced, always had a joke to tell or a beautiful piece of art to create—if it wasn't for you, I would not have learned to dig deep into my creativity and faith.

RIP and create beautiful rainbows for everyone to enjoy.

MIMI SAFIYAH

I dedicate this book to those that walk in Faith, trust in God's plan, and surrender to the journey.

MAKENZIE ELLIOTT

I dedicate my story to those who search the world for fulfillment in things, and are willing to give Jesus a chance.

NICOLE FREEMAN

My warrior Princesses Alli and Ainsli, I am grateful beyond words for your understanding and support during the times when work keeps me away from you. Your infectious laughter, joyful dancing, and impressive problem-solving skills never cease to amaze me, and I am beyond blessed that God chose me as your mother. I love you both more than you will ever know.

NOLAN PILLAY

The first line of my chapter came from Khethiwe, "What if all of you cannot hear and I am the only one who can hear—who is the one with the disability?"

Heartfelt gratitude and thanks to the late Khethiwe Madi, Mrs. Deaf South Africa 2019, for inspiring me and leaving me with words that are changing lives globally.

XILA C. HOPE

The story: Bullies, Broken Wings, and a Bullhorn is dedicated to people who want to listen to what silence has to say.

VANESSA SARACINO

In honor of my late father, Rocco, who carried me when my life fell apart. Grazie mille per tutto quello che hai fatto per noi. Non possiamo ringraziarti abbastanza. Questo e per te.(Thanks a million for everything you have done for us. We can't thank you enough. This one is for you.)

TESTIMONIALS FROM AUTHORS

Writing with Ignite was a journey full of inspiration in itself! The whole team was caring, honest and took the time to listen to your message and help you enhance it! Not only did they become my publisher—they became my family!

—Bobbie Kowalski

Holding space for a writer is a gift to the soul. We each want to be held and to be heard. Ignite offers a world-class community, a high standard of care, purpose, and promise. We are treated like bestselling authors from day one, lighting the path toward success at every step, never questioning the mission accomplished come publication time.

—Becca Rae Eagle, M.S.Ed.

Working with the Ignite team is an experience that allows for growth and exploration of your inner being.

—Jeanne Bundy

Coming into this experience, I had already finished writing and publishing one book and was finishing up a second. Hands down, this editing experience blew my other one out of the water while also teaching me valuable education for editing my second book. I can say with full conviction that I have grown in previously weak areas. I am blessed and humbled by the entire process and proud to be a part of such a beautiful community of people. Thank you, Ignite, for everything.

—Natasha Rae

The actual learning made all the difference. Each stage of this process was elevated via increased knowledge. Listening to the editors and following their guidance provided the roadmap for my story.

—Joanne Latimer

The platforms we use to share our messages are just as important as the stories. The opportunity to work with a publishing company like Ignite allowed me to work with a company that has similar ideas and beliefs. This was important to me. The collaboration between authors when using Ignite is remarkable.

—Jammie Matheson

Journaling and sharing are my way of coping with the stresses of my life, and over the years, more and more people have been telling me that I need to write my story. Even though I had illustrated and written several adult coloring books, I didn't know how to start the process of writing a story of my own. I believe a series of synchronicity events took place to bring me where I am today. I had been following JB Owen for a long time via social media and was fascinated with her story and how she was igniting everything she did. One of her posts caught my attention about looking for authors who wanted to publish their stories, and I knew I had to act. Signing on with Ignite Publishing has been transformative. It helped me move past my blocks and my doubt about my writing abilities. Each of the editing sessions, pushing me to refine my story, was part of the amazing Ignite process, and the community she created through masterminds and other coaching made the "Ignite" process so valuable. I cannot express my gratitude enough to Ignite™ for showing me how to bring my story out. I look forward to seeing where my story will take me in the future.

—Kathy Strauss, CCFC

I was introduced to Ignite Publishing after reading an anthology from its collection. Soon thereafter, I was asked to become an author. Although writing a book was one of my goals, I didn't think I would accomplish it at this point in my life. This has been an invaluable experience for me and my brand. In a nutshell, it helped me create future goals and allowed me to put words to paper in order to bring light to a subject that is dear to my heart. This subject centers around children, especially those with cognitive deficits, who must navigate through opposition. My story was not an easy one to share, but because of the streamlined process with Ignite, it reduced some of the unease I felt with reliving experiences (that you can read from my lens, as an advocate, in the story: *Bullies, Broken Wings, and a Bullhorn)*. Additionally, a strong community of authors supports you every step of the way. Everyone was pleasant to work with, and they were willing to provide whatever you may need as your story was being developed. My favorite activity was when we had the opportunity to share our stories with a partner—this was a rewarding experience as it allowed me to connect personally with other authors. Overall, I am pleased that I decided to go on this journey with this publishing company.

—Xila C. Hope, MS, MBATM, DCPM

The writing experience has always been cathartic. With a great team behind the scenes tightening up my story and the exceptional changes made that made me think outside of my then-narrow thoughts to create clarity of flow—I am so grateful to the entire Ignite team for their support, patience, and understanding. Thank you, JB and everyone involved. It truly takes a village, and the proof is in each of the Ignite books. What an honor and privilege. Write! Get it out of you; the world is waiting to hear your story!

—Karen L. Rudolf

I'm so thankful I had the opportunity to share what means the most to me in my life. Writing with Ignite helped give me confidence in my abilities and share something with the world that holds a special place in my heart.

—Makenzie Elliott

My writing journey with Ignite has been inspiring, rewarding, and impactful. The process has been seamless because of the heartfelt, loving, generous staff. All of the editors are knowledgeable, professional, and absolutely amazing at their craft. The Ignite family is warm, inviting, patient, and, most of all, made me feel like I matter and what I have to say matters. Lady JB is the most generous person I know. This opportunity is truly incredible.

—Nicole Shantel Freeman

Writing with Ignite was an amazing experience. I enjoyed and learned a lot from the editors. Like how to overcome writer's block and breaking down a story without losing the story and its flow. I now have some new skills under my belt.

—SCAN The Goddess

As a three-time collaborative Ignite Author who has been elevated in these amazing experiences to create my own Solo Book through Ignite. This Company always lives up to its name: IGNITE!

—Dr. Jo Dee Baer

When I was presented with the opportunity to write my story about Faith, I was intimidated by the thought of opening myself up to the world. I thought, *I'm not a writer,* but I knew I had a story to tell. I took a leap of Faith and never looked back. Writing in the *Ignite* Your *Faith* book was the perfect platform for me to be vulnerable without judgment and share my story with the world. The Ignite team is with you every step of the way and provides the tools for success when writing your story. I encourage everyone to take that leap of faith and tell your story. You will be happy that you did!

—K.R. Rosser

I hadn't considered my story important enough to share with others. During the process of writing, I realized the healing that transpired in me. Working with the team at Ignite created a safe space to dive into the details and my creative side. Their joint effort made the process easy, fun, and enlightening. If you are questioning your writing abilities, let that go and jump in with the confidence this team has in you to craft a brilliant story.

—Cheryl Viczko

Being a first-time Author and writing my solo book did not afford me the expertise and guidance I received with the Ignite Team when writing my chapter. The entire team played a major role in bringing the chapter to life, and this will always be appreciated. A special shoutout and thanks to Lady JB Owen, Steph Elliott, Sarah Cross, Alex Blake, Michiko Couchman, Mimi Safiyah, AnaMaria R. Navarrete, and the entire Author community for holding my hands on this journey. I have written previous chapters but never got special attention compared to what I have received from the Ignite Team. When one experiences a sense of belonging in a community like this, one becomes part of the family and never wants to leave. I would highly recommend any Author to become part of the Ignite Team. Thank You. Much Love and Light.

—Nolan Pillay

I am astounded to personally experience how much love and care is put into every Ignite Moment story. The dedication and commitment to excellence each Ignite team member brings to every process, from the story discovery to the book launch, makes every chapter of an Ignite book an absolute masterpiece.

—Ava V. Manuel

It has been an amazing experience writing with Ignite. I am so happy that I shared my story with the world, and I know that through Ignite, the impact will leave a footprint in the world.

—Mimi Safiyah

The journey with Ignite is inspiring and motivating toward a better world.

—Ash Bhadani

This has been a fantastic experience! Working with the team of editors and the community generated by JB feels like a warm hug, making it easy, joyful, and professional. If you get the chance, do it!

—Judy 'J' Winslow

The process and support from the Ignite team was amazing. I felt fully capable, excited, and championed by all. Thank you for igniting my faith.

—Lea Barber

Writing with Ignite is such a healing journey. Great teamwork, amazing community, and JB queen rules always.

—Caroline Oettlin

As a Project Leader, I had a firsthand view of what makes each story so great. It is the intentional way Ignite designs and directs every aspect of the writing process. In *Ignite Your Faith*, I'm elated to have this Ignite experience as a Project Leader but also as an author.

—Jameece D. Pinckney, JD, M.Ed.

It's amazing to work with the entire Ignite team. They were masterful at helping me edit my story, which in turn extracted my story better than I thought possible.

—Jacki Semerau Tait

My experience writing *Ignite Your Faith* with Ignite Publishing has been transformative, thanks in large to the inclusion of a chapter about my mother, Cindy Gilman. Her story added depth and emotion to my writing, and working with Ignite Publishing and JB Owen has been nothing short of exceptional. The Ignite Publishing team, led by the inspirational JB Owen, provided invaluable support, guidance, and encouragement throughout the process. Their expertise helped me craft a compelling, authentic narrative resonating deeply with my readers. Writing about my mother's impact on my faith journey allowed me to connect with her more profoundly. This introspection fostered personal growth and strengthened my spiritual connection. Ignite Publishing maintained a collaborative approach and commitment to preserving my unique voice making this transformative experience possible. In summary, my journey with Ignite Publishing has been life-changing, and I am eternally grateful for the opportunity to share my story with the world.

—Dan Gilman

My dreams came true to Ignite Faith to the nation. The Ignite team and Visionary JB Owen operated in excellence. I received a community of faith igniters and mentors whose impact will stay with me for a lifetime. Thank you, Ignite team, you are AMAZING. If you are considering writing a book but are uncertain of which publisher to choose to assist with your story—I highly recommend Ignite Publishing for its world-class experience with excellence.

—Candice CpoeticStew

Writing with the Ignite team has been a wonderful experience. They are professionals and know how to keep you moving forward, motivated, and on track regardless of what may be standing in your way. The team is encouraging and skilled at ensuring your voice comes out as they suggest ways to engage your audience. I highly recommend working with this team if you have a story in your heart that you'd like the world to hear.

—Christine Ebeltoft-Bancalari

Contents

WHAT IS AN IGNITE BOOK? – by Lady JB Owen   18

IGNITE YOUR FAITH – by Lady JB Owen   22

THE STORY WITHIN THE STORY – by Lady JB Owen   30

WHAT'S FAITH GOT TO DO WITH IT?
– by Jameece D. Pinckney JD, M.Ed.   40

FAITHING THE WAY THROUGH – by Ash Bhadani   48

FINDING FAITH-FILLED TREASURES IN EARTHEN VESSELS
– by Joanne Latimer   56

WHY ME? – by Jacki Semerau Tait   64

ON THE OTHER SIDE OF F.E.A.R. – by Judy 'J' Winslow   72

CLIMBING TOWARD MY PURPOSE – by Nolan Pillay   80

OWNING MY PART – by Nicole Shantel Freeman   88

FEATHERS OF FAITH – by Lea Barber   96

WHERE I BELONG – by Makenzie Elliott   104

HOW DID I GET HERE? – by Ava V. Manuel   112

WHAT'S A DREAM WITHOUT FAITH? – by SCAN The Goddess   120

FAITH WITH NO BORDERS – by Natasha Rae   128

MY FOREVER VALENTINE – by K. R. Rosser   136

SURRENDER TO YOUR JOURNEY – by Mimi Safiyah   144

THE POWER OF FAITH AND HEALING:
THE LEGACY OF CINDY GILMAN – by Dan Gilman   152

ANCHORED BY A STAR – by Becca Rae Eagle M.S.Ed.   160

MOVING A MOUNTAIN THROUGH PAIN AND TEARS – by Karen Rudolf   168

ONE RED CARNATION – by Cheryl Viczko   176

GOD IS BIG – by Vanessa Ciano Saracino   184

TRUSTING MY FAITH – by Jeanne Bundy   192

THIS LITTLE LIGHT OF MINE – by Bobbie Kowalski   200

MAKING AN IMPRESSION – by Kathy Strauss   208

RISING FROM THE ASHES – by Caroline Oettlin   216

BULLIES, BROKEN WINGS, AND A BULLHORN
– by Xila C. Hope, MS, MBATM, DCPM   224

MESSENGERS ON THE SHOULDER – by Dr. Jo Dee Baer   232

NO PASSPORT REQUIRED – by Christine Ebeltoft-Bancalari   240

STAGES OF GREAT FAITH – by Candice CpoeticStew   248

THE WHISPER – by Jammie M. Matheson   256

RESOURCES   266
PHOTO CREDITS   272
AUTHOR CREDENTIALS   274
THANK YOU   275
WRITE WITH IGNITE   277

WHAT IS AN IGNITE BOOK?

BY LADY JB OWEN

Ignite Publishing has been the leader of Empowerment publishing for the past half decade. We sprung onto the scene with a desire to disrupt the publishing industry with books that only tell powerful, authentic, heartfelt stories designed to change lives. As we hit our twentieth compilation book, with over seven hundred authors published, we feel we are doing just that: empowering others, igniting lives, and making a massive difference on the planet that will inspire generations for centuries to come.

The very word *Ignite* signifies the intention of our books and describes the goal behind every story we share. We see our books as gifts to the world, igniting ideas, thoughts, feelings, and desires. Every book we publish is created with the intention to inspire, uplift, and *Ignite* the reader toward something greater within themselves. We believe that our books, and the stories inside them, connect hearts, foster love, bridge gaps, and form a deeper understanding within us. Each story inside our books that is divinely shared becomes a beacon of empowerment for every person on the planet.

Ignite believes that stories, and the genuine sharing of them, is the key not only to bringing people together but to healing humanity on a global scale. Stories speak directly to the heart of the reader and touch them in a profound way. Honest and authentic stories open the mind and expand compassion, connection, and joy for the life that we all desire. Stories showcase our commonalities and show how we are more alike than different. They speak of the common denominator we all know, the beautiful human experience.

Each story in this book has been created to inspire you on a deeper level. They are designed to awaken your mind while speaking directly to your heart and instilling a new sense of opportunity and possibilities in you. As you begin reading an Ignite story, you will find that each one begins with an inspiring *Power Quote*. It is an empowering statement designed to push you forward and encourage you to break outside your comfort zone. Power quotes are phrases that offer insight and hope. They are meaningful statements intended to Ignite ideas, spark actions, and evoke change. Every power quote is written to activate something in you, so you can be all that you desire to become and ideally ignite another life.

Since this book is all about faith, each power quote is designed to inspire a deeper faith inside of you. They are written with the intention that whatever you have gone through, or are going through, you can use your faith, lean into your beliefs, and move forward to overcome what might be in your way. The wonderful thing about faith is that it is individual, personal, and intimate. A person's faith is unique to them, but the power behind their faith is universal amongst us all. Regardless of religion or doctrine, these stories show a connection to something greater. They shine a light on the divine connection with the hope it will inspire you.

After the power quote, you will find the author's personal *Intention*. These are the individual insights and genuine wishes the author wants to share with you, as well as their intention for what you will gain from reading their caring story. Each author came into this book with a desire to IGNITE something in you, and they share that lovingly in their opening intention. From the very beginning, they want you to know they hope their story will indeed Ignite Faith in you.

After the intention, you will read the author's transformational *Ignite Moment*. It is a genuine sharing of the author's journey and how they emerge through it with a greater understanding of themselves. Through their unique experiences and circumstances, the authors explain how their Ignite Moment transformed them, awakened them, and set them on a new trajectory in life. They reveal their honest feelings and share their personal discoveries. They give an insightful account of an exact moment when a deep internal faith created a valuable connection to something greater than themselves.

We all have Ignite Moments that change us, define us, and set us forth on a wonderful new journey of inner exploration. The stories in this book are derived from those moments and are told in the most endearing and empowering way. They show us that *life-altering* situations are designed to impact us in a way that inspires us to step into the person we were born to become. Ignite Moments are universal and transcend all barriers. They allow us to be more connected on a deeper level, showing how we are all One in many ways.

To be more than just a story, you will discover the author's share exciting *Ignite Action Steps* at the end of every chapter. They want to provide doable actions that you can use to benefit yourself. Each action step is an idea, process, or practice they have used to succeed in their own life. The goal is for you to implement an action step into your life and provoke positive change. Each Ignite Action Step is different and unique, *just like you*, and each has proven to have amazing results when done diligently and consistently.

As you sit down to read this book, know that it is not required that you read it in the traditional way; by starting at the beginning and reading through to the end. Many readers flip to a page at random and read from there, trusting that the page they landed on holds the exact story they need to read. Others glance over the table of contents, searching for the title that resonates with them. Some readers will go directly to a story recommended by a friend. However you decide to read this book, we trust it will be right for you. We know that you may read it from cover to cover in one single sitting or pick it up and put it down a dozen times. The way you read an Ignite book is as personal as every story in it, so we give you complete permission to enjoy it in whatever way fits you.

We ask that if a story touches you in some way or inspires your heart, you reach out and tell the author. Your words will mean the world to them. Since our book is all about igniting humanity, we want to foster more of that among all of us. Feel free to share your sentiments with the authors by using their contact information at the end of the book. There isn't an Ignite author who wouldn't love to hear from you and know that somehow their story positively impacted your life. And, if a story speaks to you profoundly, we encourage you to share it with someone special who may need to read it, as that story may just be the exact thing they need to help Ignite their life.

Inside the pages of this book, we know you will find a part of your story reflected in the thoughts, worries, wishes, and dreams of the many authors here. Somewhere within these pages will be a reflection of *your* journey and the Ignite Moments you have felt. We know this because Ignite stories represent the stories in all of us. It doesn't matter where you live, your skin color, your gender, or how much money you have in your pocket, Ignite stories reflect everyone. They are stories of the human condition; they touch the very essence of what makes us human and our powerful human experience. They bring us together, showing us that our stories do not define us but, instead, refine who we can become.

As you turn the page, we want to welcome you to the Ignite family. We are excited for what is about to happen because we know the stories in this book will inspire faith in yourself and others. As you dive into the upcoming pages a million different emotions will fill your heart and a kindred spirit with our authors will be established. We know that this will be a book that both awakens and inspires, transforms, and motivates.

May you be loved and supported from this page forward, and may all your Ignite Moments be filled with both joyful lessons and heart-filled blessings.

Introduction

INTRODUCTION

BY JB OWEN

It is always wonderful to dive into a book topic that has so much substance and evokes so many feelings of interest and a deeper desire for understanding. Faith is one of the oldest topics in existence. Since the beginning of time, faith has been present in all races and has served as a major cornerstone in the progress and evolution of the world and its inhabitants. Faith goes so deep that one would be hard-pressed to find a culture, civilization, or time in history when faith was not contributing to the very fabric of life itself. Faith has no boundaries, no limitations, and no end to its vast expansiveness. And yet, faith itself is the most intimate, personal, and divine notion of knowing possible in the human experience. The power of faith is so vast and never-ending, and at the same time, it is so internal and uniquely personal. Its many complex facets and regard have promoted hundreds of books over the ages, all searching for a better understanding and a clearer picture of what faith truly is in the heart of everyone.

"Sometimes beautiful things come into our lives out of nowhere. We can't always understand them, but we have to trust in them. I know you want to question everything, but sometimes it pays to just have a little faith."

— LAUREN KATE, TORMENT

What is Faith?

It has been an exciting endeavor to try to encapsulate the very essence of faith and try to unravel the precious 'silver' thread that surrounds the very meaning, impact, and interest faith creates. It seems that faith is not one thing but many things, and looking at it one way requires you to look at it in a multitude of ways. Faith can not be truly defined with one definition because it means so many things in various ways to so many diverse people. Christians believe that faith is the means by which believers come to God and put their trust in Him for salvation. Jehovah's Witnesses believe Faith is a powerful force for good—it can give stability and a reliable hope for the future. In Islam, faith is to believe in Allah, His angels, His books, His messengers, and the Last Day, and to believe in providence, both good and bad. According to Judaism, faith is about allowing our soul to experience what it remembers and what it essentially is. Faith is that dimension of ourselves that helps us connect with our true reality.

It has been said that there are nearly forty-two hundred different religions in the world, which can only mean that each is likely to have its own definition, interpretation, and understanding of what faith is. Yet, if we were to put them side-by-side and look at each idea of faith, the one common denominator would be they all include a strong personal conviction from the person who is practicing it. Faith is as individual as eye color and fingerprint. It comes, grows, and activates on its own path and in its own time. Faith rides the waves of life and is influenced by changing circumstances and the unfolding of one's fate. As much as we try to define it, its indefinability is what makes it all a part of every one of us.

In search of knowing faith, each story in this book shines a light on how faith showed up, appeared, transpired, and became the most important thing in that person's life. Faith was like a charging inferno as much as it was a fine, gossamer thread of knowing. It came in surges, whispers, trembles, and visions. It was spoken, shown, felt, and heard. Each person experienced their faith differently, yet they felt it all the same; life-changing and profound. It seems that is where faith is consistent, it touches our very soul and encompasses every part of our total beingness.

To one who has faith, no explanation is necessary. To one without faith, no explanation is possible.

— Thomas Aquinas

Why is Faith Important?

Faith has been defined as *belief with strong conviction; firm belief in something for which there may be no tangible proof; complete trust, confidence, reliance, or devotion.* That means faith is the opposite of doubt. It is the antithesis of worry, and those with faith will happily say, "I had the faith all along; I knew it would be okay."

To have such knowledge and such conviction has created miracles, changed trajectories, saved lives, ended wars, solved issues, and moved people in such a way that mass results were made. Faith has been a driving force for centuries, and millions of actions have been taken on faith alone. Therefore we *must* acknowledge its importance. We must see how vital it is in what we do and how we act; few other things can compare. Nothing but faith runs this deep and reaches this wide, touching so many while inspiring this much effort in the lives of everyone. That reality is, in times of need, sorrow, worry, and fear—faith overcomes them all and shifts everything. In the darkest moments, faith shines its light. In the toughest challenges, faith offers its hand. During the worst of the worst, faith gets a person through. And not just one person, but many. In fact, faith is present throughout all of humanity.

Since faith has all these attributes, it is not just important, it is vital. It is the life force of the very existence in all of us. Now that may seem extreme, but since faith reaches every corner of the globe and is infused in every cell of the human body, it is not just important... but fundamental.

As we face the future and the many changes unfolding in the world, we all need to have our faith, for that will bring us closer. We need not abide by someone else's faith but lean into our own. Faith does not require that we follow a certain doctrine; it simply asks that, without evidence, we believe with utter confidence. It never forces or demands; faith trusts us. When everything feels as if it is crumbling, faith is the one thing that will stand strong.

> *"None of us knows what might happen even the next minute, yet still we go forward. Because we trust. Because we have faith."*

> — Paulo Coelho

WHERE DOES FAITH RESIDE?

For many, faith has been thought to be found within the scriptures of an old text or amidst the halls of a shrine-like place. Some have been *told* to have faith and pressured to believe the ways others do. Many have been taught that faith only appears in the realms of religion and one must follow a doctrine to access faith. What is true is that faith resides in each of us in its own way. It's not transposed through an object, forced upon us by a sermon, or injected via a building filled with gold. Faith resides in the heart, the mind, the soul, the spirit, the body, the cells, and in the very air we breathe. It is inside us, not around us. It is a part of us, not something we must pledge toward. Unlike many other things in the world, faith is not an intellectual process or a concept we *simply* agree to adhere to. Faith is something that lives as we do.

If you are looking for your faith, you only have to look within yourself. Then, recognize your past, your skills, talents, and experiences to know that all of that has been gifted to you to form your faith. Everything in your life is laden with your faith. Faith in your abilities. Faith in your love. Faith in your dreams. Faith in the knowledge that you are unlike any other and that your presence on this earth is magical and Divine. To have faith is to simply look in the mirror and see how precious and spectacular you are; that despite all the odds or the possible complications, here you are, ready to show the world exactly what you are made of. You have the ability to foster and nurture your faith how you see fit, in your own way. Faith resides in you, in your unique attributes. That absolute knowing inside of you is the generator of your faith.

In this book, you will find twenty-nine stories of faith from various authors, deep in their convictions, permeating through their lives, yet each one different, unique, and personal. None of these authors shared that they found their faith anywhere else but within themselves. Look no further; your faith resides in you.

Faith is not something to grasp, it is a state to grow into.

— MAHATMA GANDHI

How to Ignite Faith

Since faith is so important, in all of us and for us to access it anytime, we each have the ability to Ignite it even more inside ourselves. There are several different ways we can grow in faith.

1. **Connect with Self.** Know that you are the ultimate manifestor of your faith. You turn up the dial and open the floodgates; you accept, increase, and allow more faith in. Just as you reject, doubt, or negate, you can also trust, believe, and increase. You hold the control. You determine the output and the outcomes. Get connected to your faith. Immerse yourself in it, and ask yourself how you can increase to feel it more.

2. **Focus on being your word.** No one is perfect, and we all make mistakes, but if you focus on following your word and living according to your values, your faith will grow naturally. You must do what you say and follow through. You have to honor your promises and live by a noble code. You need to find value in being honest, kind, and giving. When you be your word to yourself and others, your faith in who you are builds more faith within you.

3. **Notice faith in others**. Like attracts like, and when you surround yourself with others who have faith, you increase your own. Witness others in their conviction, living by their own code, believing that through their understanding, good things will unfold, they will be heard, and what they aspire to do will be given to them. Surround yourself with faithful people, and your faith will richly unfold.

4. **Take stock and recollect all the times faith got you through.** Look back to the many situations in your life when something bigger and greater was at your side. Search your memory bank of the many times you used your faith to guide your life. Notice how you acted, what you said, what your behaviors were, and how faith showed up in the way you asked it to and were open to receiving. Many times we ask and receive differently. Recall all the times you wanted it one way, yet through your faith, it turned out better than you ever imagined. Taking the time to see where and when faith has already shown up in your life will bring more faith into existence for you.

5. **Show gratitude for what your faith has done for you.** One of the greatest ways to create more faith is to thank faith for when it showed up in your life. Create a strong connection between you and your faith by recognizing all the times faith supported you. Thank your faith,

appreciate your devotion, acknowledge your convictions, and hold thanks for the work faith has performed in your life. When you give more life to your faith through gratitude, more faith will show up and shine its blessings on you.

It takes vision and courage to create - it
takes faith and courage to prove.

— OWEN D. YOUNG

HOW TO CALL FORTH FAITH IN TIMES OF NEED

As you read through this book, you will find many stories reflecting the power of faith in times of need and trouble. Each author vulnerably shares those moments when they needed their faith to deliver them from something difficult. They tell how they found their faith when they felt lost and how faith showed up in the darkest, most painful moment. Often faith is the light that cuts through the darkness and shines a beacon to a greater place. Many of us cling to our faith when we need it and lean into its comfort in times of desperation.

Faith is not a switch to be turned on and off. It is not here for now and parked for later, when needed, like it has hidden access. Faith is something we carry with us daily, work on, and curate in our hearts endlessly. In those times when our faith is challenged, stretched, and put to the test, we are asked to use our faith and hold tight to our beliefs.

If you are needing more faith in your life right now due to troubling times, here are a few ways to Ignite the faith in your life and increase its flame.

1. **Know that you are being heard, cared for, and supported.** With deep conviction, know that you are loved and supported and that what you desire is being given to you… just maybe not on your timeline. Keep the faith.

2. **Trust that you deserve only good and blessings**. Every great entity in the world wants to take care of and support you. You are designed to receive, and your Maker wants to give. If the smallest creatures are taken care of, you will be too.

3. **Give more.** You must give to get. Even in times of trouble, we all must give. It seems counterintuitive when you are struggling to give and not receive. However, when you give to someone else, you are also blessing yourself. You are creating the frequency of giving as you want to be given to.

4. **Choose a positive outlook.** Sink into what you believe and hold tight to what you know. Then take every negative thought and turn it into a positive one. Flip the thought from what isn't working to what *is* working, and know that faith is on your side.

5. **Put your hand up.** When we are hurting, we need help; we need to lean on those who care about us the most. Coming together with others increases our faith, making it stronger and more formidable. One of the most important things you can do in difficult times is to rely on those who love you. Share about your situation and allow those who care to support you in the ways they do best.

6. **Get connected.** Being connected to others who are strong in their faith is essential. Expressing your faith, and listening to others express theirs, builds a stronger faith in everyone. We are all part of the collective, and when we come together, we forge a more powerful connection of faith and miracles.

7. **Help others.** So many people are hurting, maybe some more than you. Doing service work and helping those in dire need will help you see the solutions to some of your own problems. Giving a part of yourself to someone who desperately needs it will help you stay connected to your faith and devotion.

8. **Seek peace.** If you truly want to feel your faith, you must be peaceful enough to allow it to appear. Find solace, silence, and moments void of all distractions to connect within yourself and the epicenter of your faith. When you are willing to be still, your faith will show itself to you in grand and wonderful ways.

9. **Avoid begging.** We don't beg for something we already have. Don't ask or command your faith to show up, be with it and immerse yourself in it. Your faith is with you at all times, and you simply need to connect with it and begin to use it. Faith wants to be of service to you, so it is available at a moment's notice.

10. **Be intimate with your faith.** Share your deepest secrets, wildest dreams, true desires, playful muses, and moments of great despair and challenge. Faith wants to be your closest ally, so it knows how to serve you best. Share openly and intimately with your faith, for then it will be your greatest supporter.

One of the things I learned the hard way was that it doesn't
pay to get discouraged. Keeping busy and making optimism
a way of life can restore your faith in yourself.

— LUCILLE BALL

EMBRACING FAITH

As you dive into this book, know that one or more stories will specifically speak to your heart. Something in that story will spark more faith in you. You will feel lighter, stronger, more connected, and affirmed in your choices and behaviors. Your faith will be invigorated and inspired, and a feeling of contentment will wash over you. These stories will be the catalyst for awakening more faith in you.

Living in faith means that you are willing to go into the unknown. It's trusting even though you don't know where you're headed or the results—you will carry onward. You will preserve. You will continue despite the path not being clear. The Bible gives a short definition of faith in Hebrews 11:1: Now faith is being sure of what we hope for and certain of what we do not see.

You may not see your faith rising like a thermometer or increasing like a container filling to the brim, but you will feel your faith more inside of you, more solidified in your thinking, more entrenched in your heart. Faith is a beautiful feeling that will grow expediently as you read this book.

You can accomplish anything that you dedicate yourself to. Think how
many people struggle across the world, across the country. Anything is
possible if you set your mind, your body, your soul, and your faith to it.

— HENRY CEJUDO

Lady JB Owen

LADY JB OWEN

"In faith, we find ourselves."

It is my intention to share a story of faith embellished with qualities of friendship, love, laughter, and fun, yet, laced with sadness, sorrow, and hurt. I want to share how faith is one thing, but at the same time, so much more. Faith resides so high and yet also can be found so low. Through my journey and the events that unfolded, I was tested and shown that faith is in everything. Faith is the moments that take your breath away and the moments that breathe life back into your spirit. Faith is like a trusted guide, a loving support, a comforting hand. In my story, faith stands as a marker and becomes the beacon that leads the way. Faith is constant. Faith is assuring. Faith brought me closer to myself and allowed me to finally be free.

THE STORY WITHIN THE STORY

Few people realize there are many stories within one story. There is the pre-story, back-story, sub-story, post-story, story markers, story points, and the rise and fall of the story. What one story tells, another story withholds. What is important in one story seems lost in another, and if you knew the *full* story, it would be a different story completely. A story is one point of view, a single look through the viewfinder of the author deciding what to reveal and what to relinquish, and what to expose. Many see the story that they *want* to see or *miss* seeing the story that was unfolding all along. The many layers of a story are seldom fully known, and most stories have much more to be revealed.

In your hand, you hold the book that holds the story that reflects another story only a few people know. It is the story that was unfolding in the background, the story that shaped the future and impacted many. It is a story that now wishes to be told.

I looked over to see the clock showing 4:03 AM. I had to get up. The excitement was simply too much. I had been sitting on an idea for a few days, and every part of my body was electrified with anticipation of what it might become. I had attended an event a few days prior that sparked an idea that had grown into a flame and bubbled to the surface, ready to Ignite. I slipped quietly out of bed so as not to wake my husband and ambled off to my office to formulate a plan. With inspiration on my side and aspirations swirling in my head, I mapped out, graphed out, drew columns, made lists, and formed ideas of exactly what I *knew* my business would be. I was on the verge of something amazing and felt a flame surge from within. It wasn't going to be easy, but I wasn't worried; I had all the faith I needed, and I knew it was going to be exceptional.

With so much ignited energy, from an ignited Source, via an ignited situation, the listening yet responded unphased and unmoved, proving to me they weren't. This particular designer seemed interested, intrigued, and excited. She had been listening intently to my ambitious projection to set a record and publish over four hundred people in a single year.

I can't say for certain what Dania Zafar, born in Pakistan, living in Toronto, passionate about book design, and a wiz at production, thought of my idea at the get-go. But I can say how she made *me* feel. The questions she asked and the interest she showed kept the conversation going and the ideas flowing, and before I knew it, I felt she was the one. I got off the phone, eager to start working with her, and told my husband we may just have found our magic jewel, our secret weapon. Any publishing house knows that your books are your *everything*. The way they look, the colors, and the feelings they create—the company just had to be called Ignite™. And the idea was galactic, to *Ignite lives, enliven hearts, and impact humanity.* With the fury of a dozen rocket engines, I took on the task of making sure I was indeed going to Ignite others. I started with stories: personal, heartfelt stories of perseverance, dedication, and accomplishment. Stories that would heal, inspire, and transform. Stories that needed to be told and stories that would change people's lives simply by reading them. Such stories, that right out of the gate, hit international best-selling status, in multiple countries, with authors from around the world. I had taken my idea out of my head and proved it was possible; it was time to do even more!

"I want to do twelve best sellers in twelve months. Do you think you can handle that?" I blurted out, half asking, half telling the young, up-and-coming talented book designer I was speaking to on the phone. She was a potential new hire and about to become an integral part of my vision, and I wanted to see if she was shocked by my claim. I had scared off a few potentials before her. It seemed my big ideas and broad vision were a deterrent to the many millennials working in the graphic-design field. Most had scoffed at my plan, a few said it wasn't possible, and some acted as if they were provoked. The uniqueness of the pages, the words, and the letters all speak to who you are as a brand. It was time for Ignite to show up in the literary circles, and I felt Dania would help me get there. I had all the faith in the world in her despite her young twenty-seven years. I believed that we had been brought together divinely and that with her help, I indeed would accomplish what I had set out to achieve.

For the next year, Dania dazzled me with her designs, concepts, and creations. We'd collaborate on everything, and there was a systematized flow and ease. She was calm in her disposition, grounded in her ideas, and welcoming of modifications, enhancements, and my forever "tweaking" of ideas. I seldom had reason to criticize her work. She took to my style quickly and seemed to be able to see what I could see. A small doodle on the back of an envelope was enough to get her started. A picture I'd gathered for reference or something I penned out in my journal was always just what she needed. She was open, creative, and eager to try new design concepts, innovations that pushed convention, and anything that screamed JB. There was also a comforting assuredness about her. She never panicked, stressed, or blamed anyone for her workload, backlog, or list of changes. She did her work perfectly and with ease, implementing my requests often better than I ever thought they could be.

In that first year, Dania was the one who made sure I reached my goal. Despite a million circumstances against us, we hit the target and launched twelve books in just over twelve months, publishing four hundred and thirty-four authors. Dania had the same faith that I did. We rallied and pushed and got there, patting each other on the back with deep respect and appreciation when we reached the finish line.

As we plowed into year two, I came up with a new goal: *Spark Success.* I wanted to produce a monthly magazine about success strategies from our authors, so Dania immediately jumped on board and began putting articles and stories into a digital masterpiece. It was a magazine of the highest caliber, including innovative techniques that other magazine designers hadn't considered implementing. Dania helped incorporate interactive workbooks and hyperlinked paths the reader could go on to make the experience that much more enjoyable. Once again, she had taken my vision and turned it into something better than I had ever dreamed.

Before that year was over, I thought up another epic idea: *Ignite Possibilities™*. I wanted to cycle my tandem bicycle across Canada with my husband and raise money for charity. Dania was still producing all our books, and now I had new things added to her plate. She was responsible for designing banners, flags, postcards, decals, and jerseys. Ignite Possibilities was going to inspire people to believe in and have faith, that *anything and everything is possible—* Dania had the job of putting that on all the collateral we needed. She even displayed my vision in a twelve-foot tall by thirty-five-foot wide, 360-degree decal we plastered all over the motorhome that followed us across the country to share the message with everyone. I remember one late night, working with her, designing the precise words and exact phrases that we would place on this spot on the motorhome below the window, to the left of the door, away from the air vent, just above the wheel well. We laughed at how tedious it was and how the wrong positioning could look catastrophic if it were out of place. She was one of the few people who cared as much as I did that everything came out just right. No matter how many times I wanted to make a revision, Dania agreed. She was willing and would stay up late with me to ensure everything was complete. We forged a deeper friendship over that project. I could tell she wasn't just working or doing a job; she was with me, supporting me, and loyal in a way money can't buy.

I'll say in year three, Dania got her stride. She was heading up our entire book production division and pretty much designing whatever crazy idea I was thinking up. I wanted Ignite™ *everywhere:* on the side of candles, t-shirts, card decks, journals, bike jerseys, and tote bags. There was never a wish or a whim Dania didn't say yes to. There was never a wrinkled nose from the wrong color or raised eyebrow from a risky choice that she didn't smile at and try to improve. She interpreted my wild ideas from late-night text messages, a series of photos from my phone, a windy call from the back of my bike on a Sunday morning, or a screenshot of something I'd seen and sent to her saying, "Can we do that?!" It was like she knew, accepted, and got me. She understood how I thought, how the wheels turned in my head, and those wacky wonderful ideas that would whirl around endlessly; she created them.

Dania was a prominent sub-story in my main story. The world saw the outcomes; the awarding-winning books year after year, the charity bike rides to Alaska, and the Maritimes. Everyone saw the magazines we were producing, the book covers we were creating, and the products we were selling. People were participating in programs, buying from the pitch decks and sales sheets Dania was helping me to create. Behind the main story was an additional story: her commitment to Ignite and me. I often say that God brought her to me, and if I could clone her, I could take on anything.

Like a conductor motioning to the orchestra, and the music playing in perfect harmony, Dania allowed me to close my eyes and have faith that everything would work out. She helped me springboard my charity initiative: *Ignite Humanity™*, to build schools overseas. With one hundred percent of our online book sales going to constructing schools, Dania jumped in to ensure we attracted donors and supporters who aligned with the project's vision and focused solely on the kids in need. She had a soft spot for children, wanting to help create a curriculum and support girls in impoverished nations. Her giving nature always seemed to radiate outward. Dania even made my wedding invitations when my husband and I renewed our vows over the summer. She created t-shirt designs after I cycled to Newfoundland and found a town I loved called Heart's Content. She made lapel buttons for me to pin on the shirts of the children I would meet at a speaking engagement I did in India. There wasn't a thing I could think of that Dania would ever decline. If I wanted it, she wanted it also.

As we entered our fourth year, she began sharing her talents with our solo authors in their personal books and coaching clients through their book creations, infusing her sparkly dust of creativity upon them. I knew it was not a coincidence she was in my life. We had developed our own communication style, private lingo, and trust that went beyond working colleagues. She became like a daughter to me; she was alone in Canada, with all her family back in Pakistan. We went through COVID-19 together. We'd meet daily on our team's scrum calls. We celebrated birthdays and holidays, all remotely but united nonetheless. We laughed, cried, pushed, and climbed; she was always there to ensure my dreams were being shared with the world. And, I took it upon myself to make sure I was there for her.

Then it happened. The story completely changed.

While I was living out my story in India, Dania had taken a few days off to go on a girl's trip with a friend and create a story of her own. She set Ignite aside to travel to Montreal and spend time with a friend she had known since childhood. My story was playing out as planned. I was traveling, promoting my initiative, posting, doing social media, and meeting with clients, while Dania's story… took a different turn.

I arrived home to find out Dania had missed a few appointments, a couple of meetings, and was not answering her phone. That wasn't like her. I could almost set my clock on her timeliness. But I allowed her youth and my own stories of a girls' weekend to forgive her lack of checking in. In four years, she had never missed an appointment or not shown up. My motherly sentiment was hoping the fun had overtaken her, that she was engulfed in so much play she simply lost all track of time. I even had to smile thinking she'd be back at work with some wild, fantastical tale of a story that would excuse her absences. But as the days accumulated and she did not return, I asked another team member to call hospitals and check news reports. I held onto my faith that she was fine, maybe a fender bender that resulted in her phone being lost at the scene. Or, a bad bout of food poisoning and a drained battery with no way to charge.

I was not prepared for the story I did receive and the hyperlink to a shocking news report. *A fire broke out; people were trapped, fire trucks were called, and no one had been found alive.* It's amazing how a story can be told with so few words. As I dug deeper, more stories surfaced. *Dania Zafar has been declared missing by her father when she and her friend did not return. Fire officials are looking for two women in the wreckage of their Airbnb, which had tragically burned down. A devastating fire claims victims as windows were locked and there was no way out.*

The two girls were staying in a heritage building in old Montreal and were set to come home but planned to stay an extra night. *Seven bodies have been recovered, but identification will take days.* I am unsure which part of me started operating first, the part that envisioned her okay, or the part of me that believed if she were okay, she would have called me by now. My desire to steer the plot of her story kept me hoping they'd find her huddled in the rubble, pinned under concrete, unconscious, slightly burned, but alive. It is amazing how we will weave our own stories to help us strategize and cope. My faith kept believing she was tough, determined, and could survive this. We all hear stories of people who've been in earthquakes, trapped in buildings, only to be pulled from the rumble and survive. We cling to those stories, wanting our loved ones to be like those people, our situation to be the miracle story in the bunch. If a story isn't working out, we try to manufacture a new one. Tell ourselves a story that seems easier to understand. Yet as a week passed and they were still demolishing the building, I knew with no food and water, her chances were diminishing. The story was unraveling, and I couldn't think straight, breathe right, or hold a conversation with anyone. At 3:30 in the afternoon, I went to bed, unable to carry on further. She was my Dania, my dream-maker, my budding seed, a flower blooming in my garden, a light that had been igniting me.

They say we are the makers of our story, and I needed to do something to help define mine. I needed to know... the waiting was so unfair. I closed my eyes and asked God to take me to her... "Take me to Dania!" I demanded in a way only one of extreme faith can ask of the Great Maker Himself. "Let me see her; show me where she is!" My command was so strong it shook me to my core, and I knew I was being heard. Within seconds I saw her lying still, burned, unrecognizable, hand bent upward across her chest. God had shown me her. She was gone; she was no longer my Dania.

Unwilling to accept that as the final chapter in my memory bank, I lovingly asked God in my grief to *show me* Dania *before* the fire. He took me to the night she arrived at the *Airbnb*™. I saw her and her friend pushing their suitcases down the sidewalk. They were laughing, excited, and filled with joy and anticipation. I saw Dania happy, relaxed, and carefree. Before yanking her suitcase up the stairs, she stopped and, for a moment, looked down the sidewalk; directly at me. I knew God had allowed me to time-travel back to that moment and see her look in my direction because at that moment, the night she was there, she thought of me. In a fleeting moment, before she passed, I came to her mind, and that thought allowed the Universe to open up and let me be there. Let me see her. Let me get one last look at her in happiness. Witness her loving life and joyous attitude, and know *that* was my Dania. That was the girl who had imprinted herself on me, and together we had done a mountain of goodness in our joint desire to Ignite Humanity.

Depending on your faith, you may or may not believe this part of the story; that's up to you. That's the great thing about stories, they deliver, and you get to receive. You take from them what you need and allow them to change you willingly and fundamentally. They become a part of you even if you don't fully agree. Choosing to believe a story does not change or negate it; the life of a story carries on even beyond its readers.

God lovingly allowed me to write a different ending to this story, and I knew without a doubt that He had deeply blessed me. He had brought Dania into my life and shared her gifts in ways beyond measurement. That inspired me to continue her story and carry on Dania's legacy. I decided since Dania was a part of our school initiative, the perfect thing to do was build a school in her name, for her parents and family in Pakistan to have more to remember her by and a place in which to create new stories. *The Dania Zafar School of Hope* is a place for brilliant minds to be creative and shine brightly in life. I wanted a place where her parents could go to carry on *their* story of the daughter they loved, the sister her brothers adored, and the cousin so many of her cousins admired. They each have a story of their own, with their beautiful woven circumstances and picturesque memories of Dania. Every story is unique, I have my story and they have theirs, but what is common among us all is the love we felt for her. The faith we clung to when we found out we lost her, and the connection we have built with each other since then.

I have felt everything in my story with Dania. Every emotion possible, every high and low. I have basked in the joy of her gloriousness and shriveled in the grief of her loss. Like all stories, ours is full, radiant, and robust. It has endured everything, and I feel the vast expansiveness of it all. And... that is what makes a great story, great. A chance encounter, a gleeful connection, a mutual under-standing, an adventure with a mission and a dragon to slay in the end, followed by a hopeful ending and a new chapter just waiting to begin. To be a full and rewarding story, it has to have its arc, many points, and final farewell.

There are so many layers to *every* story. So many twists and turns, moments of reflection, times of need, and seconds of surrender. All stories are packed full of emotions of loss, love, need, joy, gratitude, and exhilaration. Everything happens in a story because a story is a slice of life. It is a reflection of a relationship, a movement, or a brilliant encounter. Stories create feelings on top of feelings and call forth a faith that can not be explained. Everything you need is in your story to strengthen your faith and bring forth blessings of the greatest consequence. Embrace your story in all its varieties and many layers. Trust that your story matters because it is undoubtedly a part of someone else's story. Your role in their story is more important than you may ever realize. The part you play may just be a subplot, a B-line, or a plot twist, or your story may be the very thing that awakens their heart and allows them to finally be free. Your story is a part of my story; for you reading it right now is a layer in a story that started years ago and will divinely carry on.

Make your mark in your story and make a mark in someone else's along the way. Have faith that every day you are weaving a story of your own while interweaving another, and another, and another. The lives your story touches go on for infinity.

With the deepest love and gratitude, I am so thankful for every moment of my story with Dania Zafar. She made me a better storyteller. I am only remiss in that all the years that Dania was at Ignite, she never wrote her story in one of our books. I can only feel that her story was not meant to be in words but in bricks. If you want to add to her story that is yet to unfold, please donate to the *Dania Zafar School of Hope*. Every dollar buys one brick, and your donation will be not just part of her story and my story, but a part of the many children's story who will attend that school. Please be a part of building it. Go to daniazafarmemorial.com to be a contributor to a story that still needs to be told.

IGNITE ACTION STEPS

- **Close your eyes and picture your story.** Who do you want to be? Paint out in your mind the perfect, most wonderful life you could ever dream of, and when you get there, go even deeper, and brighter, turn up the volume to make it beyond your wildest dreams. Only you define your story. Only you cast the characters, pick the place, and perform the plot. Make your story exactly what you want it to be.

- **Choose the cast in your story carefully and only let the right people into it.** People don't just get to show up and be players without an invite. No one writes the plot but you.

- **Be the hero in your story.** A story will have all the plot points, the arc that includes the protagonist and villain, and the challenges and hurdles to overcome. Be the hero each and every time. Overcome the barriers, push through the storms, rally the troops, and claim back the castle. It's all yours.

- **Help others in their story.** Be the helping hand. Be the character that adds to the story, not takes away from it. Move the story forward and ensure that you are there when you are needed. When it's your time to vacate, do so… you can't be in someone else's story forever.

JAMEECE D. PINCKNEY,

JD, M.ED.

"Faith is my strength and hope for tomorrow."

This story is written to share a miraculous story of faith. I hope it brings power to your voice to speak to those mountains that seem unmovable, encourages you to believe in those things you cannot see possible, and inspires prayers you didn't realize could be answered. I pray my journey of faith brings you strength and hope to keep walking in *your* purpose.

WHAT'S FAITH GOT TO DO WITH IT?

Faith is the window through which we climb when reaching for those things unseen. Faith is a catalyst that sparks fire in our hearts and inspires us to believe. Faith says no matter what it looks like, you can still achieve it. *Oh faith, oh faith, are you there in my darkest of days?* When we fall, faith encourages us to get up and stand tall so we can continue to rise! It will never forsake you. Faith gives us hope, guides, and lifts us as we climb. Faith waits on us to lean in and implement it in all of our ways.

You may ask, What's faith got to do with it? I will tell you everything!

It was a month before my forty-fourth birthday when I was attending a conference in Houston, Texas. It was hot and muggy outside—the heat seemed unbearable that summer. During the conference, I was on a committee hosting one of the workshops being offered. The conference was seven days long and coming to an end. My stress levels were at an all-time high because I was being pulled in so many directions. I told my husband I wasn't sure if I was going to make it to the end, but he said, "You're in the home stretch, so just keep pushing through."

My scheduled workshop was on the last day of the conference. I had woken up, started preparing for the day, and noticed in the mirror that my face was drooping on the left side. I immediately exclaimed, "Dear Lord, what is going on?" I didn't know how I ended up that way; I hadn't felt any symptoms the day prior or throughout the night. After staring at myself for a minute, I asked my husband to come into the bathroom and tell me what he saw. He observed there was a slight slur in my voice and encouraged me to consider going to the emergency room. I did not because I was insistent on showing up to assist with conducting the workshop that day. I said to myself, "Lord, I trust you and I am walking by faith that nothing more will go wrong."

While the workshop went well, I found myself rushing back to my room so that we could start packing to travel the next morning. My condition started to worsen, and I was trying to hide the disfigurement in my face. While on the plane home, I told my husband that we needed to go straight to the emergency room. Upon arrival at the emergency room the doctor took one look at me and said, "You have Bell's palsy." Unfortunately, I knew what that was because my mother suffered from Bell's palsy years prior, so I was familiar with this onset. The doctor asked when I first noticed a change in my face, and I told him it was the day prior. She was glad to hear that because she told me I had a seventy-two hour window to take medication to reverse the reaction. They gave me medication to take overnight and told me that within a few days, I should be okay. I said "Thank you, Lord," because I had made it to the hospital just in time.

I was contemplating *why* that had happened to me. The Lord reminded me that in 2013 I went in for a procedure on my knee, and the surgery was aborted by the doctor due to anesthesia complications. That experience scared me so much that I had not been to see any of my doctors for nearly two years. I was sure that God intended for this episode on my face as a way to get my attention, a way for me to slow down, and to recognize that *nothing in life is so important that you forsake your own self-care and health.*

I then picked up the phone and began making my annual appointments, and in doing so, the Lord again reminded me that I should start with my OBGYN. I remembered her telling me on my last visit (two years prior) that I needed to get a pelvic exam. I scheduled my appointment, and as they were doing the ultrasound, I began praying because I felt uneasy. My doctor informed me that my endometrium was enlarged, and additional testing was required. I was fearful of what an enlarged endometrium meant and wondered if a biopsy was the next step. At my follow-up appointment, my OBGYN told me that she had reviewed the pelvic exam results and wanted to do a biopsy right there on the spot. My anxiety went from zero to ten in seconds. While the procedure was being performed, I was laying on my back while gripping the sides of the bed, when the Lord reminded me how I got to that place. With tears streaming out of the sides of my eyes, I quietly said to myself, "Thank you, Lord, I remember." It was the Bell's palsy incident that got me here.

As we were wrapping up the appointment, the doctor told me that once she received the results, she would call me. The results were back in less than two weeks, and I returned to her office. I was watching her mouth closely to see if she is getting ready to form the C-word. With bated breath, I waited. She shared with me as directly as she could that cancer cells were present, but she would have to do another procedure to take samples from my entire endometrium and uterus; that would require mild anesthesia. *Oh no,* I thought, *not anesthesia.* This triggered my fear of surgery again, and I wasn't sure if I could do it. The Lord reminded me of the scripture, (2 Timothy 1:7) *I did not give you the spirit of fear but of power, and love, and of sound mind.*

In December, I had the procedure and awaited the results. About two weeks before Christmas, I received the call from my OBGYN. My heart was hoping for the best, but my head was expecting the worst. She said, "Jameece, you have cancer." At that moment, my world went dark. As did my faith.

My doctor said, "I have a referral for you, but there is nothing else I can do for you at this time." The conversation concluded in less than five minutes, and that's all it took to turn my world upside down. I had a ton of emotions flowing through me and just had to sit back and take a breath. I had to accept the fact that I had endometrial cancer in the lining of my womb. There were a plethora of questions, *What did this all mean? How would this impact my ability to have children? Will I overcome it? Will I need to have treatments? Will I survive this?* While I didn't know the answers, the Lord reminded me to surrender to my faith and trust in Him. I had to focus so that I could stand and push myself forward despite the doctor's report. I was reminded I had to trust the report of the Lord, and all would be well.

That was the beginning of my miraculous faith journey.

After sharing this news with my husband, he held me close, and I cried into his shoulder like a baby. I felt my entire world was shattered because after being married for six years, I still had not given him a child. So, we began strategizing on our plan to start connecting with doctors to get a second opinion and see where the road would lead us. By the time January rolled around, I had seen two oncologists in Virginia and was seeking guidance on how we move forward. My overall health was in question, not to mention I was forty-five by then, and my ability to bear children was hanging in the balance.

Amazingly, we were referred to one of the top oncologists in Maryland and during our first meeting he immediately assured us that everything would be okay. He reviewed my medical files and also the results of medical procedures performed by my OBGYN and concurred with her diagnosis. However, he said, "You have options, and after going over those options, whatever you decide, we will get through this together." It was a vast difference compared to the information I had received from the first doctor. This doctor's compassion sparked a glimmer of hope and peace. He was an answer to a prayer I didn't have the answers to and restored some of my faith.

I prayed for that doctor. No matter what was happening to me medically, he saw me and had compassion for what I was experiencing, bringing calm to my spirit. This was important considering how my OBGYN had delivered the devastating news to me. I needed a bedside manner that would help me manage the stress of the situation. I thought my angel had arrived, and I immediately thanked the Lord. During our consultation, the doctor reviewed four options with us: I could do nothing and wait six months to see how the cancer was progressing; I could have a partial hysterectomy and leave my ovaries, but then there was a chance the cancer had affected my ovaries which could mean two surgeries eventually; I could have a complete hysterectomy, and by removing all my female organs, there would be a high chance that the cancer would be completely removed; and finally, if I wanted to go the path of trying to have a child, I could wait and go through the IVF process, but this could take up to two years, and there were no guarantees that I would get pregnant.

With tears falling down my face, the doctor handed me some tissue to wipe my eyes and said, "I will leave you two to discuss these options." My husband turned to me and said, over and over again, "I choose you." I fell into his arms, and the decision was made, we would be doing a complete hysterectomy. We shared our decision with my new oncologist because, at that point, we were selecting who my new doctor would be to take us on this faith journey. He asked his nurse to step in to review his calendar and the date we chose for the surgery was March 3rd, 2016. So far things were lining up, and I seemed to be doing a good job of overcoming fear by *walking in faith*. I had to somehow let go of the idea that I would not become a mother, but I found solace in knowing my husband had two older daughters from a previous marriage that I call my own.

As the date for my surgery approached, I met with my Pastor and First Lady to share this news so they could pray with and for me. During our prayer, my Pastor prayed that although I was losing my ability to bear children, the Lord would fill that void. He didn't know that I was wrestling with not being able to bring a child into our union, but in that prayer, as I was listening to those words, the Lord reminded me of my eight nieces and nephews, and the eleven godchildren I had who brought joy to my life. I felt a sense of peace when he concluded the prayer and was comforted knowing God cares so much He makes provisions even when we cannot see the path clearly.

The night before my surgery I played the old hymn, "How Great Thou Art,' and covered myself in a blanket as I sang and listened to the words. How great is the Lord to cover us, protect us, and even when we receive news that is not of good report, how great is He to bring people into our lives to help bring healing and encourage our faith? More importantly, I had to speak up to any mountain or obstacle that would prohibit a successful outcome.

Going into the surgery I was anxious because of my prior experience with anesthesia, but it's amazing how the anesthesiologist came to see me and said that all was well, he had reviewed my prior hospital report, and I had nothing to fear. My oncologist stopped by to say, "We've got this," which made me feel at ease. When I woke up in recovery, my husband was standing by my side. He told me everything went well, and the surgery was a success. It had not yet hit me that a part of me was missing. I was so concerned with my recovery, I was not fully grasping what I had lost. I was trying to listen to the doctor's post-op instructions, especially since this was my very first surgery, but all I could think of was the care I would need once I got home and for the weeks ahead.

When I arrived home my husband helped me to the bathroom, and it hit me like a ton of bricks; *my womb is gone!* I completely lost it and began crying uncontrollably! My husband didn't know what to do, so he called my mom and stood there shaking because he felt helpless. I was crying and praying to the Lord to increase, restore, and amplify my faith because all I could think was, *What have I done? Have I lost my womanhood?*

It was then, in a still, small voice, I heard the Lord say, *You have the faith of a mustard seed, it is planted, and through this experience, your faith will continue to grow and be stronger than ever.* I was in great pain, so I asked my husband to help get me to bed so that my recovery could begin. I asked the Lord to just let me wake up; if I woke up, I would no longer doubt my faith in Him.

I awoke the next morning with the curtains slightly open so I could see outside. There was a deer near my window walking in the newly fallen snow. *How great thou art,* I thought to myself *How great is our journey, our life, our trials, and tribulations.* I knew my faith journey could continue as God had me in a place of healing. My faith was strengthened. So much had to happen to get me to this place, and I knew then my walk in faith would carry on and inspire others.

It's been seven years since the surgery, and for seven years and counting, I have been cancer free. Praise be to God! Faith has had everything to do with my outcome and every aspect of my life. There is no question about it.

Faith is now my strength and remains my hope for tomorrow.

I shared with you a faith journey that went from stress to strategy to overcoming a difficult diagnosis in my life. Had I not been impacted by Bell's palsy, which led me to the doctor to be tested and diagnosed with cancer when I did, who knows where I would be today? My fear kept me from going to check on the welfare of my health, but my faith led me to move forward and trust my intuition to act and care for myself.

God allowed me to see myself disfigured so He could *reconfigure* what was happening inside my body. The day I was told I had cancer ended up being the darkest day of my life. Yet ultimately, His light awakened me to have the courage to be cancer free and live the best days of my life; with faith.

I pray my story resonates in a way that stirs courage in you to move beyond fear when facing challenges. Let faith guide you along the path to victory. Let faith show you how *the power in your voice enables you to speak to mountains that seem unmovable.* I hope faith encourages you to see that by believing in those things which you cannot see possible, they can come to pass. I hope through your prayers you will receive answers that demonstrate God's love for you. I pray my journey brings you strength and hope to keep walking in your purpose and faith.

When asked, "What's your faith got to do with it?" May your response be, "Everything!"

IGNITE ACTION STEPS

- **Try not to let stress interrupt your well-being.** Stress can be self-induced, or it can sneak up on you. Don't let the stresses of life overwhelm you to the point that it impacts your health. Do your best to live your best life stress-free by faith!

- **Be intentional about self-care; it's your welfare.** Sometimes we ignore the signs. Sometimes we don't make those medical appointments the way we should. But just as the Lord wakes us up each day and gives us another opportunity to excel, be sensitive to your health, and pay attention when your body speaks to you. Walking in good health is a faith walk, and no one knows you better than you, so be intentional about your daily self-care.

- **Overcome your fears with faith.** It can be challenging walking in faith, but God will not take you on a journey you are not prepared to embrace. Walking in faith can sometimes bring about fears. In those moments, let your worship speak louder than your worry. Let your praise speak louder than your pain. Let your faith speak louder than your fears. No matter the journey, you got this by faith!

- **Pay it forward by helping others and the community.** Nothing is more gratifying than your success, except when you help others. No matter your story, always remember to pay it forward. Find a dynamic nonprofit that you can connect with, such as The OPHELIA Foundation, which I founded and established on the principle of helping others. Refer to the references to find out more.

Ash Bhadani

ASH BHADANI

"Faith is the beacon of hope that shines through the darkest of times."

My heartfelt intention is to inspire and empower my readers with the life-changing truth that faith is the ultimate shield against all negativity. I want you to feel the transformative power of faith as an impenetrable armor that will give you the courage and strength to face your innermost fears, overcome challenges with ease and safety, and live a life filled with hope, joy, and love.

FAITHING THE WAY THROUGH

Being a child is hard work. I vividly recall stomping my feet in frustration, trying to get the grown-ups in my family to understand my seven-year-old burden. I needed an assistant to help tackle the endless list of chores the grown-ups assigned to me. It was exhausting to be the sole child amidst so many adults. I yearned for some support, and, most importantly, I needed information on how I could welcome a new addition to our family. My classmates had younger siblings, and I was desperate for tangible aid to acquire one of my own. Seeking guidance, I turned to my confidant—my grandpa (who I lovingly called Dadu in my native language of Punjabi). My pigtails bounced as I stomped toward him; I asked, "How can I get a baby brother?" Dadu's advice was, "Go and ask."

I was utterly taken aback by his response. For me, Dadu was always the go-to person for any query, as he never failed to have a satisfying answer. I inquired, eager to clarify, "Whom should I seek out for guidance?" But he chose to guide me by finding the answers for myself, like a person shining a flashlight down on a path rather than leading by the hand.

In my bewilderment, I asked him again, "Who should I ask?" He replied that I should ask God. Now, I was even more perplexed. I tried to engage my young mind and said, "Dadu, but how can I ask God? I can't see Him; I don't know where to find Him." He explained that just as I can feel the air and smell flowers from far away, I can also sense the love or anger of our loved ones without being in the same room. If I chose to believe in God, I could feel His presence also. His presence is always with us if we seek Him. Dadu gave me the task of talking to God whenever I felt confused about a situation or needed love and support.

The entire week passed by, and I persistently asked God various things. Sometimes, I implored Him just to provide proof of His existence. After a week of my monologues or one-way conversations, my faith dwindled. I approached my Dadu with disbelief and frustration. I inquired whether or not there was a specific location where God resides so I could be certain that I could communicate with Him and He would lend an ear to me.

Dadu informed me that while God lives within all of us, there are certain places where His presence is especially potent, and where devotees go to seek His guidance and assistance. When I asked him which places he was referring to, he responded that one such place was a Gurdwara, a Sikh Temple. It's a sacred place of worship where individuals express their love and faith in God, and where people gather to honor and connect with the Divine.

From that moment on, I was determined to visit the Sikh Temple as soon as possible. As it was already quite late when Dadu shared this wisdom, I went to the Gurdwara early the next day. I was stopped at the entrance by the caretakers and construction workers. My path was blocked by iron bars and tools being used for renovating the space. I explained to them that I had important business inside the temple, determinedly refusing to leave without talking to God. But the construction workers and helpers were equally resolute in not allowing me in. Luckily, one of the helpers wanted to provide me with some solace and suggested that I could communicate with God through acts of service. Seeing this as my way through, I insisted that I wouldn't budge until they permitted me to perform service in the temple.

For my small hands, washing bricks before their use in constructing the temple was a fitting and secure task. With great love and care, I began washing the bricks, and something ignited in me through that process. Although my primary motive for coming to the temple was to get a little brother, I discovered a great sense of calm, peace, and unity while truly connecting with my faith.

After some weeks went by, Dadu called me after school to have a chat. He inquired about how my conversations with God were progressing, and I informed him that I was communicating with Him regularly. Although I couldn't hear God's voice, I felt a unique happiness and I didn't like being late for my daily visit to the temple to talk to Him.

My daily routine was fixed: wake up early, complete household chores, prepare for school, attend school, return home, finish homework, help my mother, and head to the temple at precisely 6 PM for the service. Time seemed to crawl by, but I was content. After almost two months, my grandmother (Dadi) called me just as I was about to leave for the temple. She advised me to pray to God for a younger brother, as God will bless my mother with another baby soon.

I reassured Dadi that I had already been conversing with God and that I had envisioned what my baby brother would look like. I promised her that I would love him with all my heart. After 7 months, my mom gave birth to my long-awaited 'personal assistant,' who we named Nishu. He came into our lives and changed everything. With the knowledge that God was watching over me, I began to see the world with newfound assurance that a Higher Power would take care of my desires. I started and ended each day with unwavering faith.

At that point, I was unaware that my mother had faced multiple miscarriages after my birth, leading her to lose all hope of having another child. Years later, I discovered that my unwavering faith not only blessed me with a brother, but also gave my mother hope and acceptance for her body, restoring her feminine pride. I was bestowed with the gift of a baby sister named Eesha just two years after the birth of my brother Nishu. I had only asked for one sibling, but God had gifted us with two, allowing us to experience the unique bond of siblings. I began to cherish them as my own babies, loving them unconditionally. They were my miracles, the first of many to come.

Yet, miracles are also framed within hardships and challenges, too, and faith only grows stronger when it is tested. As time went on, I faced those tests. One day playing with my beloved baby brother resulted in the excruciating pain of fracturing both of my ankles, one after the other. Still faithful, I asked God what the lesson was with this experience, and if He could lower my pain.

Life kept moving day-by-day, year-by-year, with different experiences filled with blessings and lessons for me. Through the highs and lows, I remained grateful that every moment had something valuable to teach me. While faith can bring comfort and solace, it can also be a difficult and demanding path, continually testing to see if we are willing to walk the walk, not just talk the talk.

Heading into my teenage years, I strongly desired to become a pilot. But my father had different plans for me—a career in medicine. He began coercing me to prepare for the medical entrance exam. However, I refused to follow his path and stood my ground for a year, fighting for my dream career. Despite my efforts, nothing changed, and while my mind remained fixated on my ultimate desire, I finally resigned to his wishes. I was out of resources and hoped medical school could be the way to a better life. It wasn't until later that I learned that things happen when we surrender ourselves peacefully and joyfully to the Universe.

I traveled to Russia to pursue my medical degree. It was there that I met the love of my life, who is now my husband. My life has become bigger than my wildest dreams. I came to understand that the path we desire is not always meant to bring us peace, joy, and happiness. True faith provides peace through surrender to a Divine power. It always guides us to a place of safety and peace. People often ask God, "WHY me?" whereas I have always asked God, "Why not ME?" even when I was asking for a baby brother or a career as a pilot.

I have endured my fair share of harrowing experiences, each leaving its mark on me in its own way. In my early adulthood, I came to know the searing agony of being burned by fire and the heart-stopping terror of surviving deadly car accidents. They were among the many challenges I faced that tested my strength and resilience.

When Nilesh (my husband) and I arrived in the United States with just $20 to our names, we were forced to rely on our faith and the kindness of strangers to build a new life for ourselves. And yet, time and again, we were met with miraculous opportunities and encounters that allowed us to thrive and prosper in this foreign land. I have never been alone. Whether it was the reassuring presence of a loved one, the kind words of a stranger, or the unwavering support of a community, I knew that there was always someone there by His grace to hold me up when I felt like I was falling apart. And God was granting me strength and protection as I was creating my reality.

Against all odds, I was able to pursue an education in a foreign country, thanks to my family's unwavering support and generosity. And, despite the pressures of societal norms and familial expectations, I had the courage to break free from tradition and forge my own path, charting a course toward a life of meaning and purpose. But perhaps the greatest miracle of all was finding love and marrying someone with whom I share a deep and abiding connection, a love that fills my heart and soul with joy and contentment. We are now the proud parents of two incredible boys: Anish and Ansh. Each one is a testament to the power of love and faith. They are an echo of the first miracles I knew when in the face of my mother's heartbreaking miscarriages, I was given those two precious gifts of a brother and sister, living proof of the power of hope and perseverance. Now, Nilesh and I have built a relationship grounded in mutual respect and open communication, allowing us to parent with a shared sense of purpose and vision. Along the way, I have discovered hidden talents and unexpected passions, including becoming an international best-selling author and a certified empowering life coach. These experiences have allowed me to help others on their own journeys of self-discovery and empowerment. And, through it all, I have learned to trust that every experience is a stepping stone on the path toward my greater purpose, guided by the loving hand of God. As long as I have the courage to take the next step, I know He will be there to light the way.

Life is an unpredictable journey full of ups and downs. While it may not be easy, it is also not as complicated as we tend to make it out to be. After all, we are mere blips in the grand scheme of things, with the earth being around for over four billion years. Yet, somehow, even as blips, we hold the power to imprint, shape, and completely transform those we touch. In the fleeting moments that we are in this world, we can become the beacon to so many people. That is the incredible power God has granted each of us, and it is that same power that lets us grow and learn to navigate the world with greater resilience and wisdom each time we are tested.

Each person that has graced my life is part of a divine plan; each moment is a sign of Him. I constantly sense the presence of God in my life through signals, inspiring phrases, compassionate individuals, and miracles. I don't burden Him with excessive requests; simply knowing that He is attentive and protective was enough to bring me contentment. God's vision is greater than mine. He sees the world with a wider lens, while my perception is limited. Walking in faith requires surrender, but it brings a sense of certainty that enables me to navigate through life's ups and downs. I can traverse any valley or mountain with faith as my guide.

We are all on a journey to becoming the person that God intended us to be. Every experience we go through is a stepping stone toward that ultimate destination. And, while the journey ahead may be fraught with uncertainty and obstacles, I take solace in the knowledge that I am never truly alone. By living in the present moment and being aware of our divine presence, we can approach our experiences with a sense of openness and acceptance. When we let go of our resistance to these experiences, we break down the walls that separate us from them and start to see them for what they truly are. We begin to recognize that these experiences are not here to harm us but rather to teach us important lessons and to help us grow. As we drop our resistance, we also release the negative emotions that often accompany these experiences, such as anxiety, anguish, pain, and depression. By fully embracing and learning from our experiences, we can become the best version of ourselves and fulfill our purpose in life.

My faith taught me that the ultimate goal is the well-being of everyone. The Universe pays attention to our words when they are infused with love, not when they stem from fearful thoughts. Faith is for the highest good of all. People sometimes think that God is a supplier of materials and resources—they only pray when they need something tangible. But faith is about giving and receiving. This is why I begin each day with unwavering faith and end it with the same conviction. I trust that the Universe supports me as long as I have faith and surrender to its divine will. My task is to align my actions with my faith, in the peaceful knowing that the Universe will guide me to where I need to be. The outcome the Universe delivers as I am faithing my way through, is for the highest good of all.

Ignite Action Steps

- **Start a gratitude jar** at the beginning of each month and add a note every day expressing how someone's kindness made you feel grateful.

- **Initiate a miracle jar annually,** where you include a slip of paper with details about when you experienced a wonder and how it came to you, along with money inside the container.

- **Access both jars whenever you encounter challenges** that put your faith to the test. When you feel adversity and require hope to remind you of your blessings, you can rely on the money you've collected in your miracle jar to sustain you as the Universe continues to send you more miracles.

- **Every morning, make a conscious decision** to put on the armor of love as your safeguard instead of wrapping yourself up in a bag of fear.

- **Surrender yourself to faith and align your actions with it.** Acknowledge any fear you may have and remind yourself it is only temporary. Remember that when you call on God for help, He will dispatch assistance to you.

Joanne Latimer

Joanne Latimer

"Faith says: Keep (Your Mind) In Spiritual Serenity: K.I.S.S. Your Mind!"

It is my desire to touch your heart. It's your time to be free indeed! Declare your liberation! Your faith vessel showed up, bearing ample strength to support you in every area of your life. Anchored in truth, you unapologetically embrace your personal faith-filled treasures of peace, which are Comfort, Compatibility, and Clean Hands. These treasures await your arrival every time. My hope is that my story helps you discover your own glorious faith-filled Ignite Moments! Let the blessings overflow!

Finding Faith-Filled Treasures in Earthen Vessels

During the mid-sixties, almost every night on the evening news, I saw brutal images of my people being hosed down by the police, as well as being viciously attacked by police dogs. It was an era when black people marched and died for racial equality. Their courage was contagious and spread rapidly among most black youth from high school to college. I strongly believed in the cause. My generation knew we were up next to do our part in the fight for equality. We did not want to let our elders and ancestors down, so we fought to maintain our integrity.

Facing the changes that the civil rights movement embarked on, integration was inevitable. It found its way into my neighborhood in 1965. At age thirteen, I was amongst the first group of negro children who were bussed to an all-white middle school. It was an experience I shall never forget as I found out first-hand the truth surrounding ignorance and prejudice.

In the fall of 1969, I enrolled in a local university. My close friend and sorority sister exercised our beliefs and became student activists. It was monumental seeing my faith in action. The voter registration campaign and other issues of injustice emboldened the Civil Rights Movement. As momentum accelerated, scores of us college youths joined in unity on one accord. Where I attended school, the students' demand was to have a full curriculum for African American Studies be offered in the subsequent semesters.

Following the assassinations of most of our brilliant, fearless leaders, young and old, we suddenly found ourselves feeling emotionally gagged with both hands bound. We never got the chance to see our vision come to fruition. Despite everything that had transpired, some still held onto the belief that we would overcome such inequalities one day. Many others just stopped believing; like Fannie Lou Hamer said, we were all "sick and tired of being sick and tired."

Amid civil unrest, outrage, and rioting, the National Guard was dispatched to restore order and enforce martial law.[1] I was nineteen years old, watching the convoy of military tanks rolling in, but I didn't know what to think. Black people everywhere were petrified. At the end of the day, the message was clear[2]; acquiesce. Student participation dwindled rapidly. New Federal legislation financed summer jobs and vocational programs as "pacifiers" to bandage up the wounds of despair they caused.

I ended up withdrawing from college in the middle of my sophomore year because I had a baby, followed by marriage. My morale and spirit for activism were broken, my own faith and hope felt shattered in the wake of the racial disturbance. All of that devastation left me wondering, *Now what?* I made the necessary changes to my daily routines, but nothing was ever the same again. The city streets suddenly became saturated with heroin causing overwhelming negativity. Chaos and criminal activity heavily increased and affected all of our neighborhoods. Thousands of lives, homes, and families were ruined, including mine. My marriage did not survive, and my heart was crushed. Many years later, I awakened to a brutal truth. I had lost value in myself as the jewel I truly was because my harsh reality had blinded me.

Finding the strength to return to my feet was always tied to the black church. It was my lifeline. With five little girls, Jameece, nine years old, identical twins, Denise and Dana, five years old, Jessica, four years old, and Mya, two years old, there was no other way to survive except by faith. We were homeless. My sister and a couple of close friends opened their doors. Several weeks had passed when a family member told me about a house that would be available to rent. The owner was being placed in a nursing home, and the building had become a dope house. So, I rolled up my sleeves, took a long deep breath, and got to work along with a few ladies from church. That's what we did back then, we genuinely helped one another. I'm immensely thankful to the other ladies in the village who helped raise me up when I needed it most.

The house needed serious repairs. A rope and a necktie held the back-door jam closed and a piece of cardboard served as a windowpane in one of the bedrooms. The first thing I did was pour bleach all over the floors in every room, followed by ammonia (and I lived!). For days, we cleaned this house until it was finally ready for us to move in. None of my girls were happy—not at all.

On the first evening, strangers knocked on the front and back doors. I told the girls to stay in their room. I explained to the strangers that I was the new tenant. I was terrified by the fact that, most likely, these people were looking for drugs. Then came fear trying to bully me, to torture me with panic. By slowly inhaling and exhaling, inner strength rose inside me with boldness. Thankfully we were never violated the whole time we lived there. Faith was our pillar of fire, guiding us through that dark space in time.

In the corner of my eye, I saw the first mouse. I had already bought traps, so I set six of them. Shortly after that, I heard them all go off. In shock, I crept over to see and sure enough there were six dead mice. Nervously, I put on my rubber gloves, emptied all six traps, and kept resetting them until the traps finally stopped snapping. I found all of the holes where they were coming up from the basement. Using metal lids off canned foods, I covered every hole and nailed them shut. Thankfully, family members who were carpenters and plumbers eventually upgraded the most important necessities.

After six years of living there, the furnace broke down completely and the water pipes froze. It was the dead of winter with freezing temperatures, so I took my girls to family and friends. My faith treasure discovery was this: I learned how to be content in whatever state I was in. When difficult situations arose, I had to focus on the solution to the matter at hand and not get distracted worrying about the things I couldn't change.

Unforeseen circumstances prevailed, and I became homeless for the second time; I was faced with making another crucial decision. I was working for the *Better Business Bureau™*. Under the pressure of my heavy burden, I broke down in tears. Coworkers and managers were trying to console me when I received a phone call that completely changed my life and my children's futures. Our next-door neighbor, whom we had come to love as family, came to our rescue. They offered to relocate us to Georgia with a new home and some financial support. There will never be enough words to express our utmost gratitude and never-ending love for them and their family!

Looking back, I realize my first unexpected breakthrough came the day I was strong enough to take my five children and run away from the home I had built with their father. My second awakening came when I decided to stop running and become the outstanding black woman I was born to be. The unavoidable crossing of all those paths created conditions for my divine Ignite Moment to arrive undeniably! Looking fear straight in the eyes, I screamed out loud, "Fear, I will not be afraid of you any-more, ever!" That was it, my true Ignite Moment! Joyfully, I had let my own ears hear my own voice, I hugged my soul, and I kissed my mind! The lesson I learned after being hidden under a blanket of despair was to love myself unconditionally. I purposed to keep my mind in spiritual serenity by being gentle and kind to myself. That moment of spiritual liberation was truly uplifting!

Then, years seemed to pass at warp speed. All five daughters had married. Only three of them became moms. Over decades, watching their lives unfold, I have witnessed the promise of God come to pass. They have all succeeded far beyond anything I could ever conceive or imagine. They each have successful business operations through their creative visions and hard work. With the support of my 'bookends,' Jameece and Mya, 'my pillars,' Jessica, Dana, and Denise, they all lifted me up! To God be the glory!

In my early sixties, I started working at *H&R Block™* (HRB) world head-quarters, located in Kansas City, Missouri. There I met who would become my new spiritual connection. She was my corporate trainer and team lead, Mrs. Angel Williams, Senior SME (Subject Matter Expert). Instantly, I discerned her realness. She was extremely astute and had a vast range of knowledge. We worked together for the next five years. She was very impactful in my life. Angel and I concluded there was no doubt that God predestined our paths to cross. We soon learned that we both had a mutual faith and hunger to know more of God's purpose for our lives.

I listened as she shared how her faith had been shattered and her heart broken because of the people who said one thing, but their lifestyles did not match their words. Seeing hypocrisy in bold display in the place of worship, and hearing Bible scriptures being manipulated to deceive and misuse people, without hearing any remorse from anyone made her angry, even at God. Yet, as only God can, he revealed Himself through His love. She told me, "I don't mean this selfishly, but I now have the true revelation of knowing that, before the foundation of the earth was laid, I was the focus of God's LOVE!" Amen. Angel was a divine treasure God placed in my life as we became iron sharpening iron together!

While I was still working at HRB, I graduated Cum Laude from DeVry University. I earned a Bachelor's Degree in Human Resources Management. Walking across that stage at age sixty-two and hearing my family screaming my name was an exhilarating Ignite Moment!! Pure mind-blowing joy!! Need I say more?

In the previously published book, *Ignite Your Wisdom*, there's a story about a little nine-year-old girl gazing out of the kitchen window while washing the dishes. She was imagining how big the world must be on the other side when suddenly, her energy shifted as she nervously detected a presence looming nearby. Sorry, no spoiler alerts! You will have to read my daughter, Jameece Pinckney's story to find out what happened. As her mom, I can say with a surety that God refined and preserved Jameece for a time such as this. When she was preyed upon as a little girl, she did not allow dark spirits to corrupt her heart. The power of her faith equipped her to forgive all of the transgressors of her past and her present. God bestowed upon her how to turn her pain into purpose. Having set ablaze the trail to where she is today, I am proud beyond words! My beloved firstborn is truly an amazing and wise woman of God who possesses that indestructible kind of faith!

I am overjoyed about this "real-time" Ignite Moment that's in progress! I would be remiss not to mention that God used a friend who insisted repeatedly that I should listen to the voice of Mr. Les Brown, which is how I first learned about Lady JB. After storing up weeks of his videos, I went on a marathon watching and taking it all in. I felt moved to learn more about this greatness Mr. Brown spoke so passionately about. I believed and embraced that *"It's Possible," "It's Necessary," "It's You," "It's Hard," "It's Worth-it,"* and *"It's Done."* I cannot find words to describe how elevating it was to attend those powerful live zooms! Mr. Brown's son, John-Leslie Brown, coached me and pinpointed exactly what I needed to do to find my voice, which also equipped me to tell my story. I owe the father, the son, and the entire phenomenal inner circle family for my birthing and breakthrough, which enabled me to be here right now.

I am honored, Lady JB, that you have blessed me with this once in a lifetime opportunity! My heart is in amazement to share my story, along with dozens of stellar authors, in this marvelous book! You are the quintessential extraordinaire as you fulfill your earthly mission and your spiritual calling! Much gratitude to Lady JB Owen and the entire Ignite Team!

From my perspective, faith requires the belief that God exists. According to the Book of Life, God gives every person a measure of faith. Similar to raising children, faith must be nurtured and tended to with steadfast focus. With each passing decade, time unfolds its own way of keeping track of our faith journey. Gold is refined by fire. Diamonds are created by pressure. Faith to believe you *can* endure the pressure and the fire is priceless.

Now approaching age seventy-two, I marvel in awe daily over God's majesty. I indeed bear witness that by having faith in God, I went from enduring grueling circumstances to remarkable triumphs! I learned to take God at his word and how to "Be Extra" over my faith. The ability to live in peace on purpose is, again, priceless! I am thankful for my healing and for my heart being made whole. For the remainder of my days, I shall continue to *fight the good fight of faith.*

In its simplest form, faith shows up as a vessel that transports us from a negative mind filled with doubt to complete persuasion. Each deliberate leap of faith empowers us! We overthrow indecisiveness, and we overcome the fear of the unknown. Ultimately, even when we are lacking in faith, we can ask God, anytime, to help our unbelief and increase our enduring faith!

My suggestion to anyone who feels their faith has let them down is this: Make self-accountability the primary standard for governing yourself. Have clean hands and a pure heart. Your words must match your actions, and your actions must bear witness to your words. My self-accountability power quote is my golden rule:

"Never lie to yourself, especially about yourself."

Remember, this is a process. For faith to be effective, you must spiritually align with God. Through this, you will find faith-filled treasures within the beautiful earthen vessel that is you.

IGNITE ACTION STEPS:

"BE EXTRA" Over Your Faith!

Bear witness to your truth, the good and the part that's hard to admit.

Exhale slowly.

Elevate your ways of knowing.

Xenial behavior goes far (being hospitable goes even farther).

Treat others always with fairness .

Respect (it's a two-way lane; don't forget to respect yourself)

Acknowledge the little things; they all matter.

JACKI SEMERAU TAIT

"The most powerful place to be is in a state of surrender."

My hope for you as you read this is that you will know and understand that God is there for you. He is there in the good times, and there through the hardships. He has placed within you a desire for a relationship with Him and the power to move the mountains you face. So, place your faith in Him.

WHY ME?

"Why me?" As a girl of fourteen years old, I sat on my bedroom floor, broken by the events of the past several weeks. I angrily asked that question of the God I was raised to believe in, the God who seemed to have abandoned me.

Before that point, I was a self-confident girl growing up in the suburbs of Chicago. While I certainly faced hardships and challenges, I would admit that my home life was as idyllic as it could be. My parents loved each other, loved their three children, and loved God with all their hearts. I was raised to believe I could do anything I wanted to do, given every opportunity my parents could muster to chase my dreams. For me, that meant dancing. I was a high-energy child, and my stay-at-home mom knew I needed a way to channel that energy. Seeing that I loved dancing, she signed me up for a beginner's ballet class at four years old. We weren't well off by any means, but I really didn't know that. My parents would stretch to pay for my dance classes. Even my grandma would support me by buying my ballet shoes. That was the environment of loving effort I grew up in.

My days as a ballerina intensified, and I ended up getting hired as a student teacher for the beginner classes to help pay for all the lessons I was taking as a teenager. I was so focused on becoming a professional ballerina that it maintained the majority of my focus. Sports, events, and even dating were all on the back burner. The one other thing I allowed to take priority was following Jesus. I was raised in a Christian household and intended to remain a virgin until I got married. It was important to me, and I was strong-willed enough that I never thought it would be otherwise.

Then I started high school. It wasn't really high school in and of itself that changed the trajectory of my life. It was one more tragic event that my fourteen-year-old self had no idea how to handle. A childhood friend—a goofy kid from Sunday school who always made me laugh—died in a motorcycle accident. A few weeks before he died, he told our mutual friend that he "liked" me. Not knowing how to handle that, I said some mean things about him behind his back so that our friend wouldn't think I "liked" him in return.

If we're honest with ourselves, we can look back at our teenage years and know that we said and did a lot of toxic things. It's the nature of the beast—that time when hormones start to wake up and rage through our changing bodies. We don't know what to do with ourselves or how to handle these new situations. It's a time where we learn a lot, but let's face it: it's often awful.

That was me. Awful. Then my friend passed away. It was the first time I realized we might never get a chance to apologize, make amends, or set the record straight. Sometimes the bad choices we make in an instant can leave us with sadness or regret that will never really go away.

All of that led me to depression, a feeling of being out of control, which led me to try alcohol for the first time. I was at a party with friends I trusted, and I never thought that I may put myself in danger. I just remember the feeling of relief when I was drunk. For a brief moment, the tragedy that had me spiraling out of control was no longer in the forefront of my mind. I started looking for more parties, more opportunities to drink. I wanted to keep going to that place where my mind shut off my regret and sense of loss. I was able to find a couple of chances to do exactly that. I knew enough to stay with people I trusted. But I never thought about what would happen if the people I trusted were also making bad choices.

Two weeks after having my first taste of alcohol, I was out with friends at a party by a firepit in the woods. After a few drinks, a new person showed up. He was older than the rest of us. When he got there, he turned his attention to me, which was as distracting and intoxicating as the alcohol itself. I liked the way it made me feel.

That is until the weather turned. He took me to his car to "get out of the snow." And that's where he sexually assaulted me.

So, there I was the next day, sitting on my bedroom floor, angry at God. At the man who took everything from me. At myself for being so stupid as to be in that situation to begin with. I was a child dealing with adult situations of loss, guilt, and sexual assault. Three weeks was all it took for me to go from confident and focused to depressed and out of control. All I could do was shake my fist at God, asking, "WHY?! Why me?! Why didn't You stop this from happening? Why did You bring that person into my life? Why did You let my friend die?" No answers were forthcoming.

At that moment, I told God to leave me alone. I was done with Him. What had believing in Him done for me? It didn't keep me from the pain, so what good was He? I can still remember the feeling of utter hopelessness in that moment. But I was stubborn, and not about to take it back.

I began searching for a new religion to believe in, for meaning in my life. I checked out all sorts of religions. You name it, I researched it. And, like trying on clothes to see if they fit, I tried on new belief systems to see if they felt right.

All the while, my life continued to be dictated by one bad choice after another. I let dance go by the wayside. I struggled in my academics at school, even though I had been a straight-A student previously. With no anchor of faith to reign me in, I made a mess of myself.

After three years without Him, I felt God call to me. I was lying in bed one night, trying to make sense of all that had happened, when a song popped into my head. It was a Sunday-school song based on 1 John 4:7-8. The sing-song chorus echoed, *"Beloved, let us love one another. For love is of God, and anyone who loves knows God. He who loves not, knows not God. For God is love."*

That's when I knew that love was the answer. I needed God's love for me and needed to find a way to love myself in spite of everything.

Of course, remember that I'm stubborn. I was seventeen when I recalled that song, when I felt God calling me back to a relationship with Him. But I was thirty-six when I finally surrendered my life fully to God. In the years in between, I got married, had two beautiful daughters, and went through a divorce. Becoming a single mom was the best and worst of times for me. At first, I enjoyed financial and professional success, but then the 2008 Great Recession hit my professional life like a Category 5 hurricane. We lost everything and ended up moving in with my parents. Over the next two years, I was able to get back on my feet financially and find an apartment for the three of us. Things were great for a while.

Then it all came crashing back down around me. Within two short weeks, I lost all three sources of my income. As it all dried up, I found myself scrambling to figure out how to keep us from repeating the hard times we had just overcome. For weeks I would wake up every day and get to work trying to generate business: cold-calling, networking, and even applying for jobs waiting tables, anything I could think of to bring back my financial security. I continued to try every day. If there's one thing I can say about myself it is that I'm tenacious. I don't think that is an inherent trait. I believe that it's one that every mom learns when she becomes the sole head of her household. A single mom will do whatever she needs to do to provide for her children, and most try to do it in such a subtle way to keep their kids away from the struggle.

Yet, by the first week of January, I could no longer pay the rent. The first time I lost everything, it had been scary. Losing a house you have a mortgage on is a long process. Being evicted from an apartment is fast and furious. This time was TERRIFYING.

January 15th dawned with a knock and a piece of paper taped to my front door. It was my official eviction notice. I had ten short days before my children and I were left homeless. Moving back in with my parents was no longer an option since they had downsized and moved to a retirement community. There was nowhere left to go.

The knot in my stomach that had been growing day by day now grew hourly. I was in constant panic, trying to hide it long enough to make phone calls and set up interviews. With the eviction notice delivered, I didn't know what more to do or who else to turn to. I was afraid. Alone. Desperate.

I had been praying to God every day. But my prayers were wrapped up in asking God to fix the problem; "Lord, help me find a job." "Lord, help me find the money." "Lord, bring me a client." But on that day, my prayer changed.

I simply surrendered. I was in my living room with tears running down my face when I gave it all to God. Falling to my knees, I cried out, "Jesus, I have tried everything I know to do. And still, here I sit with no hope for my future. But God, I know you are in control! If homelessness is something you know I need to experience, so be it."

It wasn't just a prayer—it was a true surrender in my heart. I imagined myself with nowhere to live. For the first time since my chain of financial battles began, it didn't scare me. Instead, I started to see it through the eyes of my future self. God gave me a vision of telling my story to others on a mission to bring healing and hope. I asked myself, *Do I need to walk the path of homelessness for my story to bring glory to God, to reach in and help others walking that path?*

There, on the floor and speaking to God, I felt the knot in my stomach loosen. My mindset started to shift. What if this was a temporary situation that needed to happen to bring me to a future that God had planned? What if my children needed to go through this with me to learn empathy for people down on their luck?

It was on my bedroom floor where I rejected God... and on my living room floor twenty-two years later where I fully allowed my faith to reignite. My impending tragedy turned into a great adventure in my mind, and I knew that the Lord would bless me with everything I needed to get through it.

In Isaiah 55:8, the Bible tells us that the Lord declares, *"My thoughts are not your thoughts. My ways are not your ways."* I decided to stop trying to get God to see things my way. Instead, I prayed for God to help me see things through His eyes.

I stood up, not one penny richer, but with hope in my heart I cannot explain. I knew that one day I would be able to point to this time as a catalyst for my success. A success I could see no evidence for at that moment but the success I knew would become my reality because I would never stop fighting for it, even in the midst of getting thrown out on the street.

Once I surrendered, things began to change. Within days, a friend lent me the money to pay my past-due rent, ensuring the ability to stay in our apartment. I had submitted my resume to a mortgage company where one of my dear friends worked. I was hired as a marketing consultant representing several loan officers. Not only was I hired into a company in my chosen field, but it was an ideal fit where I could use the combination of my real estate background and my marketing expertise.

We didn't have to walk through homelessness. But I think God was bringing me to a lesson I needed to learn. I had to be willing to go through the hardest thing I could imagine. God was showing me that I needed to lean not on my own understanding but to trust in Him fully and completely.

The relationship I now have with God is intensely personal, no longer just something I was raised to believe. It is something I believe wholeheartedly because I have lived it firsthand. I lived the decision to surrender my life and my heart to God, and I've seen the difference ever since.

My journey hasn't been a straight trajectory, but it has been primarily uphill since that moment. I can point to the lessons I learned during that time as the catalyst. Without faith in God, I tried to drive my own life. And I was driving it right into the ground. But once I placed all my faith in the Lord, things did turn around for the better. And as long as I live in faith, God blesses me.

I asked the question, "Why me?" throughout all the hardships. I wondered where God was, only to learn He was there all along. I just needed to make the decision to trust in Him. To have faith that God created me on purpose for a purpose. That all the hard times were necessary in order to reveal what I was made of. Without the hardships, I would never know what true contentment even was.

Just a few years ago, I stood at my bedroom window overlooking the beautiful view. We live on a hillside in a mountain town, and from my bedroom window, I can see a gorgeous view over the tops of the ponderosa pine forest behind our home. I watched as a storm rolled in. There's something about the sounds, sights, and smell of a fresh rain that reminds me of possibilities. I stood there, taking it all in, and a feeling of peace overwhelmed me. I realized how blessed I have been, and how far my life's journey had taken me.

Tears began to roll down my cheeks, and I found myself once again asking the question, "Why me?" Only now, I wasn't asking from a place of self-pity and helplessness. I was asking from the point of feeling blessed beyond measure. I was asking, "Why me? Why, oh, Lord, have you chosen to bless me so fully when I had spent so much time making a mess of things?"

Like the song that had played in my mind at seventeen, once again, I was reminded through a Bible verse of the power of love, how love is at the center of faith. Ephesians 2:8-9 states, *"For by grace you have been saved through faith. And this is not your own doing; it is the gift of God, not a result of works, so that no one may boast."* It is through faith and the gift of God's love and the sacrifice of His Son that is the answer to the question, OF COURSE ME! God chooses to love us, to bless us, and to call EACH of us into a relationship with Him. We simply have to choose to receive His gift in reverence. When I surrendered all, I opened up the possibilities.

Let me ask you, are you on the floor? On the floor in victimhood or on the floor in surrender? I would encourage you, when you find yourself there, choose to surrender all to Him. Because the answer to your "why me?" is "OF COURSE ME!" God's gift of love is yours to receive; you just have to know, believe, and walk in faith with Him.

Ignite Action Steps

Live in a state of surrender. When you give it all to God, you are assured that your actions will perfectly align with your higher purpose. When we live for ourselves, we often oppose what is truly best for our lives. What action items can you take to do the hard work of surrendering?

- **Choose your focus.** If you find yourself focusing your attention on what is going wrong, you're living in a state of victimhood. Ask yourself, "How can this moment be used for a higher purpose in the future?"

- **Accept the struggles.** Instead of fighting against the hardships, lean into them. Look at who you desire to be in one year, and ask yourself how the Lord will use this current hardship to achieve that dream.

- **Get into a personal relationship with God.** If you read this story and want to explore the kind of relationship with the Lord that I experience, start by reading your Bible. It's God's love letter, instructional manual, and personal development book. It's how God speaks to us. Also, pray. It's how you can speak back to God.

JUDY 'J' WINSLOW

"We are forged in the fires, then molded with magic."

My deep desire is for you to understand your own power, that your thoughts are things as alive as anything you can imagine. We are energetic beings here to experiment with all that we call life. My wish is to motivate you to use your story to write an amazing adventure. You, my dear reader, can create success by design, allowing you to have all that you envision to leave a legacy that is as beautiful as you see in your mind.

ON THE OTHER SIDE OF F.E.A.R.

They say that after evading death, most are thrilled to be alive, feeling they have a new chance, a new perspective, and treasure life in a new way. But I didn't feel anything like that. Life felt meaningless. Empty. A silly chase of the "things." I was asking myself, *Why bother if we were just going to end up gone? Why strive and push only to be snuffed out faster than a candle?* No matter how much money, impact, or imprint we made on this earth, it's all gone in a second. That just felt so sad.

There I was, laying in bed, looking up at the ceiling fan spin endlessly. Covers up under my chin. I was in a *bad* place. It was one of those dark nights of the soul. I couldn't seem to pull myself out of it, even though I knew better;

after all, I had spent the last twenty-plus years learning about personal growth, which certainly changed my life in positive ways. But on that day, with the sun shining brightly through the palm trees, I saw only darkness. Something had changed inside me, and at that moment, I couldn't figure out what that was.

I dragged myself out of bed because I knew I had to, or I would continue to sink into this big murky, messy abyss.

Reading a chapter in yet another personal development book to make myself feel better left me shaking my head. It just wasn't making any sense. Have faith that all will work out... blah blah blah; come on, people, why? That felt like a *Big Lie*. Really BIG.

Then I had an idea; what if I tried an experiment? All this talk of having faith was making me have less faith. Maybe it was time to consider what could happen if I was a believer for the next six months. Starting that day, I was committed to believing everything was working out for me. That life was happening *for me* rather than *to me*, that there was some reason for this madness; that if I could hang on, I'd make some sense of it all, of this journey we call *life*.

Truthfully, I was fairly certain that nothing would come of it. Because I was quite clear that this "faith stuff" was complete and utter BS, and, in case it wasn't clear, I could have screamed: **THIS IS BULLSHIT!!!**

Man, oh, man, was I in for a ride! You may think that now I will share some wild story of how my life turned around and became perfect, but no, that didn't happen. What did happen is that it got worse before it got better. Whenever I would feel hopeless, I'd repeat to myself these mantras:

Hang in there.
Keep the faith.
Trust the path.
Use the tools you've gathered after decades of personal development work.

What may have triggered this crisis was an incident a few months prior with my parents. We had been driving down a super highway in England, called the M5, heading from London to Gatwick airport after a fantastic holiday. My dad was dozing in the front seat while my mom and I chatted away in the back. Suddenly another car nudged us from the side, and our driver tried to correct the vehicle, which sent us into a spin that lifted us off the ground and tumbling toward the median.

I remember thinking that if we crashed through the median strip and guard rail, all was over and we'd be dead. I had this flash that it didn't matter. It didn't matter how much money we had, how much we had accomplished in our lives, or even if we were good people. We would soon be gone in an instant. I turned toward my mom to protect her out of instinct, only realizing later that my glasses would lacerate her forehead, almost causing her to lose an eye.

There we were, crashing not only through the median but across the additional four lanes of traffic in the other direction. We came to an abrupt halt on the shoulder of the road with all of the glass blown out of the vehicle, tires no longer on the car, and our luggage strewn along the highway for about half a block.

It was an absolute miracle that we were alive. The adrenaline was so intense I was running along the highway, easily lifting our bulky, heavy suitcases and bringing them to the side by our car while the other three passengers stood in a glazed shock, seemingly unable to move. We were all quite shaken up, but intact. Somehow there was an "interference" that saved our lives. There was NO traffic on the four lanes we were pushed across. We were all so rattled it didn't occur to us to wonder why. Later we found out from the police that all cars had been halted for a bit because of some construction. The bit that would have killed us and who knows who else as we were tossed across those lanes. To this day, I believe Angels saved us.

Through the aftermath, I knew we were going to be okay. My dad was taken away on a stretcher, not a hair out of place—something that was VERY important to him—and we joked about it for years after, that no matter what, his precious locks were in place.

After an additional week of laying in bed at an airport hotel, I could finally sit and board a flight with my bruised body and cracked ribs. My dad had punctured a lung, so they took a cruise home to the United States because he could not fly. A brilliant idea of my mom's, it was the last cabin on this fancy transatlantic cruise ship that took about two weeks to cross the Atlantic to the U.S. Some would think a cruise is an amazing treat, but this was a medical necessity rather than a joyful event. Mostly they said they were stuck in their rooms being visited by the ship's doctors, needing to heal. All of us were discombobulated for many months following that event; our systems were in shock from the impact. There's little I recall about that trip; all I can vividly remember is the accident.

That event was twenty years ago this year. It is hard to believe how much life has happened since then. Now, I can reflect and see that, in that moment, I wasn't simply depressed as much as my internal chemistry had been deeply affected by the accident. Some "stuff" that had been dormant was activated, including some hormonal depletions and other issues that most traditional doctors don't even know how to diagnose or address.

It was my own journey through darkness and into the light that made a difference. When life feels so fragile,you think you won't emerge from it, and despair will win somehow. And it will; only if we allow it to. But, damn it, that wasn't gonna happen! I was determined to make my life mean something, if not to anyone else, then to myself!! This may not have been conscious; it may have been my natural human tendency to thrive because that *is* truly our natural state. Whatever it was, it has taken me on a fantabulous trip of a lifetime.

Years before, as a teenager, I had been ready to check out. Ironically, during those years my biggest fantasy had been a fatal car crash. Well, here I had manifested that—finally, *yet, really Universe?* The result wasn't what I had expected. It was not my time after all. This was another hint from the heavens that although I may not have been thrilled to have been spared, there was more for me here to tap into; more to contribute.

That entire experience, not only living through the accident but actually realizing what it had done to my health, became a defining chapter in my life. The aftermath of that event lasted for years; the journey wasn't a straight line, nor was the destination one I could have predicted.

Have you heard the story of the fly that was trying to get outside but was blocked by a screen on the window? He keeps hurling himself at the screen, desperately trying, again and again, to escape into the fresh air and bright blue sky. Yet, nothing is working. He is so intent on getting out, he exhausted his little self and fell to the sill. Sadly, he's unable to see that only a few feet to his right was an open door. A door that would have easily allowed him to move into the freedom and light he was so hungry to attain.

We're like that also. Science backs up this idea as well. When we are in fight or flight, *aka* problem mode, our brains constrict the blood flow, limiting access to solutions we would see if we just took a breath and thought about challenges rather than problems. Brain science indicates that we interpret each word in its own unique ways. We search for solutions like a computer rather than break down and stop. A challenge is interpreted differently than a problem, problems we want to fix; a challenge asks our computer brains to sort through various options.

Falling to the sill was what happened to me. My go-to since my late twenties, when I got immersed in personal growth, was to lean on what I had learned as a way to cope. When my system was battered and bruised like my body, I used the Faith Experiment to dig out of it. That was the challenge I assigned to myself.

It didn't really work as I would have liked. That darn metaphorical door wasn't a few feet to my right, it was years away. Through times of sickness, flashes of inspiration, and cool new projects, I began to move toward a new life, all while using the mantras mentioned above. It's been a wild and often bumpy ride, yet it's yielded so many gifts!

That same year, I graduated from a rather robust coaching program which gave me additional tools to work with. Partly, I learned I'd been a coach my entire life. My system of working with others to develop their brand didn't have a name. I thought it was entirely original, but then I discovered that in the 60s, this was coined *Creative Problem Solving* by Edward DeBono. Here I thought I was the brilliant one! It isn't exactly how I work, but its philosophies are integrated into my style of coaching and consulting.

I met new mentors, took new classes, read new books, and joined more positive communities. Each was a brick in this new house I was creating. Over time, life became full; the home and headspace where I now live.

The opportunity came for me to do some workshops and public speaking, which has been a blast. It allowed me to create *TEDxSarasota*™ and continue to work with business leaders in a new way. Combining all I've learned about design thinking, personal growth, and the joy of stepping onto our own unique path has helped me in immeasurable ways. Business owners may be the ultimate expression of faith as they step into a vision of *what can be*, expecting and knowing that they will use their instincts and guidance to get it going and be successful.

Each of us has our own mission here on earth; the question we all get to answer is, *Can we lean into our Faith to step towards that image rather than resist our divine design?* As I formulated this message for you, I got a solid download. That's when my inner voice speaks to me. It happens when I share with clients, also. Ideas and curious questions that come *through* me rather than *from* me. This time, I saw FAITH as an acronym. A word that uses each initial to mean something more. A way for each of us to be reminded of the true nature of F.A.I.T.H. Yet, I couldn't find the right way to express it.

Then, I went to a *Burning Man*™ event in Miami, Florida. These events always rock my world as they are the most creative spaces I've ever been in. Imagine thousands of people coming together in the spirit of love, creativity, and joy—a pop-up city of sorts. I sometimes describe it as Disney World™, only better and more fun. It is solely created by all the participants who attend, sharing the responsibility to generate an unforgettable atmosphere of play intertwined with education, music, and art.

One day, during the event, I took my bike out to wander around and see what was happening beyond my camp, and as I did, I could feel the love, the energy of joy, possibility, and co-creation. It was as palpable as when you walk into a meeting and know bad news is coming; something doesn't feel right. This felt as right as could be. My heart was literally FULL.

Everything suddenly clicked in. I felt warm, grounded, and clear. I've been interested in energy, vibration, and frequency for the last decade or so. My clients and I often discuss energy management and its impact on their results, how we generate with intention, manage our own energy, and how leaders affect their business, culture, and results when they are conscious of their own vibrational output.

That's when I had this awareness: **F.A.I.T.H.** is when the **F**requency is **A**ltered **I**n **T**he **H**eart, thereby changing how we radiate outwards. Like the butterfly effect, we impact the energy we emit. The signal we are now sending out is far higher. Just like listening to a new radio station, we are now tuned into one that draws what we desire to us rather than striving or pushing, or even resisting what we say we want. As the Law of Attraction states, "That which is like unto itself is drawn." At that higher frequency, anything is possible! Your life is a reflection of your energy. Stay calm. Find the fun and funny. Stop the resistance, and focus on what flow means now. Doing so in difficult moments may be difficult, but it is simple and available. Especially when we know that with this **F.A.I.T.H.** we are able to work with the energy that surrounds us all the time.

I invite you to activate your faith and begin today! This experiment could change everything for you and, consequently, the world. What a beautiful world it would be! Filled with high frequency caring souls who want each other to thrive.

Having faith isn't about God or religion, in my opinion. It's about choosing to be the leader of your own life, finding the frequency you want to embody to impact your life's experience, and leaning into your own inner awarenesses. As you move away from **F.E.A.R.** (**F**alse **E**vidence **A**ppearing **R**eal) and turn toward **F.A.I.T.H.** (**F**requency **A**ltered **I**n **T**he **H**eart), choosing to focus on the *frequency*, you will begin a new habit, form new neural pathways, and embark on creating all that you desire. Hang in there! Goodness is on the way to you! Change the frequency in your heart, and you will change your ability to succeed.

IGNITE ACTION STEPS

Do you ever wonder if you can change your own frequency? You can! It takes some practice, but it is a magic that is available to us all.

To begin: Use your own power of observation to notice how and when you speak to yourself (and others).

Notice when you are kind, notice when you are not (taking notes is helpful here).

When you are kind and loving, see if you can feel that energy. Inversely, when you are unkind and cruel, notice that energy and the frequency of that energy.

Start playing with your frequency. Identify how you'd like to radiate. Perhaps start with confidence. Practice what the energy of confidence feels like before entering a room and see if you can match that energy. Notice how others now receive you.

Once you are able to feel this vibration and SEE it in action, imagine your future self and the energy you will embody. Hold that vision in your heart and lovingly see that energy expand into the world as it expresses itself into existence.

Give yourself at least six months to try this out and see what you can create!! This is an exciting time to generate all that you desire as you *become* this new frequency on a regular basis!

Nolan Pillay

NOLAN PILLAY

*"YOU must find that place inside YOURSELF,
where nothing is IMPOSSIBLE!"*

**I want you to realize that no matter what challenge or obstacle you face in
your life, there is a reason for it. I would encourage you to use that as an
opportunity to understand *what* is happening and *why* it is happening to
you. My intention is that you don't just "*go*" through it, you allow yourself
to learn from it and "*grow*" through it!**

CLIMBING TOWARD MY PURPOSE

"What if all of you cannot hear and I am the only one who can hear—who is the
one with the disability?"

This was the question asked by the late Mrs. Deaf South Africa, Khethiwe Madi, stunning my audience and me at the relaunch of my company.
Immediately, her question touched my heart, and I felt a deep resonance and
a call to action. Was my purpose on this beautiful planet being defined right
in front of me? Surely, my belief in the power of human connection allowed
me to reach this point.

Little did I know that night would set me on a journey toward serving humanity
in a bigger way, beyond my wildest dreams.

The decision was to be the voice for the often voiceless Deaf community. During my meditations, I asked my higher purpose what I could do to serve the Deaf community. The answer was, "Find a way to give the gift of hearing to a child, allowing them to live a normal life." I was not focused on *how*; I knew something extreme and adventurous needed to be done—that would inspire others to follow.

I had an idea of what I was going to do. I wanted to climb Mount Kilimanjaro… AGAIN! I first climbed Mount Kilimanjaro in 2019 with my wife, and we reached the summit successfully. Kilimanjaro is the highest mountain in Africa, and the highest single free-standing mountain above sea level in the world, standing tall at 19,340 feet above sea level.

Back then, we raised funds for girls living in rural areas to have access to sanitary pads, which we believe should be free for every single girl who cannot afford them. I remember clearly how my Faith was tested during that climb. On a bitingly cold day, an increasing pain in my shoulder made the journey harder to achieve, yet, my mind, strength, and willpower kept me focused on my goal and allowed me to overcome the agony. Leading up to the summit during the cold, dark night, I was still unaware of what to expect. Starting the climb is something that must be done at night to endure the steepness of this gigantic mountain; if climbers see the gradient of the mountain, it could instill tremendous fear in them.

During my climb, I recall having conversations with my late Dad and Grandmother; it was like they were there with me, pulling me up the mountain and being cheerleaders along the way. It was a feeling that is hard to describe; we chatted casually, as if we were in front of each other until we made it to the summit. They made me feel protected and guided—my personal guardian angels. I was like a child, taking videos and enjoying being close to God and my other loved ones who had passed on.

The guides told us that we should be up there for a maximum of fifteen minutes, but I was able to stay for about twenty-five minutes. My wife reached the summit and I took a quick photo with her and then sent her down the mountain with the guides. Her oxygen levels were close to seventy percent at the time, a danger that could cost her life. Those are the risks one takes on this journey, but if your faith and willpower are strong enough, anyone can do it.

Thinking about Khethiwe's question, I knew what I had to do. I set out for the next climb. I decided to take seven Deaf and eight Hearing climbers up the mountain, risking our lives for a common cause. This was never going to be an easy task as I was not good at sign language. My doubts surfaced. What if a Deaf climber got into trouble? How would I be able to help them?

I spoke to a local Deaf climber and asked if I could count on him to help me, and he agreed. I also had to play my part, and decided to learn basic sign language to interact more with the Deaf community. Training together helped me connect with and better understand Deaf culture even more. My *why* drove me to make this happen; I started visualizing all climbers at the summit, celebrating our victory.

The planning stage started, and we agreed that 2021 and half of 2022 would be for training, getting climbers, sponsors, and various other activities. We decided to summit in August of 2022, a few weeks before our annual Miss., Mr., and Mrs. Deaf South Africa pageant.

Everything was going well…until I got COVID-19 in January, 2021. That was when COVID-19 was at its peak. I was admitted with fifty-eight percent oxygen levels and spent thirteen days in the intensive care unit. On day six, a doctor crying out to die received his wish; he passed on. That broke me; of course it would, I am human, after all. I called my family and told them, "I cannot go on; I cannot do this anymore." They rallied and motivated me. Telling me to be strong, don't give up, and that I would be fine. Still, I was not convinced until my daughter did something special. She sent me a picture of my 'Goal Card', something I carry with me every day in my pocket to remind me of my goals. She went on further to say, "Dad, don't forget what your purpose is!" My faith was being tested.

Facing trauma daily wasn't easy, but with my strong mindset, I focused on getting better. I felt special and needed; I knew that I had to snap out of my victim and self-pity mindset and focus on getting out of the hospital. I visualized being moved from the intensive care unit to the regular ward and eventually walking out of the hospital to our car and driving home. Unfortunately, due to COVID-19 protocol, I had to be wheeled to the awaiting car. I felt relieved, grateful, and full of bliss because I was heading home with my family.

My discharge condition was that I needed to be on oxygen 24/7, I agreed as I knew it would help me breathe better. When I got home, I started to walk around the yard, smelling the freshness of the trees, getting my oxygen from them, and grounding myself as much as possible. After two weeks, I called the oxygen company and told them to collect the oxygen bottle and give it to someone who needed it. "I will be fine," I told them; I was getting stronger.

Throughout my COVID-19 experience, canceling the climb never crossed my mind; it was not an option. The only difference was I needed to work harder to get my strength back and improve my breathing. I lost just over twenty-two pounds in total. As much as I was loving the look of my six-pack, I had overcome the worst.

During my time in the hospital, around day seven, I did a video message which I shared on social media, encouraging people to look after themselves, and also to inspire them. The video was recorded in snippets of fifty seconds due to my constant battling to breathe. Two friends saw the video and told me, "Nolan, the world needs your story."

Guess what? That painful experience, which taught me how to value life even more, became a success story, and my book, *My Covid Journey*, made me a first time author. My intention was to help anyone who'd lost a loved one because of COVID-19, and allow them to realize what a COVID-19 patient goes through. I also wanted to encourage individuals to reach peace and closure, and share mindhacks and techniques that anyone can use to conquer any challenges they might face.

Three months after leaving the hospital I was walking over three miles per day. My breathing improved, and I was back to healthy eating habits. I learned so much more about who I am as a person. The love and support I received while being in the hospital blew my mind away. People from around the globe told me they were doing healing prayers for me. I was so grateful to everyone who took the time to pray and send healing energies toward me. *Thank you, I love you all.*

Throughout that experience, I never lost sight of the climbing challenge, now called *Climb4TheDeaf*. By then, our team of fifteen climbers had been reduced to seven, fiveDeaf and two Hearing climbers, including me. I felt sad that the hearing climbers had withdrawn from an opportunity to connect with our Deaf community. We kept our training schedules and got in touch with sponsors. The momentum had picked up a lot, and everyone was ready to reach their dreams.

In December 2021, again, my faith was called to the test! I was struggling to breathe and decided to get a checkup at the hospital. When I got there, I told them, "I think there is a problem with my lungs." They did some checks and called the doctor, who informed me that I had a mild heart attack and they needed to clear out the blocked arteries immediately. It took three stents to remove the blockages. I had to stay for two days under observation. My family had been through a lot that year, and we decided that we would stay home in December, just bonding together. Overall, I was grateful for life, and knew God was sending me a message; that I still had work to do, but my purpose had not yet been fulfilled.

With nine months until the climb, I needed to get my breathing back to normal, and focus on the sponsors and the climbers; there was so much more still to do. There was no turning back. My belief that we *could* and *would* do this drove me even more. I knew so many people relied on my strength, and I couldn't let them or myself down. More so, the five Deaf climbers had been training and were already on a mighty high, waiting to achieve something that, for most people, seemed impossible. As much as we all wanted to climb Mount Kilimanjaro, the truth was that each one of us was actually climbing our own personal mountains as well. We had to dig deep within ourselves, programming our subconscious minds and visualizing being on top of the mountain. I kept motivating the team, making them realize they were powerful beyond measure.

During the next few months, I decided I needed to focus on myself as I had a lot on my shoulders, taking it one day at a time. Keeping in mind why we were putting our lives at risk. The children born Deaf needed to live normal lives, and they were counting on us.

The day had arrived. We departed South Africa on the 20th of August, 2022, got to Tanzania, spent Sunday night at a local hotel, and started our climb on Monday. The weather was in our favor, with no snow or rain in sight. As we headed through the rainforest, we experienced a slight drizzle, but the beauty of the forest kept our minds busy, breathing the green atmosphere surrounding us.

The next few days were great for bonding. We had a few uncomfortable situations, yet we knew we needed each other more than ever. Then came summit night, the plan was to start the summit at 11 PM. Bear in mind the distance from the Kibo base camp to the summit is around four miles, so it takes about eleven hours to reach the summit.

Personally, that was a challenge and a test of my body and mind. I knew my mind was strong, but my breathing started to take a toll around the 16,000 feet mark. I could feel that my body had enough, I needed to listen to it, otherwise I could put my life in danger.

I did not listen!

I continued and reached the 17,000 feet marker. I could not make it any further this time, so I called the chief guide over. We chatted, and he asked me if I was sure; I said, "Yes, I am." I went on to say, "The mountain will always be here." But this time, my life was more important. Meanwhile, two other climbers faced altitude sickness and stopped their journey. I told the chief guide, "There are four climbers left; please take them to the summit, but promise if anyone is not feeling well, please advise them to come down. The foundation will not risk anyone's life if we see that they are struggling."

Back at the cabin, exhausted, tired, and emotionally drained because I had to cut my climb short, I could not close my eyes. I kept thinking about the four climbers and praying that they could reach the summit. I got a call from the chief guide saying they all made it and were coming back down. I was excited and relieved that all went well. I closed my eyes to get a few hours of sleep before we took the long trek back to Horombo hut. The rest of the journey went well. Back at the hotel, we handed out the certificates to all climbers; it was a successful climb for all of us. The next day we headed back to South Africa.

The journey has not ended. We set out to climb this massive mountain to raise funds to give the gift of hearing to a child born Deaf and create awareness around the challenges our Deaf community faces daily.

A week later, we attended the Miss., Mr., and Mrs. Deaf South Africa pageant to hand over a check that will be used for the "Bridging the Gap" workshops together with our foundation. These workshops bring hearing and Deaf people together to socialize and understand each other more. I learned from a few hearing people that it's not that they don't want to communicate with the Deaf community; it is that they don't know how.

The most rewarding phase of that beautiful journey happened when I got an email from the Foundation for Children with Hearing Loss manager saying that they had two donors, a seven and fifteen-year-old, who were desperate for hearing aids. I had goosebumps and started to feel anxious. It was the most exciting part of our *Climb4TheDeaf Challenge*. My heart was beating much faster, knowing that what we put out into the Universe was finally becoming a reality. Our faith and belief in achieving what once was impossible was undeniable! We watched the recording of the first implant with tears running down our cheeks, delighted that we gifted a seven-year-old the ability to hear for the first time in her life.

A week later, I had a similar email inviting us to witness the hearing aid fitting for Kwazi, a fifteen year-old-girl who was blossoming into her teenage life. What we saw will live in our hearts forever. I get emotional as I relate that experience to you even now. Once the hearing aid was fitted, her reaction was immediate and we saw it when she quickly turned to her mother and said, "I can hear you!" We all burst into tears; such a heartwarming Ignite Moment to enjoy; a child hearing for the first time in fifteen years! We will do this repeatedly just to see that magical smile on a child's face; it is priceless. Kwazi opened up her heart and explained that because of her hearing disability, she was bullied at school. I decided to start coaching Kwazi. She tells me that her confidence has grown and the bullying is not as bad. Even her teachers understand her better now—she wants to become a lawyer.

Surviving COVID-19 and climbing the majority of that glorious mountain nine months after having three stents in my heart showed me that my *Faith* and *Belief* will never let me down. The key is *having* Faith in a Higher Purpose and acknowledging that nothing is impossible.

Remember that everything starts with a thought when you decide to do anything in life. When you take that thought and attach it to an emotion, it pushes you to take inspired action. Whatever mountain you might be climbing, allow yourself to surrender and receive guidance from above. Let faith be your compass and belief be your guide, and trust that they will show you the divine way.

IGNITE ACTION STEPS

- **Find your Purpose** - Go back to your values and find what relates to you at this moment. Every painful moment or obstacle could be your sign to finding your purpose.

- **Connect to your Purpose** - Do a short meditation, connect to your Higher Purpose/Spirit Guides/God/Angels or any Higher Power you are comfortable with, and ask deep questions about your purpose.

- **Take Inspired Action Steps** - Write down all the steps you would need to take to transform your purpose into a reality. A few examples of mine were learning basic sign language, training with the team, creating a mental image of the outcome, creating an intention statement, and focusing on the *why*.

- **Contribution to Humanity** - Ask yourself, how is your purpose contributing to Humanity? You should be feeling excited that you are making a difference to another life. In the process, you awakened your true potential; you have found that place inside yourself where nothing is IMPOSSIBLE!

Nicole Shantel Freeman

NICOLE SHANTEL FREEMAN

"Trust the plan and process even when you cannot see the path."

My intention is to support you toward pivoting when what you envisioned doesn't align with God's plan. I am sharing my story to offer hope, encouragement, and support for you to move forward in the midst of chaos and despair. Embrace and enjoy the beauty in the journey by surrendering to God. God doesn't make mistakes, and He makes all things a masterpiece. When you find yourself in a place of hopelessness, hold onto the truth, and please know that I hear you, I see you, and I stand with you.

OWNING MY PART

I was completely blindsided. I sat in the doctor's office on that cold, rainy day and heard the nurse say, "Nicole, you are pregnant." I nearly fell onto the floor in disbelief. What was supposed to be a joyous occasion turned out to be one of the most devastating traumatic events of my life. As a forty-year-old single mother of a teenager, and a leader at church excited about ministry, finding out I was pregnant was not only embarrassing but also shameful.

Dang, it happened again; I was having another child without being married. What will people say? Am I a hypocrite? How will I afford to take care of another child? Am I too old? Those were just some of the questions that ran rampant in my head. I began to not only weep but wail, with a pain that went all the way down to my core. As though there was no hope in sight; I felt a soul-crushing feeling of failure in the pit of my stomach. I felt like I disappointed God, my teenage daughter, the church, and myself. I cried so much that the nurse grabbed a chair, sat beside me, and simply held me. She stated that this pregnancy may have taken me by surprise, but not God. At that point, I cried even more with anger toward God. I thought to myself, *God, you could have stopped this; you could have caused the sperm to miss the egg (*yes, I know, that's a bit much; I did have a little something to do with getting pregnant)! But, I wanted to feel like God, in some way, had my back.

As I sat in my car and the rain beat against the window, I wondered how my life was going to look: how it was going to change, how I was to share my love between 2 children, and how I would afford a baby. As the days went by I began to think of a plan. I thought about having an abortion because that way no one would have to know. My life would not have to change and I could pretend everything was fine. The only problem with that was I am pro-life. I have always referred to children as blessings, and there I was, contemplating aborting that blessing. Did I really want to get rid of my baby just because of embarrassment, guilt, and shame? No, of course not. I made the decision to go through with my pregnancy and have my blessing despite the emotions tugging at me from every direction. Huddled on the painfully cold floor of my tiny bathroom closet, I cried out to God in desperation for his forgiveness; for him to take the emotional pain away; for him to change my situation.

Yet, my pregnancy continued, and I was forced to come to terms with stepping down from the positions I held in the church. I leaned on the faith I had in the relationship with my boyfriend. I envisioned us catering to each other's emotional and spiritual needs as our child was developing. I anticipated us laughing and giggling when we would feel the fluttering kicks and see the weird shapes from the tumbling somersaults of the baby's ultrasound. I visualized us browsing the baby aisles and creating a mile-long wishlist of necessary things. I imagined us attending informative birthing classes and playfully picking baby names.

Then came that gut-wrenching feeling again. I was hit with the realization that my boyfriend didn't want to marry me just because I was pregnant. We had been dating on and off again for almost five years so when he told me that marriage was off the table, I was overtaken by my steaming emotions. I became enraged. I mean, I was livid. And in that moment, my faith in our relationship completely disappeared. I became deaf to his explanations. I simply could not understand his reasoning, or I did not want to understand his reasoning because I was not getting what I desired: a marriage to the man I knew was destined to be my husband. I couldn't come to grips with this truth and became so frustrated that I began to lash out at him in every conversation. I treated him so harshly that he broke off the relationship with me. I assumed he couldn't handle my cruel treatment any longer. The feeling in my very pregnant stomach was overwhelming as I felt he was abandoning me.

My heart was deeply damaged, like someone reached into my chest and savagely ripped it out. I had never felt heartbreak like that in my life. The emotions of abandonment, betrayal, and rejection rolled out like a flood. I was dumped by the man I thought was destined to be my husband. I was dumped by the one person I thought loved me. *How could he do this to me? How could he abruptly walk away from this relationship? How could he desert me while I was caring for his child? Oh my, will that horrible, hurtful feeling in my heart ever leave?*

With my oldest daughter graduating eighth grade, and my baby showing up as a bump under my clothes, I distinctly remember hearing God say to me, "I have graced you for the journey." Little did I know what I was about to embark upon: the unplanned pregnancy, the fact that every prenatal appointment came with a reminder that I was high risk because of my age, feeling on display for being pregnant and not married, and the recent breakup from the father of my unborn child. I didn't realize and couldn't see that I had turned into an unrecognizable, bitter, angry victim. I never thought about what my ex must have been going through and how my ugly attitude was affecting him. My only thoughts were that *I am pregnant and alone, and God doesn't care.*

Looking back, I can see that I was not alone, and God is faithful. But seeing is much harder with tears in your eyes. I cried all day, every day. I still don't know how I functioned because I cried at work, I cried in the carpool lane, I cried while cooking, I cried in the shower, I cried myself to sleep—I cried all the time. I cried because I wanted my relationship mended. I wanted my ex there, to go through my pregnancy together. My sister told me she could hear my heartache when I cried; it was more than crying—it was the sound of someone who was genuinely heartbroken and hopeless. My sister would always say, "Nicole, your story will become a testimony to bless others." At the time, all I could think was, *Girl; I don't wanna hear that!*

While I was feeling despondent, depressed, and weighed down by my pregnancy, my vehicle malfunctioned three times in a span of two months. The third and final time, with tears rolling down my face, I screamed to God in frustration, aggravation, and anger, "God, do you not see me? Do you not see that I am very pregnant in the scorching heat, and my car has stopped on me again? What is going on?" I started coming apart spiritually, emotionally, and mentally as if I was mimicking my broken relationship through my vehicle. I chose to concentrate on everything going on around me as opposed to having faith in God's Word. I chose to focus on the collapse of my relationship, and my disabled vehicle. At that point, I was ready to end it all. I became so depleted; I felt weak like a brown paper bag blowing in the wind and thought maybe I shouldn't carry on. I wanted desperately to escape from all of it, my pregnancy, my heartache, my vehicle, and my responsibilities. I was torn between love and anger for my ex-boyfriend mixed with guilt and shame. I wanted relief. It felt like the pain and weight of the world would never ease up on me, and I struggled to see the lifeline I felt God was hiding from me.

My support system kept me encouraged in any way they could. Though some days it seemed like empty words, they held me when I couldn't hold myself. What I didn't know was that God was holding me, also.

God began speaking to me about conducting Bible study. I was so upset because I was trying my best to hold it together for my teenage daughter and at my job. It was extremely difficult because I couldn't stop thinking about the fact that I was forty years old, single, and pregnant. I was feeling regret and embarrassment. I was so focused on the high-risk pregnancy, the vehicle, the relationship, and like everyone else, COVID-19.

When I first learned of COVID-19, I was in disbelief. I felt like I was in a suspenseful horror movie. There was that excruciating pain in my stomach again. As my eyes welled up with tears, I looked up at heaven and said, "What in the world is going on?" It took every fiber of my being to picture God as bigger than COVID-19. I had to muster up the strength that I didn't know existed in me so as not to lose my mind and be present for my daughter and baby. I was bombarded with so many negative thoughts running wildly through my head. I stood in the middle of my living room floor and felt water drops on my feet, not realizing that tears were rolling off my cheeks. I was trying not to cry, but the tears kept flowing. My emotions were all over the place as I thought to myself: *I am seriously afraid. I don't know what to do. I am pregnant. I can't let my emotions affect the baby or allow my teenage daughter to see me in a panic. Lord, I need you!*

And… that is when He spoke back to me! God enveloped my heart and gripped my spirit with the message; *You need to conduct a Bible study.* Despite my desperation, my anxieties telling me to run away, and the reservations that I wasn't strong enough, I surrendered and said, *Okay, God… yes!*

The Lord's theme of my Bible study was *Faith Over Fear*. I began researching scriptures on faith, and as I thought through those powerful words, my eyes
finally began to open. My ears finally began to hear again. The blinkers finally
came off, and I noticed when I took my eyes off of Jesus and lost my faith in
God. I struggled when things didn't look like what I thought they should and
my situations seemed too big to handle. I soon realized that Bible study was
meant to help activate *my* faith. I was so consumed with looking at my situation
negatively I did not realize that God was trying to help me. He wanted me to
recognize His love and see Him in everything.

I felt like God left me, like he didn't care about me. But the truth was that God
was with me the whole time. He was showing up for me by having my ex show up
for me. My ex would graciously offer to support me periodically throughout the day
while maintaining his job, managing *his* emotions, and dealing with my selfish anger
toward him. Each time he reached out to me, he was met with bitterness, rage, and
anger. It seemed that the nicer he would be, the meaner I would become. I could not
understand why we couldn't get back together and do things as a couple. This notion
plagued me. Yet he kept showing up. He bought everything I needed in my house for
our unborn baby. He not only bought the baby's crib, but the extremely expensive
one that I so badly desired. He bought the stroller, car seat, and many other needed
items. Not only did he buy them, he came over and assembled them as well. He was
doing the Lord's work in the best way he could.

God revealed Himself also in the intimate moments with my teenage daughter.
God gave me quality time with her throughout the pandemic. We would go on
breathtaking walks in our neighborhood while the sun delivered a light that was so
inviting. We would spend countless hours on the couch binge-watching movies.
Many times we just sat and reminisced about great times we had shared; other
times, we would just be silly, telling jokes that didn't make sense, and laughing
at our goofy selves. We danced, baked, made music videos, and we made the
most out of COVID-19. God was with me in spite of my horrible attitude. He
still loved me despite my anger and victim mentality. God's love is truly unconditional, unfathomable, and unimaginable. God never left me; the truth was He
was loving, protecting, and guiding me the whole time.

Things started looking brighter once I relinquished control and waved the
white flag, and activated my faith in God by looking up at Jesus and trusting His
way, His plan, His process, and His timing. It's like I could actually hear God
say, "Nicole, how long will you mourn that relationship?" I pondered on that for
a few days. Then I was reminded of the scripture when the Lord asked Samuel,
"How long will you mourn Saul… Fill your horn with oil and be on your way."

That hit me like a ton of bricks. Basically, I had been mourning a relationship that the Lord had denied at that time.

It was time for me to dry my tears and MOVE FORWARD. And that's what I did. I repented to the Lord for being angry with Him. I started journaling and had a healing conversation with myself for holding on to something that was no longer serving me. I enrolled into therapy and got a personal trainer to assist me with my healing journey. I finally made the life-changing decision to surrender to God. I shifted my focus onto Him and His Word and not on my current situation as a single mom of two daughters. I did an exercise to help me with my process; I had a funeral for that relationship. I took a moment to visualize myself dressed in black from head to toe. I wore an oversized black hat, huge black sunglasses, a black form-fitting, sheath dress, and a pair of black ankle strap stilettos. As I stood confidently over the grave marked with our names, the sun beamed down on me ever so brightly; I gently placed a dozen beautiful red roses on the grave that held my dead relationship and forgave both of us. At that moment, I realized that I had finally released that relationship, the good, the bad, the ugly, all of it, that had been dead for almost two years.

Forgiveness is truly transformative, and I can attest to that from personal experience. The exercise I went through was nothing short of empowering; it ignited a spark within me that had been dormant for far too long. Even though my situation hadn't changed, I had. I began to feel strong, confident, powerful, and fearless; like I could conquer anything that came my way. I was grateful to God for this newfound joy and happiness that I felt deep within my soul. People could see the transformation in me, and it was amazing to be able to share that positivity with others. Whenever I felt lost, I would reach out to my sister, friend, or therapist, and they would help me regain my focus and redirect my eyes to God. I was determined to keep celebrating my progress and moving forward with my two children by my side.

My life was far from what I had envisioned, but somehow I am hopeful and enjoying it! As my ex and I began co-parenting our baby daughter, we developed a cordial relationship. I can recall one day asking him to engage in a conversation with me, and he humbly agreed. As I began to speak, I was greeted by a huge lump in my throat because I didn't know if he would receive what I had to offer. As I sat there, I looked him in his eyes and warmly placed my hand on his hand, and began to say, "I apologize for my awful attitude, treatment, and words toward you while you were only attempting to support me through my pregnancy." We both began to cry as I asked him, "What were your feelings during those times? How did you endure my brutal attacks?" He explained his experience, and I heard him with both ears and my whole heart.

Our conversations from that point onward were open, connected, and compassionate. We grew in friendship. We let go of who we used to be and allowed ourselves to become who we are today. I became a woman who trusted God amid chaos, gave grace to myself as well as others, and listened as opposed to demanding my way. Ecclesiastes 3:11 states that God makes all things beautiful in his timing, and that's exactly what happened with my ex and I. God resurrected a dead, messy, ugly relationship and miraculously turned it into a beautiful masterpiece. Above all, I opened my heart to own my part in it all, so I could trust the process and have faith as I awakened God's presence in me.

IGNITE ACTION STEPS

Here are action steps that I implemented to activate my faith and I believe they will help you on your faith journey:

- **Fixate on God:** As you surrender to God, His plan for your life and His timing, you will notice a shift in your perspective. Keeping your eyes on Jesus will bring you peace.

- **Forgiveness:** Forgiveness allows you to gain control of your life. It releases you from the hurt and pain to allow you to move forward with ease.

- **Gratitude:** Practicing gratitude will help you gain a more appreciative perspective on life and promote your emotional well-being.

- **Journaling:** Journaling is a powerful tool for your emotional health. As you are journaling your thoughts, feelings, and daily activities, this process is helping you gain insight, self-awareness, and personal growth.

- **Give Yourself Grace:** Be kind to yourself. Practice self-love. Celebrate yourself. Remember, it's a marathon, not a sprint.

Lea Barber

LEA BARBER

"Flow with life's goodbyes and show up in the hellos."

It is my hope for you to see, feel, and experience all of the beautiful messages around you. A whisper in your ear, tickling you to say, "I have never left you; I am here! Keep showing up, darling; the world needs your light." Embody your faith; allow its essence and presence to illuminate your path into purposeful movement. This is where change can take place, and bold steps can happen. This is where songs can be heard and felt in every cell of your being. This is where rainbows appear; birds can *caw*, and feathers land. My wish is this: May you find your rainbows, experience the whispers, and dance in joy and reverence to the songs our souls sing to one another... in this life and beyond.

FEATHERS OF FAITH

As she took her last breath, I held mine. Her last breath was stuck in my own throat. Overwhelmed by the sensation, I left the room and went to the rooftop garden at the Hospice; gasping for air, tears streaming from my bloodshot eyes. My body was trembling with grief, and something caught my eye and ear. "CAWWW, CAWWW!" A black crow perched itself right in front of me, its call piercing through my being.

Persistent in getting my attention, an unexpected roar of laughter exited my body. Suspended at that moment, my stepdad joined me, and we both laughed through our tears as I spewed out, "An old crow! She's back, so soon, as an old crow!"

Three and a half years before my mom left the earth, I was excitedly awaiting the arrival of my first baby. On that particular September day, my mom was on her way to purchase a plane ticket to be present at his birth. As she left the house and was driving to the travel agency, a sudden burst of sneezes exited her body. On the tenth sneeze, pain began to permeate her chest, and she knew she needed to seek medical help. Faced with the choice to continue driving forty-five minutes to the hospital or stop at the ambulance rest stop, she courageously chose to keep driving. Once arriving at the hospital emergency room, she was ushered swiftly to surgery and the Intensive Care Unit. Her lungs had collapsed.

The day she got out of the ICU was when I gave birth to my son, and I could finally speak to her on the telephone. That moment was a blessing, and yet more news was to follow. Her lung collapsing gave us more information: Mom had lung cancer. The cancer was removed during the surgery, however, my mom was not quite right.

After a few months of my mom not feeling herself, I traveled with my newborn to Victoria, British Columbia, to be with her and allow my son time to know his Nana. Shortly before Christmas, we sat in the doctor's office together and were gut punched with the news, "Christine, you need to get your affairs in order. You have aggressive metastatic brain tumors and, without radiation, a possible three weeks to live." In true Mom style, she lifted her chin and said, "Screw that! I got grandchildren to be with."

I packed up and moved to Victoria, 4,000 kilometers away, in order to be present and close to my mom on her transitional journey from this life to the next. One day while taking the bus to be with her, I stopped at a mall and found a music box set with a beautiful picture of a dove on it. Inside was a CD containing a beautiful song composed from the poem "The Serenity Prayer." I took it to my mom, aunt, and sisters and requested that when she took her last breaths, she would cross over with music. We made a CD of "I Believe in Angels," "Morning Has Broken," and "Serenity Prayer." We knew she was hearing those precious words while they carried her to the *higher side of life*.

As my mother's child, I had been allowed to make peace with our goodbye. My son Spencer was not given the same gift. The day she passed was the only day in those three and a half years he did not come to visit his Nana; I thought

I was protecting him. Perhaps, I was protecting myself. In any case, there was my little boy who didn't get the opportunity to speak his goodbye on the day he lost his Nana.

After I moved back to Toronto, he was struggling emotionally, so much so that one day I asked him in exasperation, "What is WRONG?" He looked right into my eyes and said, "You never let me say goodbye to Nana." He was right, and I knew he deserved that closure one way or another, and I knew I had to act immediately. "We're going to pretend Nana is here," I said lovingly, asking him what he would say to her knowing she was going to die. He replied, "Nana, I love you; I'm going to miss you." I transcribed the words coming from his three-and-a-half-year-old heart, creating a love letter to his Nana. Then we walked to the store, got a helium balloon, and tied his note to Nana onto the string. We walked hand in hand to the schoolyard, and he folded his hands to say a prayer. Then he sent the balloon flying up to Heaven. I was a puddle, convulsing as I wept. But he simply said with an exuberant tone, "Okay, Mom! I'm ready to go play now." In an instant, he turned my tears into joy.

The joy would multiply for me with the birth of my second child. By this point, I was settling into a thriving career, working my way up into senior management. I was living a life of fulfillment when one day, my body spoke. I arrived at work and suddenly found myself in the parking lot, too paralyzed to get out of my car. As I rubbed my hand over my head, I felt an unexpected patch of balding, the size of a prune, at the nape of my hairline. Simultaneously, I heard the radio playing one of my mom's favorite Rod Stewart songs and started crying inconsolably. I decided at that moment I must take action and make an appointment with my doctor.

The 'angel' nudging happened to be divine timing as my doctor was retiring the following week! He was concerned about my thyroid feeling slightly enlarged, so he set me up very quickly with an ultrasound. My whirlwind started. The ultrasound was followed quickly by a biopsy which then led me to see a specialist and a surgeon. Two surgeries and iodine radiation to abate any lingering… cancer. Yes, I had cancer. I was told I had good CANCER; what does that even mean? Did they know my mom died of cancer?

I was caught in an inner wave of anger, sadness, and confusion. I put on my armor, a mask, in hopes no one would glimpse the fear that was crashing inside of me. I was trying to cope with the inner conflict of emotions that were wrestling for a voice, for an outlet. This was the beginning of a turbulent time. I was becoming a passenger on a speeding train, not really aware yet of my destination.

As I entered the room at the hospital, ready to receive iodine radiation, my eyes were fixated on all the tactile objects in the room covered in plastic. Every door knob, fixture, and even the phone was covered in what looked like saran wrap. The nurse who came into the room only entered as far as the bold line taped on the floor. She began to speak, informing me no one would enter my room until the radiation was low enough for their safety. If I threw up or made a mess, it would remain in the room until they were safe to come in. My ears stopped listening, my body froze with fear, and I was imagining vomiting and the pressure of this, causing me to pee my pants. I wondered if I should sit on the toilet to puke so I could vomit in a bucket and pee at the same time. I was literally planning my process to avoid a mess in the room and soiling my clothes. All the "just in case moments" a person could conceptualize entered my tired, scared head, but I was also filled with resolve. The trick to getting out of the hospital was to drink massive amounts of water to wash the radiation out of my body. I was ready; I had my plan mapped out. I was a competitive winner in my mind, and I put on my "I got this!" mask. A doctor, fully covered in astronaut gear, opened a metal dome-shaped container containing the pill I was to swallow. It was passed to me with great big steel tongs. How powerful is this little pill? No one could enter the room; I was to be left completely alone!

But was I alone? The next two days were a journey of prayer and fragility. I was feeling lonely but never really alone. In the middle of the night, my stomach was twisting and twirling as I was overwhelmed with nausea. Feeling excruciating pain in my tummy, I rang for the nurse to bring me medication, but my persistent ringing was ignored. I fell in and out of a sleep state, yet I felt I had moved outside my body, watching myself from above. I sat with God and the angels while coming in and out of this life and a higher dimension of creation. I pleaded with God, the guides, my ancestors, and my mom to help me out of this situation. I heard them gently whisper, "Keep drinking your water, dear one." I awoke to a nurse throwing an anti-nausea pill under the door. I gave a small thank you of gratitude. Under the surface of my thanks was also a whimper; a cry for my slipping dignity as I picked up the pill off the floor and guzzled it down with more water.

The speeding train kept going, and as it rolled on, I felt compelled to lean into my faith and follow my inner guidance. Me, my partner and my children were all impacted. I was in hormonal, emotional, and spiritual chaos. Movement was needed, and as a result, I separated from my then-partner, quit my job, went back to school and had to show up in advocacy for my daughter who was in dire need of support during this tumultuous time. Vertigo sent my body spinning faster than a roller coaster. It left me laying in bed for days, unsure when the dizziness would end. I breathed into faith, leaned into Spirit and asked for guidance… no… *pleaded* for guidance. I flowed with the goodbyes and then boldly showed up for the hellos of new beginnings.

My last child, Mckenzie, was born when I entered my forties and had reconciled with my husband, fifteen-plus years after my Spencer sprang into this world. Without a doubt, I knew my mom was still supporting me and my family. In the first week at home with my new daughter, one night, I purposefully and thoughtfully decided to put the bassinet at the head of the bed. Always being someone who is self-aware and safety oriented, the placement of the bassinet was important. That particular night I was sleep deprived, and once my head hit the pillow, I was out like a light. I woke up hours later, and my little one was not in the bassinet and not snuggled closely near my heart. I panicked and called out to my husband. I shifted my body to get a better look across the bed. I saw her, my precious baby, perfectly swaddled in a blanket I didn't recognize. Seeing the blanket and, more importantly, *how* she was wrapped, made me burst into tears. It was the same way Mom swaddled Spencer when he was a newborn. I faithfully believe my mom held a safe space that night. I pulled my baby into my arms and held her snugly to me.

My friend Shannon was arriving that same morning for breakfast. As I pulled on a sweater I hadn't worn in months (if not a year), there on the front, right where my heart resides, was a white feather. A feather, perfectly woven into my sweater by the sharp edge of its quill.

When Shannon walked in, her first words were, "Lea, on my way here, your mom's song was on the radio, and I felt her presence with me. Then when I looked at my passenger seat, a feather was on it!" She went to the car to retrieve the feather; it was gone. That is when I saw a new feather land right at the foot of my front door.

I shared with Shannon the story of my night, about finding Mckenzie swaddled the way Mom used to do it. We shared many stories about our connection with Spirit and our loved ones who have died. We laughed and cried together while reminiscing and re-telling how their love shines through the mediums of music, nature, and feathers. I knew through the signs my mom was with me. *Lea, trust what you can't see. Be bold!* Her strength was mine; her vulnerability was mine. Unexpected help always arrived when needed. That was my test of trust and faith.

I am often in awe and wonder at all the messages of hope, love, and faith that surround us. As EE Cummings wrote, "The eyes of my eyes are open."

Happily, my partner and I had reunited our relationship before having our last child. We had a beautiful wedding ceremony in our home. Our officiant, my mentor, and friend, asked for a book we had in common. The only book my husband reads and loves is the Bible. I searched for one and discovered an old box of memorabilia from my mom. To my surprise, a small Bible in a handcrafted white case was inside the box. Inscribed inside of that Bible was my mom's handwriting,

"To Lea Marie, For you on your wedding day."

As a sacred gesture and heartfelt symbol, the officiant placed our vows and the script of our ceremony as a keepsake of our day between the pages next to her loving message.

As my husband and I said our vows and signed the marriage certificate, the doorbell rang… a delivery my husband had ordered months prior and forgotten about. We were all in total disbelief as we unwrapped the package, for it was The Holy Bible.

That, too, was a sign of the energy flowing between him and I, the energy flowing from God to us, and from my mom to our family. Despite the fact we had said our goodbyes, I felt her presence as if she was saying a cheeky hello. I began to see all the new beginnings. I was able to walk into a new blessed experience with my husband and family.

I acknowledge that flow does not always equate to smoothness. However, I knowingly leaned into my grief and sadness and flowed with the many good-byes. My senses percolated in the hellos, and felt the sweetness of tickles on my ear. My eyes have seen the magic and mystery of the divine and Spirit. I am humbled that I can share my journey with my mom, who has left the earth, yet hasn't left my heart.

Allow faith to illuminate through the cracks if and when you find yourself in the dark corners. Remind yourself that you, too, are meant to shine. You are connected to that same Universal Source. We are all rooted in love and connection. Grace gives us permission to re-direct and fall. Faith gives us that hug to move forward. I embrace all the messages around me. Give gratitude and thanks for the songs that touch your soul, the rainbows after the storm, and the feathers that appear to remind you of your FAITH.

Ignite Action Steps

Get into the flow:
Move your body. Turn up your favorite song and allow your body to dance, move, and flow with the rhythm. Tap your body, wave your arms, and swing your hips. Move freely around your space. Glide and move at your own pace. Allow yourself the freedom to just flow.

Take a breath:
Just breathe; pay attention to when you hold your breath, and when you release a breath. Follow your natural rhythm of breath. I often would hold my breath when stressed, scared, or in pain. The easiest way for me to get my breath moving was to put on a song and just burst it out of my body like I was the lead singer. This was my starting point for inhaling and exhaling. I could then readily move on to guided breathing exercises.

Say goodbye:
Write a letter to whom you want to say goodbye, and give yourself permission to say everything in your heart. Sit with yourself and hold a loving space for your connection. Perhaps write a love letter to yourself, letting go and releasing parts of you that no longer serve your highest good. When finished, hold a burning bowl ceremony.

Say hello:
Don't be afraid to step into new opportunities, activities, and perspectives. Say hello to new thoughts, as you become more and more open to self-discovery; boldly say hi to the newness that shows up for you! Embrace the presence of others, and the lessons they may teach you. Allow yourself to notice and feel the message of music and nature. Become open to new beginnings with a welcome Hello!

Makenzie Elliott

Makenzie Elliott

"Rest in knowing that your identity is in Jesus."

If I could, I would stand on top of the tallest building in the world, for every person to be able to hear, and the only thing I would shout is, "Jesus loves you!" That's the passion I have when it comes to knowing Jesus and wanting to share what He has done in my life. As you read my story, my wish for you is that you would feel bold enough to take a step toward Jesus. You were meant to be in relationship with Him and He longs to have a place in your heart.

Where I Belong

Everyone seems to have a big moment in their life that essentially changes everything for them—but what if you feel like you never had that big life-changing moment? *Hi, that's me.* Let me tell you a little bit about myself growing up. I was born in Orlando, Florida, which I take huge pride in, but I have lived in Maryland for most of my life. I am the oldest child in a family of five; my support system and my source of love for as long as I can remember. My family was where I belonged from the very beginning, despite the fact I didn't always have the same last name as my parents. As a child that was something I had always wondered about, but thankfully by age fourteen, it was no longer in question. The man who raised me, nurtured me, and was my father in every sense of the word, was able to legally "adopt" me, and finally all five of us in my family had the same last name.

Another person who has always meant so much to me is my Nana. One of the things I can remember most about my childhood is spending the night at her house on certain weekends, which also meant attending church with her on Sundays. I specifically remember looking forward to our Saturday evening ritual of her helping me decide what dress to wear. Church itself was also something that I would look forward to, but only if I was in a good mood. I never really understood what was being said, but I enjoyed singing the songs and sitting with her. I was using my little voice to send praises for Jesus, knowing there was something special about it, but I had no idea *what that special thing was* at the time.

When I wasn't spending the night with Nana, I was in school during the week and at cheer practice in the evenings. Cheer is something I started at a very young age, and it was a way I could let loose and do something I thought was fun. There was just something about feeling weightless and free as I was thrown up into the air and the support of being caught and wrapped in my teammates' arms. I was lifting my voice up to praise people, which felt good.

It wasn't until high school that I discovered that support wasn't always there in the ways that mattered to me. High school can be a scary place where you try to figure out who you are and where you belong. I thought I belonged with my cheer teammates. I looked forward to gathering as a team for practice at the end of every school day. I felt a part of something important. As a cheerleader in my freshman and sophomore years, attention was on me as I was one of the flyers being held up in the air. Every Friday I was in a little uniform in front of half the school at football games. People sort of knew who I was, but that didn't make finding my identity any easier. I began to recognize I didn't mean as much to the team as I thought I did, and my sense of belonging shifted. I was never the best one on the team and cheer eventually became routine for me. Something that seemed so fun at one point turned into a lot of drama, getting picked on because of the people I associated with, and cheer became something I no longer wanted to be a part of. I did not feel good enough as a cheerleader or as a person. I felt angry that people had the nerve to care about my life so much when my life had nothing to do with them.

I quickly learned that friends come and go in high school. No matter how much drama I tried to avoid, it didn't help; haters and enemies somehow always existed. Once I realized my identity wasn't in having a lot of friends, I turned my focus toward something new. I learned I could get attention, and what I thought was love, from boys. I was never part of the popular group at school, but one thing was for sure, I always had a boyfriend. Putting my identity in having a boyfriend made me feel important, and I thought that was enough for me.

Once high school came to a close, my next chapter of life started: college. It was a new page in my book, but the same story. I found myself putting my identity into things that always ended up failing me. Turns out, what got me through my normal academic classes in high school was not enough in my college classes. I had to work my butt off even more than I ever had before. Defeat was the only thing that I felt. I had to ask myself, *why does nothing seem to ever work no matter what I do in this world?* My confidence was falling short more and more. I was longing to find the place where I felt that I belonged.

That was not even the trickiest part. I also had a job; well, actually, I had three. With three jobs as a freshman in college, being a naturally independent young woman became my new identity. Making money so I didn't have to ask my parents for anything was important to me. Working excessively was the start of me feeling like I never had enough, and the only way to make it through was to keep working. Although as a college student I didn't have much to pay for, I thought I had to attach myself to how much money I made.

Working so hard just ended up being another case of mistaken identity. I quickly became tired of putting my identity in my looks and ensuring I always had a boyfriend. I had been bruised by putting my identity in my grades when I was always so average academically. And, I was definitely done with putting my identity into my athletic capabilities when if I'm honest, did not exist. Now putting my identity into how much money I (didn't) have, was only making me feel worse, like I was always stuck.

Exhausted, I turned to a place that was tied to happy memories from my youth—I decided to try out this church thing again. After talking with someone who told me about different churches in the area and getting me in touch with other freshmen in college looking to find a church, we all connected.

I remember feeling nervous on the morning we had planned to meet, not only because I was the driver for four other people I had never met but also because I hadn't been in a church in a super long time. I plugged the address into the GPS and got to know these new friends over the ten minute drive it took to get there. I was feeling excited and overwhelmed all at once. As I was walking up to the front entrance, I saw three or four greeters at the door sharing a warm welcome. It was a genuine feeling, which made me feel like I was in a place where I belonged. The church was a bit bigger than I expected and had many more young people than I thought there would be. I guess it was time to get past the assumption that church was for old people.

We found a spot near the middle of the room and waited for the service to begin. As the first song began, the band started playing, and the lights grew dim. I was pleasantly surprised and almost felt like I was at a concert. The drums played loud at first, and then the voices of those singing followed, and sounded so pleasant. I was thankful that there was a screen at the front of the room with the lyrics because I had never sung about Jesus like this before. I don't remember much about the other songs we sang, but I do specifically remember singing the song "Reckless Love" by Cory Asbury. The song's main premise is about the abundance of God's love for you. I felt my heart filled with joy and loved the song so much that I had it on repeat for the next few weeks. I left the service in awe and feeling so refreshed. I knew I wanted to return the following week, no matter what!

I wasn't sure what was happening to me, but I knew something was changing. I found myself late at night in my dorm room watching Bible study videos on YouTube and finding love for more worship songs that centered on Jesus. I sang along with them, raising my voice in praise of Him. I even remember becoming bold enough to open my Bible and read it. I felt easily overwhelmed by trying to understand the words, and asking myself, *Where do I start? What does this all even mean?* And, *is this the right "scripture" that I am supposed to be reading?*

Oh, and the thought of prayer? That was something that I knew I should take part in but felt like I was only going to "do it wrong." I gave it a go and started talking to Jesus about all the stressful things I had going on in life. Naming one thing after another, I did not expect anything to happen. Yet what seemed like such a small thing ended up being so special. I was laying in my bed, closing my eyes while praying, and just felt a strong presence; like everything was going to be okay and that Jesus was right there, walking through it all with me. I felt some of my favorite sensations again: weightlessness, freedom, and a supportive embrace. Yet, I felt them more profoundly than I ever had before, and I could sense that was the beginning of true belonging.

I knew that this process of taking a chance with Jesus would be worthwhile. As a young girl, I remember hearing about Jesus and how he died for us, but I never really understood what that meant and what that should mean for me. After continuing church for a few weeks and slowly learning more about a relationship with Jesus, I was amazed. It was hard to grasp the idea that Jesus died for my sins to be forgiven and why that was so important. I found myself connecting in a way that was both new and exciting. That led to me surrounding myself with a great community of people who were as curious about being in a relationship with Jesus as I was. I learned how to read the Bible, pray more often, and grow deeper in my faith.

Needless to say, I wasn't always perfect at following Jesus. Letting go of the habit of putting my identity in worldly things like how I looked, how good my grades were, and how much money I could make was a lot easier said than done. I remember one night of junior year, my best friend and I were stuck in the library on Halloween during finals week. I was drowning in pounds of homework and feeling like I would never be able to successfully complete everything that needed to be done without butchering something. It was going to be a long night, and boy, was I letting school get the best of me. All I could think about at that moment was that if I didn't do my best, then everything would fall apart. My friend and I finally stopped and agreed it was time to take a break and pray. It helped us slow down, reminded us we could get through it, and put things into perspective. It is times like that, when I have a bad day, when I don't feel like I look my best or am failing at life, that I am able to turn to Jesus with the stress, worry, and doubt and remember that my identity isn't in those things, but in Him; in who Jesus says I am.

Fast forward three years… looking back on my younger self as I write this story as a senior in college with a relationship with Jesus that is stronger now more than ever. I would love to go back and tell myself that I am so glad I didn't let those worldly things fully overcome my identity. I started this story talking about how I didn't have this big life-changing moment, and even though that is true, what I did have was a slow experience that completely changed my life for the better. It's also what I believe to be the best story that is out there of all time. The story of Jesus and how all you need to do is to be willing to let Him in your life, to permit Him to change your circumstances—the same way He changed mine. For me, that is what faith is all about.

One thing that often gets mistaken when people turn to Jesus, is that their life will become easier, and He won't let anything bad happen. I have learned that isn't the case. Instead, turning to Jesus means learning who you are in the eyes of the one who created you. It means surrendering your good and bad to the Son of God. He cares for you and loves you more than anyone else, and when you step into His overwhelming love, you start to learn that all of those other things that are very temporary aren't worth putting your identity into. Trying to fill myself up with friends, boyfriends, school, and money, none of it would fulfill me the way that Jesus does. When you fill your cup with all of these worldly things, your cup eventually runs out and will always leave you thirsty. Here's the cool thing about a relationship with Jesus, when you start to fill your cup up with Him, you find that your cup doesn't ever run out, and you aren't left thirsty.

There is a popular verse in the Bible that has stuck with me along this journey of growing in my faith, and it's from Jeremiah 29:11. It reads, *For I know the plans I have for you declares the Lord, plans to prosper you and not to harm you, plans to give you hope and a future.* After hearing this verse for the first time, it never left me. This was what I wanted to put my faith in, knowing that the Lord knows who I am, that the Lord created me to be exactly how I am supposed to be, and only He knows the plans that He has for me. The best part of it all was realizing that I didn't have to be perfect and be a certain way for Jesus to want a relationship with me, and believe it or not, the same goes for you.

I'm not sure if you ever thought that it is too late to have a relationship with Jesus or if you feel like you have things in life that you have given a try, and it only leaves you feeling exhausted. You may be having questions that lead you to wonder if there is more to life, and if that is the case, then I encourage you to be bold and take a step toward a relationship with Jesus, just like I did. The story of Jesus is worth so much more than I could ever figure out how to put into words. Life brings us trials all the time, that we have to somehow figure out how to get through. I'm not sure what your trials are right now. Whether it be a career change, losing someone you deeply care about, addictions, never feeling good enough, or looking for something more, rest in knowing that your identity is in Jesus and He cares! He's a friend to us; believe it or not, He is waiting for you to turn to Him with open arms. I have learned that there is nothing you could ever do that would cause Jesus to turn away from you. Isaiah 54:10 states, *"Though the mountain be shaken, and the hills be removed, yet my unfailing love for you will not be shaken, nor my covenant of peace be removed."* If you take anything away from my story, let it be this. Jesus loves you.

Ignite Action Steps

- **Read the Bible!** If you don't have access to buying a Bible, or don't want to commit to buying one, you can download the free Bible app, where there are reading plans available. You can start reading little by little daily. Reading the Bible can seem overwhelming. The book of Mark in the New Testament is always a great starting place. Start with one chapter a day and read away!

- **Pray!** Prayer is a way of speaking to Jesus. Some people think there's a correct way to pray; however, if you know how to talk to a friend, you know how to talk to Jesus! A conversation with Jesus isn't meant to be super professional, but instead just normal conversation. Some of my favorite times to pray throughout the day are when I'm driving in the car, in the morning before my day gets started and when I have some downtime.

- **Worship!** One of my favorite forms of worship is singing! It's something we all do anyways, so whenever I am rushing around or need to take a break from feelings of stress, I throw on some of my favorite songs about Jesus and take a moment to show Him my gratitude! Spotify™ and Apple™ music have "Worship" playlists, so search them and find ones you like! And don't worry; they aren't always Hymns. There are plenty of modern artists who sing songs of praise.

- **Listen!** Be still and willing to feel something within you move—listen to Jesus speak to you. The world can feel like it's forcing us to be busy, and go, go, go. Set aside time to be still and slow down. Jesus won't leave you hanging; it's hard to hear His voice when we are asking for answers, but not taking the time to hear Him.

Ava V. Manuel

AVA V. MANUEL

"What you say matters to someone."

My hope in writing this story is for your eyes to open to the powerful impact your actions, your words, and even your message can have on the future of others who intersect your path. My story shows how ordinary people impacted my life, though they didn't even know it. Without those short moments of encounters, I wouldn't be where I am right now, nor will I be the person I am today. I hope that through my story, you realize that what you say matters to someone. Your message holds the power to transform their future.

HOW DID I GET HERE?

"Ughhh, my feet are killing me!" I complained playfully to my husband, who was always quick to find ways to comfort me. By now, I had been on my feet for over ten hours at our media organization's red-carpet awards.

Spending my day meeting awardees who served their communities with their families and teams on the red carpet to recognize their efforts and contributions is a fulfillment of a dream. My Coast Guard Auxiliary and Lions Club mentor, Charlie Duncan, wished for this kind of recognition before his passing two years ago. He was constantly advocating for good works to be recognized by the media.

Charlie did a lot of good and was an exemplary community servant leader. He served and gave in many different capacities starting with enlisting in the army at nineteen, mentoring and donating resources right up till he passed away at eighty-eight, yet he never received media recognition.

What a contrast today. Picture this: bright lights, red carpet, a renowned century-old media name on the backdrop, smiles from ear to ear, cameras flash, and videos roll to capture the media recognition of exemplary leaders, and I get to be a part of putting it together. The excitement on the faces of families, teams, and supporters applauding the distinction as the awarded leaders gave back the appreciation to those who supported them. Many others felt seen and recognized with each recognition, even those not physically present. Social media pinging sounds echo as videos and pictures of the red carpet recognition are shared online—all creating ripples of appreciation, praise, and celebration for thousands of miles beyond our sight. These were moments I wanted to pinch myself. *How did I get here?*

I didn't even realize how quickly time flew. I had so much fun! As we walked to the car, my husband holding onto me to ensure I remained vertical, I reflected on the moments—the awards, the interviews, the inspiring speeches, the fun and creative poses as families and teams joined the awardees on the red carpet. I couldn't help but feel so full, so grateful. My feet are aching badly, but my heart beams with joy.

This red carpet event is the fourth I've been to, and the second I've put together in just one month. Filled with awe and gratitude, I looked at my life at a glance and thought, *How did I get here?* I didn't even know enough to dream of this during my childhood. Where I came from, I didn't watch much television. I spent the majority of my time as a little girl curled up in bed with a blanket covering myself all the way to the top of my head so I could disappear.

I am the youngest of a family unit of mainly three. I spent maybe three hundred and fifty-eight days a year with my mom, who was always angry, and my troubled brother (three years older than me), who always got into fights in school. My dad was only home from his military assignments for about a week each year. Back then, in the Philippines, military personnel either didn't have provisions to bring their family with them, or in my dad's case, he was assigned to areas of insurgence where hostility was high so it wasn't safe to bring his family. During that one week that my dad was home, I was always the happiest. I think I must have made my dad believe everything was fine when he was away. But somehow, I also imagined that, to an extent, he knew it wasn't. For that one week, I became my Daddy's princess. For the rest of the year, I hoped to be invisible.

I see myself back then, a very fearful little girl. The sound of my mom walking into the house means the start of berating. She always seemed to find something wrong: whether it was that I left my slippers out of line, or I forgot to pick something up, or she heard the sound of some mice chipping their teeth on the piano, which she then blamed on me saying, I didn't play the piano enough. The reasons were random and unpredictable, but the tirade was certain when she got home. Within moments, the screaming starts, then the spanking, and then me begging for her to stop.

From a young age, I was convinced my mom didn't like me, and I was sure it was because I was a girl. Looking at myself, it was the only reason that made sense considering how differently I looked. I wasn't dressed in cute dresses with bows like other girls. Instead, I was clothed in loose shorts and t-shirts, and my hair was chopped short like a boy's. I wasn't spoken to sweetly or treated with tenderness. I was treated like a second-born son, blamed for each fight, and told to stay out of my older brother's way.

Growing up, my mom always had some type of construction going on around the house. The combination of her rage and those construction materials was the stuff horror movies are made of. I remember one particular night when her anger was inconsolable. I looked over the sink at a knife in the middle of her beating, and in my head, I screamed, *Why don't you get that knife and kill me already? You're gonna kill me anyway. You're just making it harder.* Of course, I didn't have the guts to say it out loud. Each time it happened, I simply tried to dodge her blows, shaking and terrified, begging for her to stop. In the midst of the spanking, and her fury, I cried internally, *How did I get here?*

Looking back and rationalizing as an adult, I reason that the violence probably didn't happen daily, and my mom did her best to protect me by concealing me as a boy. Nonetheless, the terror kept me company every day as a little girl. Between avoiding my mom and staying away from my brother, I curled in bed tucked under a blanket most of the time. That was my only safe place. That was, until one early summer evening.

I remember that evening like it was yesterday. As I lay there anticipating my mom's arrival, I heard the sounds of what seemed like clapping and singing from a distance. I perked up and listened intently. I had never heard a sound like that before. I thought to myself, *They sound happy*, and a feeling of excitement came over me. I crawled out under the blanket, got off my bed, and followed the sound as if it were calling to me. I found myself in front of a small side gate three houses down from ours, where the singing, clapping, and giggling were at their loudest.

Oh, I wish I could see. I thought to myself as I got up on my tippy toes, trying to peek into the yard that led to a room where the singing was coming from. The voices sounded like they were children, just like me. But they were different. They were happy and free. It didn't take long for the lady of the house to notice me and invite me to join in. Before I knew it, I was clapping my hands joyfully, stretching my arms up and down with the other kids, and marching as we sang, "Father Abraham has many children; many children have Father Abraham."

In the midst of the joy, I suddenly felt a jolt down my spine as I remembered my mom would be looking for me when she got home. I ran back at the perfect time as she had just arrived. I bolted over to my mom, still carrying that joy in my little voice, and asked if I could be at the neighbor's house where they had singing for kids. Maybe it was my excitement or the way I fearlessly asked that made her say, "Okay," and... as soon as she did, I ran back to the neighbor's and learned a few more songs.

After the singing, they served juice in small cups and gave us some crackers. This little gesture was a big deal for me! I didn't know what to make out of it. I'd never experienced generosity like this before. My heart was so full. I felt like these people cared about me, about each of us kids. I was so happy.

After we had our snacks, a young lady named Mary Ann, probably not even in her twenties, told us a Bible story. She introduced us to Jesus being a person and taught us how to pray and talk to him. Jesus isn't new to me. I was going to a Catholic school where we had a daily mass in the big church adjacent to my school. I knew Jesus from afar. But in Mary Ann's story, Jesus loved little kids. She showed a picture where Jesus had kids huddled around him and even sitting on his lap. She said Jesus is always with us, and he never leaves us. Like an explosion of warmth and light, I felt a love I had never felt in my family. I felt seen after years of trying to be invisible like my life had been crescendoing toward this moment.

I was only eight years old. I didn't understand much, but I understood my life had changed that night. I still had the same mom and the same brother, but I wasn't the same. From that day, I was never alone again. I no longer needed to hide under the blankets. The spankings were not as painful, the screaming was not as scary, and I stopped hiding in dread expecting trouble would come.

Perhaps my perception of my situation changed. Or perhaps my situation in fact changed because I related and responded differently to my mom and brother as my trust and relationship grew with God. Without anyone else teaching me, I became a Pollyanna—the girl who saw hope and positivity in everything, no matter what it looked like. I wondered less about *how I got here* and thought more about what I could do from where I was to get to my next purpose.

I still had a tough life at home through my teenage years. But even as I got into the wrong crowds and did things teenagers shouldn't do, I somehow always knew to go back to God when I found myself in trouble. I was never stupid alone. Even in my stupidity, I could run back to God.

Through all my ups and downs, even as I got myself pregnant and settled into marriage at sixteen, I have walked forward with God's closeness. I finished college, raised my six wonderful kids, and am now a grandmother. I overcame moments of uncertainty, coming to America to work as a physical therapist, advancing my career with multiple specialties, divorcing after twenty-four years, single parenting while working two to three jobs to sustain my family, and even failing in many different businesses as I hoped to give my kids a better life. Through each day, God was my ever-faithful confidant. He was there when I cried, when I dreamt, and when I messed up. He always filled my heart with joy. With God, I always felt the grace to forgive myself, let go, believe again, dream again, and retake courageous steps.

I went on to think and pursue things people said I couldn't do or that I was not qualified for because of where I am or because of my past. Anything I decided was worth pursuing, I did and did, and did, despite failing many times, and eventually, I would succeed or learn valuable skills for my next venture. This tenacity that some people call "stupidity" is still my conquering strategy today, and it first came alive in me that night I sang, clapped, met Jesus intimately, found my faith, and discovered that He wanted the best for me.

That kids' Bible study went on once a week for maybe six weeks. I found out Mary Ann was just on a college break that summer. I never saw her again, but through her words and generosity, I was impacted forever, and she didn't even know it. When I think back on people like Mary Ann, who changed the trajectory of my life and had the greatest impact on who I am today, three people come to mind first, though there are many.

The first was a marching band teacher who I briefly encountered in fourth grade. Preparing for one of our baton-twirling performances as majorettes, as moms were fixing up their daughter's hair and putting makeup on them, I watched silently in awe. I thought to myself, *I can't remember a time when my mom brushed my hair.* That band teacher took notice and offered to put lipstick on me. As she did, she delightfully exclaimed, "You have the most beautiful lips! I love the shape of your lips." I believed her, and those words stayed with me.

Through the years, whenever I saw myself in the mirror, I admired my lips. And despite not having my mom's affection or admiration, I've grown confident in my natural self, even without makeup, and comfortable on camera even today—a skill that is crucial in the media—because of her one comment.

The second was a volunteer volleyball coach from when I was a high school freshman, a very flamboyant and animated guy. As boys would approach our team after the volleyball game, that coach would interrupt or stand between some guy and me and say, "She's beauty and brains. Don't even try." Or, he'd playfully tell me directly, "You're beauty and brains. He's beneath you." He said those words so humorously that others did not take him seriously, but those words took root in me. I walked with an unshakeable sense of identity through high school. While other girls clamored for their sense of self-worth through how boys looked at them, I didn't need any of it. I walk through life even today without needing admiration from others—a cardinal trait that every progressive and risk-taking leader must possess.

The third person was a pastor who had a trial AM radio program once a week that lasted only a few months while I was pregnant with my first baby. In one of his episodes, he taught on the topic he titled, "Don't let your mind think for you. Think for your mind." That teaching saved my life more times than I can ever count. The practice of choosing my thoughts is second nature to me by now and is the backbone of every uncomfortable pursuit I 'stayed the course' with, even today.

When I think about these individuals, they didn't gain likes or followers for what they said or did. To this day, none of them even know their impact on me, my kids, my grandkids, and the lives I touch. That pastor even thought he failed because he only had the AM radio program for a few months. He succeeded in ways he did not realize, and the ripples of his words are reaching people to this day through the effect he had on me.

I would be remiss if my encounters with these people were skipped from the days of my life or if they held back from sharing and speaking. I wouldn't be the same. Navigating the ups and downs of life while believing for the best, I fell in love again and married my best friend from my twenties, who loves me so much. With my kids grown and freely living the lives they choose, I reinvented myself, moved to Los Angeles, and now live a life of adventure and contribution amplified by the power of media. That adventure began when I first heard singing and clapping and ventured three houses down from my own.

In retrospect, I would not have had the courage nor the tenacity to persist in all that I overcame and achieved, except I have the faith that in me lives an almighty force that is everything I'm not; and who can do everything I can't.

I believed He passionately wanted the best for me, and He loved me so much that He brought me a college student to teach a kids' Bible study when I was just eight years old. And, like lily pads along my path leading me out of murky waters, that band teacher, that volleyball coach, and that radio pastor delivered God's messages to strengthen my faith in one form or another, and helped form who I am today.

As I look at my life right now, my adoring husband holding on to me as we walk back to the car, basking in the glamorous lights and smiles from my red carpet event, I can see that those words those people spoke to me, from *Him*, are exactly *how I got here.*

What you have to say matters to someone. Regardless if you get no likes or no kudos, if you think no one saw your posts or heard what you said, what you have to say can be the key to someone's breakthrough, to someone's life turning around, and them finding their inner faith. What you share could cause an Ignite Moment that changes everything for someone, an Ignite Moment that influences how they see themselves or a situation.

You are important. You matter. And, it is important that you show up every day to share your gift.

Also, anticipate and be receptive that God speaks in different ways, through different people, and creatively. So… when people show up in your life, listen to what they have to say. The words and thoughts dropped your way can be the lily pads you get to bounce from to move you forward in your adventure.

IGNITE ACTION STEPS

- **Show up daily. Dare to speak.** Celebrate where you may have even thought you failed. And do that thing you've always felt you're supposed to do. You matter, and what you have to say matters to someone.

- **Speak freely. Speak boldly.** And know that you will never know the impacts you've made in your lifetime. So in speaking, remember to speak well of yourself.

Scan The Goddess

SCAN THE GODDESS

"Faith it until you make it."

Manifesting your dreams requires effort and dedication. When you're the only one who can support you, be your own cheerleader. Stay motivated, determined, consistent, and focused. Remember, no one owes you anything; cultivate gratitude for everything you have. You'll face challenges that make you want to quit: sleepless nights, broken promises, wasted investments, and disloyalty. But through it all, your faith will sustain you. Trust God and keep going, especially when the going gets tough. My story is proof if you keep the faith, you can keep moving forward. Your dreams are worth it.

WHAT'S A DREAM WITHOUT FAITH?

Growing up, music was always present in my life. I lived in a household where everyone around me loved music. My grandmother hosted parties almost every weekend. At those parties, my cousin and I would often perform on the karaoke machine for the family, and we loved it; one Christmas day, I received my own karaoke machine, which led to me creating a music group called, *The Ultimate Level*, with my cousin and that's where my musical life began. I was inspired by well-known local talent, making music about their lives. I realized, *Ohhh, I can also make music about my life!*

The problem was, I didn't know how to write my own music, so I was always looking for a ghostwriter. By high school, my cousin and I went our separate ways, and I began hanging with new people that rapped. I was asked to join their group, using the name *Scandalous*. I loved it. They helped me write a few songs, but we never got around to recording them. It was hard to find a studio, and I was busy with school and my new love, basketball.

I started playing basketball every day, with music taking the backburner. The heartbreaking passing of my grandmother (and other family members) had me feeling like a different person, shifting my focus even more. One day one of my best friends told me he wanted to join a gang and asked me to come with him. I told him a few times how stupid it was, but he kept asking, saying he didn't want to go alone. Soon I wasn't just playing basketball, I was gang-banging. Lots of gunfire, fighting, and people getting hurt or killed through gang wars. But I still managed to stay focused enough to graduate high school and receive a scholarship to play varsity basketball for a junior college team.

Then one day during practice, I injured my ankle very badly, and as a result, I lost my scholarship and had to leave college. I started spending more time in the streets and was back to doing music. I also needed more money, so I started selling marijuana and became one of the leaders of the gang, leading lots of people and commanding lots of respect. However, while still doing what I was doing in the streets, my older brother introduced me to a record label owner with his own studio, and I signed my first deal with him. That's when my true passion and faith in music came alive.

I wrote music every day so I could get to the studio and record it. I went by the rap name that I knew, *Scandalous*. My music, known as thug music, was inspired by the things I saw and was doing in the streets every day. I was a female thug, so my producer gave me the nickname "Thug Girl." It rang a bell for me, so I started going by the name *Scandalous Thug Girl*. I started performing at different venues, and everyone loved my music. As I became more popular in the music scene, I thought I was invincible. The stage and the streets were both my home, and I was living fast and enjoying my life.

I didn't see it at the time, but I was on a path to destruction. Even though I never desired to hurt anyone or treat them badly, if somebody messed with me and my crew, I retaliated. I talked about it in my music, which created an addictive fire in me. When my first label shut down, I didn't let that stop me. I got my own bookings from doing open mic venues and selling my CDs and made many new connections, including the owner of the second label I would sign with. Within months, my first album was produced and distributed. I sold lots of copies. I heard my music playing everywhere in the streets. I was 'tested' a few times because of the lyrics and the gang I was claiming in my music. I was still the leader of that gang, so I wasn't worried. I rolled deep in every show and was ready for whatever. But as music started taking me to different places, exposing me to different things, my mindset was about to shift.

I was given the chance to rap for kids, but I only had one song I could perform because the promoter didn't allow violent music. I didn't like how that felt, as I began to see that being a product of my environment was limiting me. I wanted to write more fun music to uplift people, so I started telling my story without sounding so harsh and angry just in case I was again presented with that opportunity. That challenged me to expand my mind, and vocabulary, and my music started changing for the better. Even though I wasn't the big star that I desired to be, I stayed consistent. I had faith that it would come to pass one day, which kept my fire burning. My persona as an artist was evolving away from *Scandalous Thug Girl.*

After the second label shut down, finding a place where I felt comfortable recording was difficult. I asked my mom if I could build my own studio in her basement, and she agreed. The prices for equipment were very high, but then one day, the owner of the studio that released my first album called me and said he was selling his equipment. I didn't have enough money to purchase it immediately, so I asked him to give me a few weeks. In the meantime, I hustled by cutting hair and selling marijuana. As the two-week deadline approached, I borrowed some money and asked my new boyfriend if he wanted to go half-in on the purchase. With the equipment, we created our own label and signed some of my fellow gang members and friends with talent. I used my connections to get us known, and things were looking up.

Despite the success I was achieving with my music, something was still missing. One Sunday my mom asked me to go to church with her. I had always thought church people were funny when they would fall out on the ground saying they caught the Holy Ghost. I used to say they were crazy when I heard, "The Spirit said this, and God said that," laughing to myself: *These people have lost it. Nobody is saying anything to them. They're just taking people's money.*

Then the pastor said she had a message from God for me. She said that God said I would no longer go by the name *Scandalous*, and that the world would call me *SCAN*, which is an acronym for Saving Children Across Nations. Even though I didn't believe in all of that, I went with it. I was ready for a change anyway. I was a businesswoman now, and I no longer wanted to experience limitations, so I accepted the name and no longer went by *Scandalous Thug Girl*. I was *That Girl SCAN* (though everyone still called me SCAN for short).

The pastor's message resonated with me, and I began to do a lot of soul-searching. One of the most significant changes was my faith. While I'm not religious, I started to become more involved in helping others and realized that something bigger than myself was at play. I noticed that the more I blessed others, the more blessings I received. Even though I was still drinking, smoking, and selling marijuana, I wasn't involved in any gang wars or gang activity. My focus was solely on music, making money, and helping others do the same. Despite my actions on the streets, I have always been a loving and caring person. However, I took even more pride in helping others during this new era of That Girl SCAN. I often put them before myself and gave even when I didn't have much. Seeing people happy made me happy.

The boyfriend I was in business with eventually became my husband. He wasn't involved in the streets; he was fresh out of the Marines and had everything going for him. He was my safe haven, and after we moved in together I lost interest in being part of a gang. It was stupid, as I told my friend in high school. But it had served its purpose in my life, showing me I possessed great leadership qualities and power.

I still felt that church people were crazy, and I had never heard God speak to me. So, I went to church with my mother again, hoping to receive another message. The pastor was giving everyone a message except me, and my doubts crept back in. *It was all fake. God didn't love me.* But the pastor said, "It's not that God doesn't love you; he's working on you. I don't have a message for you. Go talk to God.'"

I was so upset with her that she didn't give me a word from God, I didn't go to church or speak to her for a very long time. I had already been through a lot in my life, and as I sat in my feelings, I decided I was better off in control of my own life anyway. *I don't need a pastor to talk to God.* I started to communicate with God myself, but *nothing* came. I didn't get upset and went back to focusing on music and money.

Then one day, while putting together bags of marijuana for my customers, I heard a voice say, "Stop smoking and give it all away." There was no WOW or shock, no racing pulse or bright lights shining down. I was just calm, understanding instantly where I was being led. Without hesitation, I called up the people who had been selling with me and told them to come over. "Here, take this," I said, and I handed over a pound and a half without even flinching, no big expression on my face. Their eyes bugged out with shock as they said, "Stop playin'!" trying to make sure that I was sure. I finally got them to understand I didn't want any money, nothing. I had faith in God even when I didn't know what it meant to trust Him.

As a result of that experience, I began to see the world in a different way. I realized that life was more than just the pursuit of money and power. There was a whole community of people out there who were hurting and in need of help. I started to change and see myself as more than just That Girl SCAN. I had a purpose now, and that purpose was to help others. I started to build a network of people who were also committed to making a difference in the world.

As the years passed, my husband and I went through all the trials and tribulations with the artists on our music label; it became draining. As a result, we decided to shut the label down. My spirit was leading me to Atlanta, and that's where I became even more connected with myself and tapped into the spiritual world. I would say that I didn't have a choice. I encountered all types of people who were being used by spiritual forces: church people, spiritual people, and just everyday people. God sent them to me for the purpose of either helping them, them helping me, or, most importantly, me discerning their spirit. God was building up my faith because, in this music industry, there can be a lot of evil forces and a lot of spiritual attacks. I had to be able to hear and see spiritually what was taking place around me.

Sometimes I wanted to quit and leave it all behind. These people don't want good; they want drama. But then I realized that it's not the people, it's the spirits that are attached to them. I have to wake them up to what's really going on out here so they won't continue to be used. I couldn't give up even if I wanted to because now I understood why God told me that my name would be *SCAN*. My purpose is to Save Children Across Nations through my organization, using my music and voice to tell my story and bring people closer to God, letting them know that God and the spiritual world *does* exist. I want to wake people up to what's going on so they can spread the word to the next person and so on, living by my organization's motto: "Grab a hand, save a soul."

I have come to realize that when my pastor said, "Go talk to God," that was the best message for me. It helped me build a relationship with God and allowed me to hear His voice more clearly. Faith is not something we can simply switch on or off; it's a habit we must cultivate over time. Faith is a belief in something that cannot be seen or proven, yet is still regarded as true. It is the confidence in the unknown, the assurance that things will work out for the best, even when the odds are against us. Despite facing numerous obstacles and challenges, I never lost faith. Every setback taught me a valuable lesson and made me stronger. I learned to trust the journey and have faith that everything happens for a reason. Looking back, I can't help but laugh and say, "I guess those church people weren't crazy after all."

As I reflect, I also see the significant role my music played in my journey. It helped me see myself as a valuable member of society and gave me the confidence to keep going. I had a series of experiences that have led me to a stronger faith in God and an awareness of the spiritual realm. I have encountered spirits and entities that initially frightened me but eventually made me become more aware of the supernatural. I am guided by the voice of God, and I let the spirit lead me. As I continue on my journey, I realize that having faith is the key to pursuing my dream. It gives me the courage to keep going, *even* when things get tough. I know that having a purpose is essential. Without a clear understanding of *why* I am pursuing my dream, I would have given up a long time ago. My purpose is to inspire and heal people through my music. Knowing this keeps me motivated, even during difficult times.

I have taken action toward my goals, even when I didn't have all the answers or resources I needed. I meditate, pray more, and trust that everything will work out for the best. My faith has helped me to overcome obstacles and setbacks that I encountered on my journey. I tell myself that every failure is a learning opportunity and a chance to grow. All of my thoughts are more positive. I am still pushing even through all of the challenges, temporary roadblocks, and barriers. My strong attitude toward my goals helps me to stay motivated and focused. I have found a sense of peace and purpose that I had never experienced before. I never doubt my abilities or think about the possibility of failure. I used to care about the judgment of others, but not anymore. I focus on the positive outcomes that I want to achieve. I visualize myself succeeding and only hanging around people who support me and believe in my potential.

I know that life is about experiences. I trust my intuition and discern what energy feels positive and beneficial for me and what feels negative or draining. My sense of awareness has heightened, and I am very attuned to the energy around me. especially during times of spiritual elevation and fasting. I set boundaries and say no to people or situations that don't align with my spiritual goals. I continue to work on myself and raise my vibration so that I can attract positive energy and manifest the things that I desire in my life. God has assured me He is right there with me and gives me messages through my music. This is how I evolved from THAT GIRL SCAN to SCAN THE GODDESS AKA SCAN.

Pursuing your dreams with faith and conviction is a journey that requires commitment, persistence, and a positive mindset. By following your faith, you can achieve your dreams and live a life aligned with your passions and aspirations. Faith is the belief in something greater than oneself, a force that guides us toward our goals and gives us the strength to overcome obstacles along the way.

IGNITE ACTION STEPS

- **Define Your Dream**: The first step toward achieving your dreams is to identify what they are. Spend some time reflecting on your passions and aspirations, and write down what you want to achieve. Be as specific and detailed as possible.

- **Believe in Your Dream:** Once you have identified your dream, you need to have faith that it is possible. Believe that you have what it takes to achieve your goal, and trust that the Universe will support you in your efforts.

- **Take Action:** Dreams are not achieved by simply wishing for them. You must take concrete steps toward making them a reality. Break down your dream into smaller, more manageable goals, and take action toward them every day.

- **Overcome Obstacles:** Pursuing your dream is not always easy, and you are likely to face obstacles along the way. When that happens, remain positive and persistent. Reframe setbacks as opportunities to learn, grow, and keep moving.

- **Surround Yourself with Support:** Surround yourself with people who believe in you and your dream. Seek out mentors, friends, and family members who can provide encouragement and support when you need it the most.

- **Stay Committed:** Pursuing your dream requires commitment and perseverance. Stay true to your vision even when faced with challenges and distractions.

- **Celebrate Your Successes:** As you make progress toward your dream, take time to celebrate your successes. Recognize your accomplishments, and use them as motivation to keep pushing towards your ultimate goal.

- **Share Your Story:** Your journey towards achieving your dream can be an inspiration to others. Share your story with others, and use your experiences to encourage and support those who are pursuing their dreams.

- **Practice Gratitude:** Remember to be grateful for the blessings in your life and the progress you have made. Gratitude helps cultivate a positive mindset, which can overcome challenges and keep you focused on your goal.

- **Keep Dreaming:** Finally, remember that achieving one dream does not mean you have to stop dreaming. Continue to dream big, and use the skills and experiences you have gained to pursue new goals and aspirations.

Natasha Rae

Natasha Rae

*"I am a woman who is empowered by FAITH
without the boundaries of what is seen."*

**This is the faith story that was placed on my heart to share with you. My
hope is that it shall bring you strength, goodness, love, and the fight to have
faith; to keep believing, and to be encouraged in the gift it offers, which is
our journey. Please don't fear the challenges that come with believing, no
matter what anyone says around you. Know that through every new situation
in your life, you can learn to be strengthened and increase in faith. There
is only one of you on this entire planet; you are special, and whatever gifts
you possess are needed each and every day.**

Faith With No Borders

Have you ever dreamed of freedom? The kind of FREEDOM that makes
your heart flutter with excitement. Something you have always wanted and
dreamed of but truly never felt possible. Well, what if your faith… something
you can't see… could take you into the depths of that very freedom? I am
here to tell you that this is a true and possible feat. I am living proof. This
is a story of faith that I walked through to get to that freedom. I would have
never known in the midst of my pain and dysfunction that the tattoo I placed

on my foot, reading, "*I walk by faith and not by sight*" (2 Corinthians 5:7), would lead me into a brand-new world. Here is the story.

I grew up in a small town, on farms and horse-filled pastures with my grand-parents. Both sides of my family were Jehovah's Witnesses, but my parents did not stay on that path, and that life taught me to know God and the world. However, I discovered that although I had God, I also had an adversary after my soul and spirit who worked to keep me down. I can honestly say that I am a fighter by nature because I was raised 'in the fire.' Still, I am a lover by nature because I was knitted in my mother's womb that way.

Have you ever daydreamed as a child? Maybe you wanted to be a ballerina, save the world so there could be peace, perhaps a police officer to deal with jus-tice, or run in a huge field full of flowers and sunshine. I see now, as I am older, the things I thought about as a child in my purity were parts of my calling. I am huge on worship, dance, and exercise. I love to share the love of God and be a light in the dark. Justice is something that I have the desire to see, especially in a world longing for peace. I am also a woman who creates medicinal and natural products from the earth.

It is easier now to look at what I have done and say my dreams have come true. But that wasn't always the case. I can remember how I felt as a kid, imag-ining the life I would lead. I also remember the years of feeling that I was not on the path I had dreamed of, that my life was not what I thought it would be. That is where my faith story began, the path I didn't want to be on... the one I felt I couldn't escape.

I had always been in abusive relationships; it was all I ever knew. I saw it growing up in some capacities, and I lived it myself. I guess you can say that if you don't know anything else, that truly is your normal. I was in a horribly abusive marriage, though it gave me three amazingly wonderful children who joined the son I already had. I thought when I finally left that my life would be better, but it taught me that when you want to run to new situations, everything you never dealt with will come right along with you.

My so-called freedom also left me with post-traumatic situations. I had been broken down so much that I truly felt like there was nothing left. Yes, I had a local church family and some support, but even some of them had turned on me and did some very dark stuff. I found myself slipping back-ward, unsure how to get out. I made choices with my body and morals that were not aligned with who I wanted to be nor who I *knew* I was. In these times it seemed all the wrong people came around me. The church had called child services because of (ex) husband's abuse and addiction, and one of my children was molested by a boy at church. I was barely keeping my head above water, but I am an overcomer—so I kept fighting.

My neighbor then figured setting me up with a guy from down the street was a good idea. His wife had passed away, and he had a daughter around my kid's age. In my state of *duh*, I figured why not, so I started another dysfunctional, abusive relationship. I am laughing because, in the place I am now, I think, *Wow, girl, what were you thinking?* This man had been through unreal pain, lost his wife in an accident, and the situation around it was heartbreaking (I found out later he was always abusive and addicted, but that's for another story). We got close fast, though it was mostly sex and partying, and we moved in together not long after. There *were* wonderful things. Both places we lived in were out in the country with beautiful views; one had buffalo and a little pond we could go paddle boating on. We also had a peacock, chickens, and an amazingly huge garden. We went into the woods and would shoot guns and have wiener roasts and marshmallows, and the children loved that because they were still young. I smile, remembering those moments because they make my heart happy. We built things together, went on holidays, made amazing meals, and loved one another.

Yet, along with that life of beauty came physical violence, a lot of smoking, drugs, alcohol, and just incredible fighting. People really need to understand what these kinds of situations actually look like; that abuse can be mixed in among happy experiences. I got to the point at night when he would be passed out, and I would be crying out to God, asking Him to help me because I knew inside that wasn't my life; it wasn't the life I was supposed to be living. I was thankful to that man for taking care of the kids and me. He allowed me to attain an education and become certified in health, wellness, and fitness—but it wasn't my path.

That is when I began the healing journey; I knew I needed to get healthy, happy, and strong in order to leave and get where I needed to be. I prayed day and night for support, made changes to my health, and found more peace. I finally told him one day I thought we needed to separate because neither of us was happy or living the lives we wanted. I made a date for June when the children were finished with school, which was six months away, so it gave us plenty of time. He decided not to help me. Maybe he was hurt or angry but instead packed all his and his daughter's stuff up and took off on me, leaving me all the bills and everything else to deal with.

My first reaction was anger and disgust that he would abandon me after I had tried to do what was right. Then the fear turned into an instinct to survive. When I finished crying, I felt surrender, and peace fell upon me. That was a reminder of the FAITH that was living in me, and I knew I had to trust that God had my back and would help me get through it.

My first plan to get away and start a new life was to go to Spain. But then my aunty, with her wisdom, suggested Spain was a bit far, so, "Why not go to British Columbia, Canada?" She reminded me that it aligned with my personality and what I loved: the mountains, the flowing water, the natural living, the "hippies," and living off the land. I felt like she had a good point, so I began to look into that, keeping in mind I had very little time to move since the landlord knew I couldn't pay for the place and wanted us out. Sometimes in life, we see something as a negative, but it's a push for a positive new direction. By the grace of God, I found a possible job teaching fitness, and after speaking to the owner over the phone, she expressed interest in hiring me. I headed to tryouts, making the trip with my ex-husband's ex-girlfriend. It sounds bizarre, but that's my entire life, and the way I see it, if you can have peace and forgiveness for everyone, that builds the greatest world around us. I went to see if I could secure a home there before I brought the children. I didn't find one, but I did meet a friend of hers who lived in a smaller town closer to my destination.

I ran into an old friend who needed a place to stay, so I made a deal with him. I gave him an extra room, and he helped me pack and sell off everything I couldn't fit in my car. That was my first gift from God on my journey. Things seemed to go well; I was selling stuff to people who really needed it and was blessed by receiving cash to prepare for moving.

I was out of time, so I officially made the trip across the border to the next province with three children, a bird, and a hamster! Since I hadn't found a place to stay, we took a tent. The children and my friend came with me. We lived in the tent for four or five days, during which the children ended up having lice which followed us from home when they visited a friend before we left. I was starting to get overwhelmed and felt like it wouldn't come together. I ended up visiting that lady I had met during the first trip, and she said we could stay at her house for a bit until we found something. It was a much-needed break from our situation. I was exhausted but knew I needed to keep going and make sure I had everything ready for us to start our new life.

Then, things came full circle. Within the week of staying with that lady, I discovered that there was abuse and addiction with her partner. She wanted to leave home, which meant we needed to leave, also. I drove her to a transition house, and sitting through her appointment there I felt that might be the perfect place for the children and me as well. Being there would allow me time to organize everything, and they also had incredible resources. When I asked the intake workers, they suggested I go to the shelter closer to my job. I made a call, and if you can believe it, they said, "Yes, we have one spot available for your family size." She explained that the one space that could accommodate my three children and I had just become available the day before. I considered that a blessing from heaven and divine timing, so we packed up and headed to our new place.

In my new city it was called the Women's Shelter, and it allowed us to get things in order; I could find the children a private school that would take all three of them. Let me take a minute to share this amazing miracle… Through events outside of myself we were led to this private school after I had searched for a few others that couldn't accommodate all three kids within the same school. As I walked into the school, I noticed a painting on the wall in the shape of a tree; it was filled with so many words that aligned with my beliefs—this excited me. I eventually caught on that tuition would likely be out of my financial abilities. I voiced that to the lady giving us the tour, and she asked me if I would be willing to write a letter to the school board to get financial help; I agreed that I would give it a shot. The next day while standing in line at the bank, she messaged me and said the school board meeting happened to be that evening and asked if I could get that letter written and emailed to her before 4 PM. I agreed that I would get it done, so I prayed right in the line, wrote the email, and sent it off. The next day they called me in, and the principal told me that in her decade of working there, the school board had never done this; by the Grace of God, they decided to fully cover the year's tuition for all three children.

We ended up getting to stay in the Women's Shelter an extra month than typically allowed… again, I believe it was by faith and the wonder-working power of God. This allowed me to get all the paperwork for health care, my vehicle, the children situated in school, furniture, and all the other things you require when relocating to a new place. I was also able to make some friends and bless others in that place with my faith. Some days I felt like a light in the darkness, others, I felt defeated, but every day I kept moving forward.

Along with the many wonderful things we were experiencing, there were the same number of trials, tribulations, and tests. One beautiful blessing was this little church across the street, where the children and I could return to a blessed environment. The very first Sunday we went, I suddenly no longer wanted to smoke cigarettes, drink alcohol, or smoke weed. I was so thankful to God that day because I felt like the things I was crying out to stop had ended and I was finally free.

I began looking for a home for us to rent. I spoke to this one person, and I felt like he had our back. He cared that I was a single mom trying to make it work for my family in an entirely new world, and he wanted to help. So just like that, BOOM! Our first rental home in our new city. The shelter helped a lot with opportunities so that we could get what we needed for our new space.

One day while driving home from the children's school, I came across a lady experiencing homelessness and found an opportunity to help both her and the local homeless shelter. I began volunteering for haircuts, which opened other community opportunities, including support systems for the children and me. It's truly amazing how God can line up events. As I sit here and write, tears roll down my face reminding me of the pain I endured, and yet, I am in awe of how Papa God showed up and my faith increased, even while wavering from time-to-time. I am empowered by how I remained strong while walking us through that huge transitional time in our lives.

Every day as I would wake, with the sun shining in my window and the mountains right behind it, I felt a smile on my face of thankfulness for where I was. As I would drive to work across the bridge, with this incredible view and glistening water, my heart would be filled. I would thank God for the beauty and majesty of His creation.

We all have great purpose and reasons to be here on earth; sometimes, we spend most of our lives searching for it. I did until I found my savior Christ Jesus. Unfortunately, life doesn't come with a *Why-you-are-on-the-earth* manual, and you still have some soul healing and generational curses to overcome... I think about how far I have come, and I know I will never be going back, that I speak with faith.

I found the strength of faith and realized faith could take me into the unknown to overcome things I never thought possible. By walking in faith, I created a world of *freedom*, a world that Jesus died to give me, a *knowing* deep within my soul. I knew that I was truly supposed to be *free*. I believe my *faith*, which is based on my life and what I have overcome, is definitely the supernatural kind, a gift from heaven.

Faith for me has been and continues to be a challenge. It's not like when you say to someone, "Hey, just have faith it will happen," and suddenly they do. I want to convey that having faith is something that will surely come to pass even though you can't see it, even if, by human standards, it seems impossible. Surrendering to faith takes a lot of courage and strength. I am here to tell you, from years of seeing miracles, signs, and wonders, that your faith truly will cause God to move mountains, open doors, and help you to overcome any obstacles. Be Blessed, and *"Keep Walking by Faith and Not by Sight."*

With love,
Natasha Rae.

Ignite Action Steps

- **Remind yourself** every day that there is only one of you on this entire planet, and whatever you hold, whatever gifts you have, they are needed here each and every day.

- **Remember** you are more than a conqueror.

- **Take some time** for yourself, take deep long breaths, dream the kind of dreams that bring a smile to your face, and don't take everything so seriously. Let there be joy.

- **Never forget** that you are dearly loved and have a God who knitted you together in your mother's womb, and He is so delighted by the beauty of who you are and becoming every day.

- **Be Blessed** and live every day like a playground party because one life is all we are promised.

- **Love yourself**—unconditionally.

K. R. Rosser

K. R. Rosser

*"There is no reason to ask God, Why; simply thank
him for each encounter you experience."*

**My intention in sharing my story is to allow you to see that your strength
will prevail even in your darkest moments. By sharing this story, I want to
encourage you to find your way back to gratitude through faith, trust, and
knowing that when you feel like you are on the road to nowhere, God is right
there with you. Draw strength from God, let go, and set yourself free. Be at
peace and be grateful, for God's blessings are always with you.**

My Forever Valentine

It was a typical dry evening in El Paso, Texas: energetic music pumping from cars
passing by and people filling the sidewalks as they enjoyed the warm weather, even
as sweat turned their clothes sticky and their chatter filled the air. It had been a long
day. It was later than usual for me to eat, and I had a craving for tacos, so I decided
to hit the local drive-thru for some takeout. As I drove home, with my windows
down and the radio blaring, I sang along to the tunes. Once I returned home, I sat
quickly to enjoy my tacos. I noticed the blinking light on my answering machine.
I thought that was odd. *Who would be calling me this late?* I continued to eat. As
I sat there, I thought to myself, it must be work. *Oh, what now?*

Unbeknownst to me, it was a message that still haunts me today. It was a call from one of my mom's dear friends.

"Your mom is very ill.
You need to get to her quickly.
Please call me immediately, no matter the time.
I will be waiting for your call."

I was frozen in disbelief; the tacos I so much wanted to enjoy weren't desirable any longer. I dropped to the floor and started to cry and scream out, "God, why me? Why my mother?" No one from my family called to tell me something was going on with her. *Did they know?*

It took me a minute to get myself together and get my mind right to make the call. When my mom's friend answered, she said hello and then asked how I was doing. I responded with, "I'm not sure how I'm doing right now." She went on to explain the reason for her worry. She had been trying to reach my mom for days, and no one would answer the phone. When she had asked someone to knock on the door, there was still no answer. Normally, she and my mom would speak daily, so it was very unusual that they hadn't talked; my mom had not returned her calls. "Have you spoken to your mom?" she asked intensely, sounding almost out of breath. I let her know that recently each time I had called my mom, our conversations were very brief. Often my stepfather answered and would say she was asleep. I didn't give it much thought; I just figured she was resting or I was calling at the wrong time.

Now the feeling began to sink in that something was off. My mom's friend shared that when she went over to my parents' residence and tried to enter the building, she was denied entry by the guard because no one buzzed her in. So she came back the next day and was able to come in with a group of people who were entering the building, making it past the guard onto the elevator. She rode up to the twenty-first floor and knocked and knocked, and eventually *banged* on the door, at which point my stepfather opened it. She pushed past him and suddenly saw my mom. My mom had lost a lot of weight and looked very ill.

That was when my stepfather said my mom was going through cancer treatment.

It felt like a gut punch in slow motion. I was frozen in time while the pain of this surreal news washed over me. Not my mom. Not cancer. It couldn't be.

I hung up and immediately began talking to God. I asked again, "Why my mother? What have I done to deserve this?" I felt like I was being punished. I cried the remainder of the night until, at some point, I finally drifted off to sleep.

When the sunlight came through the blinds, I hopped up, got a shower, and packed a bag. I waited until 8 AM to call the doctor's office. That would be the first of a few calls to that office that day. I was told to leave a message for the doctor. Two hours felt like two days, and there was no response. I called back and got that same cold receptionist telling me she would take another message. I had already left a message, what was another message going to do? We got into a contentious back and forth as I asked questions about my mom, and she quoted me the HIPAA laws and statements about doctor-patient confidentiality. I went into a verbal rage and told her: "That's my mom. If you don't have the doctor call me back, I will be on the next 'thing smoking' to Chicago, and you'll see me in person!" I slammed down the phone and screamed. How could they ask me to just wait in line when my world was falling apart?

The next call I made was to my stepfather. I asked to speak to my mother. He told me she was asleep. I said, "I know she is sick, and I would just like to speak with her." He said, "Baby, she's asleep—I don't want to wake her." He refused to put her on the phone, which made me so angry. I started cussing and fussing before throwing down the phone onto its charger.

A few more hours passed before the doctor finally called me. I explained who I was, that I was my mom's only child, and I was in the military stationed in El Paso, Texas. He began to give me the bleak news that my mom had lung cancer and that it had metastasized to other parts of her body. She was receiving treatment to prevent the spreading. I asked the dreadful question: "How long does she have?" Feeling the weight on my shoulders get heavier, I waited for his answer. All he would tell me was that he "really couldn't say at this point."

With his vague answer ringing in my mind, I packed my car and headed to my office to notify my command that I would need to take emergency leave. I was not looking forward to the twenty-plus hour drive to Chicago but had already mapped out my route, determined to get to my mom. Although I had driven that route many times, the drive was noticeably longer, and felt like I was on the road to nowhere. As I drove across Texas, the only thing I could think about was that my mom needed me and I wasn't there for her. I kept asking myself, *Why didn't I see the signs?" Was it because I was so wrapped up in what I was trying to accomplish in life?* My mind drifted back to the previous year when she visited me in Alabama prior to my move to Texas. She had always been vibrant, the life of the party. But that visit was different. She didn't want to do much of anything but relax and sleep. I asked her if she was okay and she said yes, that she just needed some time to get away and relax. That was the first sign I missed. Then I reflected on my numerous calls to her and my stepfather telling me she was asleep, taking a shower, or in the bathroom. I didn't question any of that at that time. That was the second sign I missed.

I was driving so fast that I never noticed the police car sitting in the median as I sped by. Then I saw the flashing lights in my rearview mirror and said to myself, *Now I'm about to get a ticket; what more could go wrong?* As the officer approached the vehicle, I handed him my license and military ID and didn't ask any questions because I already knew I had a big ticket coming. He asked me politely how I was doing. I said, "Not too good." Then he asked where I was headed, and I told him Chicago because my mom was gravely ill, and I was trying to get to her. He gently said, "You probably need to slow down so you can make it there." He took my credentials and went to his vehicle. He came back, and to my surprise, he wrote me a warning ticket with no fine attached. I cracked a light smile at him as he handed me my credentials, and I said, "Thank you, Officer; I will make sure I slow down so I can arrive alive." I sat there for a moment to gather my thoughts, and then I continued my drive. Nightfall started to set in, but I was determined to leave Texas. I stopped at a rest stop for about three hours once I crossed the border into the next state.

Once I made it to Oklahoma, I knew I didn't have much longer to go. I arrived in Chicago and drove straight to my parents' home, but just missed the ambulance. I made my way to the University of Chicago hospital emergency room, then proceeded to the desk and identified myself. Finally, and thankfully, they allowed me to see her.

I was *so* ready to see her, but I wasn't ready for what I saw. My mom was unrecognizable. She looked like she had aged two times over; her gray hair was dull, her skin was sunken, and she was talking out of her mind. She was staring at the ceiling, saying, "...the bubbles go poop, poop..." I went to her and grabbed her hand, and said softly, "Mom." She looked over at me like she didn't know who I was. I asked her to tell me her name and birthdate, which she did. I then asked her to name her sisters, and she named them: "Ruth, Celeste, Judy... and Karen." I corrected her, "You have only three sisters, Mom. I'm Karen, your daughter." In her own humorous way, she said, "Well, I knew she was in there somewhere." I chuckled a bit, grateful to be in her presence.

I spoke with the doctor, who informed me that my mom was severely dehydrated and not coping well with the cancer treatment. That scared me. I begged him, "Treat her like you would treat your own mother." I then asked if she could be transferred out of state to Barnes-Jewish Hospital Cancer Center in St. Louis, as it was near my grandmother's house and there was a great support system there. The doctor agreed. I stayed with my mom in the hospital and told her I would be packing some of her things so I could take her to St. Louis, where I knew she would get the best care and treatment. My stepfather was not happy with my decision, so he started telling everyone I was taking his wife from him. I sobbed as we both stood there crying, "I only have one mother, and I want her to live. She is only going to St. Louis where she can be cared for 24/7."

My mother and I arrived in St. Louis, and I settled her in at my grandma's. Knowing her appointments were set up, I felt comfortable leaving her and returning to Texas. I checked on her every day, and as the days went on she gained her strength back and returned to her more vibrant, spunky self.

Then, a few weeks later, my uncle called to ask me if I knew my mom was heading back to Chicago. I said, "No, I hadn't heard that." I hung up, called my mom, and asked her what she was doing. She stated she wanted to go home to Chicago. In anger, I replied, "If you go back to Chicago, I will be done with you; and tell your husband to call when it's time for your funeral." My heart was feeling both afraid and scared, but I let my anger get the best of me. I said something I didn't mean, but it came out anyway.

My mom was taken aback, saying, "I don't want you mad at me, so I'm going to stay." I wasn't trying to hurt her, and told her that she had to be the one who wants to LIVE, to get in the ring and FIGHT. I told her we could beat this cancer. She promised me that she would stay in St. Louis. Of course, that meant I had to call my stepfather and tell him she was not coming back to him. You can guess how well that conversation went. He insisted, "She's my wife!"

I screamed, "She is my mother, the only one I have!" I warned him not to go to St. Louis to try to take her, and then I hung up. I was so angry. I felt powerless and defeated. I was terrified I might not see my mom again.

Over months the cancer continued aggressively spreading through her body. The doctors eventually stated they could do nothing more than send her home and make her comfortable. That was a very dark moment for me. I lost hope in God and felt like my prayers weren't being answered. I took another leave from work and went to St. Louis to be with her.

A day before I was scheduled to return home, February 11th of 2002, my mom rose out of her sleep like a ghost and said, "I know you have to leave, but I want to know if you are okay." I said I was, and she smiled. She then stated, "As long as I know you are okay, I'm okay. I'm tired of fighting, tired of treatments, and taking shots."

I wasn't ready for her to give up. I told her she was doing so well and we were winning the fight. I then had to excuse myself and go to the bathroom, where I screamed and cried. All the strength in my body was gone. I felt like I couldn't continue on. I looked up and said, "God, are you with me? If you can hear me, please save my mom." I got myself together and went back in to talk to her. I told her we could make it.

Later that evening, I went to check on my mom, and I just watched her, confused. She had taken off all of her clothes and taken her breathing machine off, and thrown it. I put her clothes back on her and her breathing tube back in her nose. She was having a conversation with her friend who, she said, was sitting in the corner, but I didn't see anyone there. She also kept reaching for the sky like she was trying to grab something.

Early the next morning, my aunt gently woke me and told me to check on my mom. I ran upstairs to her room, and when I was close enough to touch her, I could hear the death rattle in her breathing. She was in another place. The ambulance came, and we got her to the hospital. I was able to ride in the ambulance with her. They resuscitated her two times. Once we arrived, I spoke to the doctor, and told him to do everything in his power to save her. She was placed on a ventilator, yet, I eventually had to make the dreadful decision to unplug it, as she was gone. That was the hardest decision and saddest day of my life. I watched my mom take her last breath on February 12th, two days before Valentine's Day.

After that loss, I was done with God for a good minute. I found no peace in Him, and I avoided church. Still, I needed something to fill the emptiness in the days, months, and years following my mom's death. I started to write to her daily in a journal, and I felt a sense of peace when I wrote to her. It was so surreal like she was right there listening to me. The more I grieved and thought things through, the more I began to change my point of view.

A conversation with my girlfriend led me to the clarity I needed and led me back to God. I was asking, *Why, why, why*, when she told me, "Instead of asking *why*, thank God! Thank God that your mother was here on this earth for fifty-six years, and you were able to enjoy her. Thank God that He gave you such a wonderful mother; she is with Him now. She is up in heaven looking down on you right now." My friend urged me to go back to church; to start praying again. And that's what I did.

As I slowly started going back to church, I felt renewed. I began to see that even though things happen and we don't understand why, God makes no mistakes. He takes us on the journey we are meant to take. In losing my mother, I was shown that I am stronger than I realized. As I kept journaling, I knew my mom wouldn't want me to be sad. She would want me to live, enjoy, and do good things; to keep up those accomplishments she had always been so proud of. I have renewed my faith in God. There is no reason for me to ask Him *why*; I simply thank Him for each encounter I experience.

We all have a mark on the calendar that is our time, and we may not get to say goodbye before God decides it's time to go. Questioning *why* does not help. But cherishing the memories, being grateful for the time you share with the people you love, and finding their presence in new ways can bring you joy. You can still see them at your favorite restaurant, in a puppy who stays by your side, or in your own reflection as you look at that nose and eyes that reflect their spitting image. Knowing we are connected, that everything is divine, trust that God is walking with you, and His love is there for you, always and forever.

Ignite Action Steps

- **Get a journal** and write to your loved one. Share with them all of the life events that they miss.

- **Celebrate your loved one** during their birth month. Cherish memories and remember the times they made you laugh.

- **Surrender to God** and release and let go of your anger. Instead of asking, "Why me, God?" consider saying, "Why not me, God?"

- **Keep your prayer life going** and ask God for direction and strength to endure.

- **Join a support group** to help you deal with the loss of your loved one.

Mimi Safiyah

Mimi Safiyah

"Your faith is your footprint."

My intention is for you to find the courage within you to be authentically you. To discover your belonging through leaning into your faith and trusting the journey and your role in it. I want you to be assured that it's okay to lay on your prayer mat crying, seeking solace and comfort through silent whispers. I desire for you to attain a knowing that despite differences, we are all innately the same. And, above all, I want you to believe in the depths of your heart and soul that if you have your faith, you have everything you will ever need.

Surrender to your journey

The smell of orange flowers fills the air in Ramallah, Palestine, as the sound of the *athan* (call to prayer) echoes melodiously through the fields surrounding me. I admire my Jeddah (Grandma in Arabic) cooking grape leaves in the kitchen and preparing for the morning meal before the first fast of Ramadan. Excitement fills my soul as I run around playing with my cousins while fulfilling the request of our Jeddah to pick fresh oranges and lemons from the fragrant trees in our garden so she can make freshly squeezed *easir* (juice) for all of us to enjoy. Ramadan is upon us once again, and I squeal in delight at the ambiance that overflows into the streets, homes, markets, and hearts of all believers. Like every other Muslim child, I was anticipating with joy all the amazing sweets I would receive, the family gatherings I would attend, and the fun I would enjoy as the festivities began. I was eager to practice the fasts with all the other children, to prepare for when we reach puberty, feeding our souls with the virtue of grace. Everything about the day was in harmony with our yearly family traditions and reminded me of the beauty of Islam.

"The greatest of richness is the richness of the soul." - Prophet Muhammad (ﷺ)

As the years passed and I grew up, Ramadan reached new meanings for me. What was once centered around excitement and fun evolved into a more mature and profound concept. I realized that the greatest blessing was deepening the connection you have with Allah. It is a quest to draw closer to Him through acts of worship, enclosing yourself in the sacred refuge of prayer and fasting. Ramadan is a sanctuary to lean into once a year to rehabilitate yourself from this worldly life and its distractions. For me, it also is a way to release any pain I have encountered, a chance to heal myself—I give my heart to Allah in all of its broken pieces, and He returns it mended, healed, and stronger than before.

"O you who believe! Fasting is prescribed to you as it was prescribed to those before you, so that you may learn self-restraint." (Qu'ran 2:183)

This year, I was especially yearning to experience Ramadan. Having just received news about my dear Muslim friend and work colleague Dania passing away suddenly in a devastating fire—her transition (Inna lillahi wa inna ilayhi raji un—to Allah we belong and to Him we shall return), merely days before Ramadan, weighed heavy on my heart. I wanted to pray for her and her family—in full faith that this sacred time would bring them solace. I also wanted to receive healing from the obstacles I had overcome during the past year and gain the strength to face the current and future ones yet to unfold. My faith is the pillar of my life. It holds me up on days when I can't stand. It motivates me to see the good in everyday moments and to acknowledge the tiny profound details that matter so much. My faith is there for me when I am weak, like a guiding light that shines and shows me the way. Whenever something goes wrong in my life, I hold on to my belief that *everything happens for a reason*—Allah guides me to what is best, even if I can not see its benevolence until hindsight. My path is *mine to walk*, and *only I can walk it*.

In Islam, there is a concept called *Tawwakul*, which means having full faith that Allah will take care of you even when things look impossible. I find myself constantly leaning into *Tawwakul* and surrendering my life to Allah's will because I find contentment when I do. Everything in life becomes better, and I release the tension and stress that overtakes me when I try so hard to control every minute detail. We want to grab hold of the wheel and take ourselves to where we believe is better. We want that promotion, desire more children, work to accumulate wealth, and foolishly believe that our health will always be at its best—until sickness takes hold of us. We fight against the plan that Allah has written for us, forgetting His wisdom and mastery in timing. As it is written in the Qu'ran, *"We plan, Allah plans—and Allah is the best of planners." -Surah Ali Imran (3:54).*

It is hard when you desperately want something, and you believe to your core that it is what you need, to simply say, "Okay Allah, I really, really want this, but I will leave my request with you; please do what is best." The truth is, we all resist and have moments in our life when we struggle to understand *why* calamities befall us, or *why* things come easily to some, and as a storm for others. It is only after we *lean in,* release all expectations, and embrace the *present* that we manage to acknowledge the wisdom. When we reflect on the years that have passed, everything makes sense. *Allah was redirecting us to something better.*

The time when I feel the closest to Allah is when I immerse myself in supplication. We perform what we call *'du'a'* which are private conversations between you and your Lord where you ask Him for help and guidance, or even just express your gratitude for all the blessings that you have in your life. Whenever I perform them I feel as though I am being wrapped in His warmth. I know He is listening to me. I am certain that when I feel distant from everyone else He is always near.

The Prophet (ﷺ) said, "Verily your Lord is generous and shy. If his servant raises his hands to Him (in supplication) He becomes shy to return them empty."

Still, I have discovered that walking the path of faith is not always an easy path to walk. I have been misjudged and disregarded more times than I can count. I have been called hurtful names, scrutinized for my beliefs, and misunderstood. A memory that still haunts me is when I was ridiculed and spat on by a group of rowdy teenage boys as I walked my newborn twin daughters to the local shops in (so-called multicultural) London. *What did I do?* I kept walking, pushing my babies in their stroller, gripping the handlebar tighter as I prayed that we would not be harmed. Whenever I have experienced discrimination, I always think, *I accept you for who you are; why can you not accept me for who I am?*

I admit that I feel deeply disappointed by the ongoing debate brought by some branches of feminism who claim they fight for women to be free, yet are against a woman *choosing* to cover her hair or face. I personally find this to be a complete contradiction to women *being free*. I want to cover myself; that is my choice and my desire—if that was taken away from me, and I could not leave my house due to having to be uncovered outside, would I be a *free* woman? No! I would never discriminate or judge someone based on how they choose to live, even if it went against everything I believe to the core of my being. However, I respect my Higher Power; I know I do not own that right to judge; only He, the Everlasting can.

In contemplation, through all those moments, I see the wisdom and the bless-ings in every step I have had to walk during my path of following Allah and the Prophet's(ﷺ) teachings. It has made me want to be the voice for the voiceless—to advocate for those who are too often misunderstood. The adversity I have expe-rienced encouraged me to write this story so that I can hopefully Ignite change and help eliminate the prejudice that is currently residing in the world. I want everyone to know that we are all *one of the same*—we all feel pain, desire love, and deserve to be respected despite our differences. We all laugh, cry, and have a favorite meal that *only our mum can make.*

The Prophet (ﷺ) said, "Whoever established prayers on the night of Qadr out of sincere faith and hoping for a reward from Allah, then all his previous sins will be forgiven; and whoever fasts in the month of Ramadan out of sincere faith, and hoping for a reward from Allah, then all his previous sins will be forgiven."

Ramadan, for me, is magic. It is filled with Ignite Moments that arrive every year to reshape, awaken, and educate me. It catalyzes me to analyze the past year, work on what I must do to become a better person, and enriches my faith and connection to Allah. It also increases family bonds, strengthens the communities, rebuilds our ties to those we love, and encourages us to stay away from what doesn't benefit us. I especially love the fact that I use my phone less during Ramadan. Hands down—I am an avid phone browser. I love watching *Netflix*™ series and *Pinterest*™ scrolling. I also love my *Kindle*™; as a book editor, it is built within my soul to read, read, read. Still, during Ramadan, I opt for less screen time to dedicate myself to worship. It is a detox for the soul, reminding me of what is *really* important.

We all search for one exceptional night in Ramadan—Al Qadr. No one knows exactly when this night will be. It takes place during the last ten nights of Rama-dan when the Qur'an was revealed to the Prophet(ﷺ). During this special night, believers worldwide seclude themselves in prayer, calling out to their Lord, and asking for all the things that their heart desires. Some pray for health, love, and forgiveness, others for help, guidance, and Jannah (heaven). We believe that

Angels descend on that night, and with them, they bring down the prewritten destiny for each person for the following year. However, Allah can change their prewritten destinies on this night, which is why we dedicate that night to glorifying Him and doing good deeds.

I remember watching my Jeddah praying when I was a child. It was transformative to witness her devotion to her Lord. She would wear beautiful garments made of the finest silk, with intricate little details sewn into them. Every movement she did in her prayers—from standing to bowing to her forehead touching the floor—you could feel her love and loyalty to her Maker. When she finished praying, she would sit with her hands out, palms facing up, and ask Allah to protect us, to guide us to what is best, immersing herself in gratitude for all that she had in her life. That, to me, was a footprint left on my soul. A memory that if I close my eyes now, I can see right in front of me. Her diligence was an example that I habitually reflect on when I am in need of guidance. She would always tell me, "Allah only tests those whom He loves, so be patient in your tests, and you will see the blessings arrive." I believe that this is what she stood by, and her life was one of abundance because of it.

Abu Huraira reported: The Prophet Muhammad(ﷺ) said, "If Allah wills good for someone, He afflicts him with trials." Source: Ṣaḥīḥ al-Bukhārī (5645)

Jeddah's beautiful eyes would glisten, as she would continue to share with me, "When Allah wants good for you, He will inflict you with trials and tribulations to bring you closer to Him. He wants to remind you that no matter where you turn on this Earth, or who you have around you—He is the one who loves you the most, and He will never leave you. For Allah, it is easy; all He says is "Kun Faya Kun"—"Be, and it is." Her commitment serves as a constant reminder that He can change our situation within a second, but we must show our devotion to Him, have gratitude for what we do have, and surrender ourselves to the most beautiful patience.

I believe that *our faith is the footprint* that we leave behind in this world. It is how we love, how we connect, how we endure, and how we treat others. It is what we will be remembered by, and the beautiful nuggets of wisdom that we share with those closest to us. It is what our children will embrace and build their lives upon. Never overlook the power of a childhood memory and the simple things in life. The money, the materialistic aspects of life—all these things are adornments of this world, but they do not *feed our souls*. The connection that you have with your Maker is your strength. How do you measure the strength of such a connection? It all lies in your faith. *Do you lean in? Do you accept your circumstances and persevere with gratitude? Do you dedicate time daily to your faith and your connection with your Lord? Has your faith made you a better person? Are you more humble, loving, and gracious? Are you kind to others?*

Ali ibn Abi Talib reports from the Prophet Muhammad (ﷺ): "Allah is kind and loves kindness, and he rewards for kindness in a way that He does not reward for harshness."

When we are kind, we enrich others. We leave footprints on their soul, even in a quick fleeting moment. It is a gift that uplifts those around us. Always choose to be kind, even if you are being judged or misunderstood. Perhaps your kindness is a gift to them from the Divine, at a time when they need it the most.

Your faith is your footprint—the legacy you leave in this world, and an example for the generations that will follow. You will touch many souls during your walk in life. Many of them won't ever see you again or even know your name. Perhaps it was the distraught lady you comforted on the train, the curious and friendly child you played with in the airport, or the shopkeeper to whom you gave back the extra change and extra gratitude. Along our path, we will leave behind traces of who we are and what we believe in. I pray for those traces to deepen your devotion, so that they become a reflection of your love, kindness, hope, and faith.

IGNITE ACTION STEPS

- **Let your faith be your compass.** When you feel low or that life is out of your control, lean in and surrender to your Lord. Have full faith that He will see you through the darkness and bring light into your life once again.

- **Treat others with love and humility**—it will come back to you tenfold.

- **Learn to embrace patience.** Patience will mold your character. It will help you to see the *wisdom within the pause.*

- **Learn to love the power in the pause.** When Allah is making you wait for something, redirect your focus to what you currently have in this moment, and all the blessings that surround you. Take a deep breath in, pray, and realize that if you were to try to count the blessings from your Lord, never would you be able to do so, the number is endless. Our eyesight, our hearing, the sky, the breeze, nature—everything is a blessing, and those who can admire and appreciate these things can also admire the pearls of wisdom that only He provides.

- **Contemplate your past** and how everything happened for a reason. Compare it with your current situation to reflect on how those experiences prepared you for today, and stay open to learning that what you are undergoing currently will also have profound meaning.

- **Study your faith.** I believe that knowledge is power, and the more that you learn about your faith, the more you will achieve a closeness to your Lord and all His Majesty. Learn about the prophets (peace be upon them), their stories will show you that even the most beloved to Allah had trials and tribulations in their life. Learn about the character that you should adopt and thrive to become.

- **Remember that your success lies in your fortitude,** your grace, and the way that you influence and lift up those around you—focus on this rather than the material world that will give and take, as it does for everyone.

- **Stand up for what you believe in**—we need more people in the world who are not afraid to embrace their uniqueness. Use your individuality as an example to others, with the intent to guide people away from judgment and harshness.

- **Remind yourself that He loves you immensely.** We are taught that Allah loves us all more than even our mothers. Whenever you feel alone in the world, take yourself to your place of prayer, and immerse yourself in solitude with your Lord.

- **Acknowledge the power of your footprint**—what do you want to be remembered for? What do you want to leave behind in the generations that follow you? Your faith is the greatest footprint that you will imprint on this earth. Use this to empower you, keep you steadfast, and guide you to who you were born to be.

Dan Gilman

DAN GILMAN

"Discover your potential; it is the bridge that connects you to the impossible."

My goal is to Ignite within you a sense of purpose and potential, while also highlighting the lasting impact of my mother's legacy. Through her inspiring story and the profound influence she had on numerous lives, I hope to demonstrate the incredible power of unwavering faith. By sharing her story, my aim is to inspire you and others to uncover your own potential and cultivate faith in yourselves, much like my mother did.

THE POWER OF FAITH AND HEALING: THE LEGACY OF CINDY GILMAN

The room was quiet, except for the soft whooshing sound of the oxygen machine and the quiet sound of my mother's labored breaths. I sat by her bedside, holding her hand and watching her chest rise and fall in a steady rhythm. I knew that the end was near, but it still came as a shock when her breathing slowed, and finally stopped. At that moment, as I watched my mother take her final breath, I felt a strange sensation within me. It was as if her spirit was passing on a message, one of faith and hope, a message that would Ignite my own spirit and transform my life.

As I sat there in stunned silence, I felt a newfound sense of purpose that I had never felt before. It was as if a spark had been lit within me, one that would guide me on a new path, a path of faith and discovery.

In the days that followed, as I received calls from over one hundred people, all sharing stories of how my mother, Cindy, had touched their lives, I realized the impact that one person could have on the world around them. It was then that I knew that my mother's spirit would continue to live on and that her unwavering faith would be the foundation upon which I built my own life.

Through my grief, I found a new sense of hope and inspiration—a belief that anything was possible if I had the faith to pursue it. I discovered that faith was the key that unlocked my potential, giving me the courage to dream, the strength to endure, and the power to manifest my greatest desires.

My mother believed that anything was possible if you had the faith to pursue it; her life was a testament to that belief. She was a woman of lifelong dedication to her faith. She was a spiritual counselor and intimate friend for innumerable people whose lives she touched in a very special way. In earlier life, she was a celebrated singer and performer, having sung with the Boston Opera Company, Lincoln Center NYC, the Miami Beach Yiddish Theatre, and Warsaw Ghetto Memorials. For years, she became a popular weekly radio talk show host and personality in Providence, Rhode Island, and continued with a livestream internet show.

Her life wasn't always easy. Like many of us, she faced challenges and obstacles along the way. However, through it all, she held onto her faith, never losing sight of her dreams and the potential that lay within her. With each step, she discovered more about her intuitive healing abilities and honed her skills—before long, she was using her gifts to help others.

My mother began her spiritual journey at a very young age. I was ten years old when she shared with me the first spiritual experience that she could recall as a second grader. She went up to her teacher and intuitively said, "I have to go home because my mother needs me. My grandfather just passed away." When my mother arrived home early from school, they were surprised to find out that she knew her grandfather was passing, and her grandmother validated that this death had indeed occurred just moments before her arrival.

At age seven, more than seventy years ago, my mother became aware of her spiritual gifts as she sang to a room full of Holocaust survivors at a memorial service held in Boston. Standing on a milk crate to reach the microphone, my mother brought tears to the eyes of many in the room. She nervously sang lullaby songs that the survivors remembered their mothers singing while they were in captivity in concentration camps.

Years later, during an interview, my mother reflected on that powerful moment of her youth; she shared a deep secret that no one knew what she was truly feeling standing on that milk crate: "As the audience's horrifying, suppressed memories surfaced, I didn't see them as they appeared that day. Instead, I saw them gaunt, with shorn heads and clad in striped uniforms like those in the camps. Shutting my eyes, my maternal grandfather materialized before my spiritual sight—young and robust, rather than the man once devastated by cancer who had passed away months prior. My late grandfather nodded, and in that instant, I realized that life extended beyond the mere physical form."

My mother told nobody of that experience for a long time, but eventually brought it up with my great-grandmother. My mother started crying, and my great-grandmother told her, "God is with you," and held her face in her hands.

Later, at a family gathering, my mother walked up to an uncle and warned him of an impending heart attack. Her mother quickly told her not to say things like this. My mother had come to acknowledge that her spiritual verbal slips may originate from her higher intuitive self or a spirit guide. Similarly, when I became aware of my own intuitive abilities, I faced a similar situation where I was advised to refrain from utilizing them. Upon hearing my mother's accounts of these experiences, I recall feeling a blend of wonder and apprehension. As I delved deeper into my talents, I encountered resistance and was advised to suppress my abilities.

At age seventeen, my mother sought formal training to enhance her musical career by attending Emerson College, where she once danced with Henry Winkler, 'the Fonz' in the show *Happy Days™*, during a college production. "We remained in touch long after our college days," she said.

My mother's journey after completing her studies at the prestigious New England Conservatory of Music involved pursuing a career as a professional musician. Through performing in a variety of cities and venues, she honed her skills and showcased her talents to diverse audiences. From the vibrant city of Miami, Florida, to the bustling metropolis of New York City, she entertained countless music enthusiasts. She also had the opportunity to perform in the scenic Catskill Mountains of Upstate New York and even ventured to the Bahamas to entertain international crowds.

At that time, before she became a professional medium, she would sometimes pick up future events about audience members and have premonitions about their lives as she performed her repertoire of songs from the stage. In her late twenties, she returned to Boston to begin to work as a professional intuitive spiritual medium.

My mother was a pioneer in this type of work. People started calling and asking her for readings. Both print and TV outlets started reaching out to her, requesting interviews to discuss her insights on spiritual understanding.

Over the course of more than twenty-three years, my mother provided solace and wisdom to thousands of listeners as a radio talk show host. Utilizing her intuitive and healing gifts and expertise in hypnosis and meditation, she helped facilitate the healing process for countless individuals.

As my mother's reputation grew, she began to attract more clients who sought her guidance and healing abilities. Her work as a spiritual medium was not limited to individual readings, but also included lectures and workshops on psychic development and spiritual topics. She also worked with intuitively gifted children and used her extrasensory perception (ESP) expertise to assist in police investigations, although she eventually retired from this service due to the emotional toll it took on her.

Despite her success as a medium and healer, my mother never forgot her roots as a performer. She continued to sing and perform throughout her life, often weaving her spiritual beliefs into her music. Her voice and presence were a source of comfort and inspiration to many, including me; she always believed that music had the power to heal and uplift. Today, I cherish a collection of her music on cassette tapes that I have converted to digital audio. These timeless recordings continue to inspire me and others who seek solace and motivation in her melodic expressions.

My mother's life was a testament to the power of faith and the potential within each of us. She believed that we all can connect with the Divine and use that connection to heal and transform ourselves and the world around us.

She believed that each person had the ability to heal and grow, and she worked tirelessly to help them unlock that potential. Her work was a reflection of her deep belief that anything was possible if you had faith in yourself and your abilities. She helped people overcome their fears, embrace their strengths, and tap into their inner power; doing so, she touched countless lives.

Her quote, "Don't ever stop believing in better times and brighter days. Too many possibilities, too many opportunities, and too many dreams to ever lose hope. When times are bad, they can only get better. When things are okay, with a little encouragement, you can help them stay that way. Tomorrow's horizon may hold surprises that will make things better than you ever imagined. Don't give up hope, and never stop believing in the things you can do—It could be that one of your dreams is just waiting around the corner. Make it come true. You can do it. I believe in you." These words of hope speak directly to my mother's life and enduring legacy.

The quote reflects the essence of my mother's journey, emphasizing the importance of never losing hope, even in the face of adversity, and believing in the possibility of brighter days and better times. It speaks to the limitless potential of the human spirit and the power of one's dreams. My mother's life and legacy continue to inspire and encourage others to pursue their dreams and to hold onto the hope that tomorrow's horizon may hold the surprises that will make things better than they ever imagined.

My mother lived a life of purpose, helping others to heal and grow, and her unwavering belief in the power of faith was a constant source of inspiration. Her legacy lives on, reminding us that we can achieve great things when we believe in ourselves and have faith in our abilities.

As her son, I was inspired by my mother's life and the lessons she taught me; to have faith in myself and to never give up on my dreams. She showed me that anything is possible if I have the fortitude to pursue my passions and the strength to endure challenges. Her life was a testament to the power of faith, and I am grateful for the example she set for me and so many others.

In my own life, I have found that the principles my mother lived by are just as relevant today as they were when she was alive. I have learned that I can overcome any obstacle and achieve my wildest dreams when I have faith in myself and my talents. I have found that having faith gives me the courage to pursue my passions and the power to manifest my greatest desires.

Over time, I also began to see my own life's impact on those around me. I realized that, like my mother, I, too, had the power to touch the lives of others in meaningful ways. I began to work in my community, volunteering my time and energy to help those in need. After my mother passed away, I took over her radio show, *Discover Your Potential*, to carry on her legacy and continue inspiring people to tap into their unique gifts and talents.

Through my work, I saw firsthand how a small act of kindness or a word of encouragement could make a huge difference in someone's life. I witnessed how faith could give people the strength to overcome their fears and chase their dreams, making the world a better place.

As I continued on my journey, I also began to explore my own spirituality in more depth. I delved into different religious and spiritual traditions, seeking to understand the common threads that bound them all together. I studied the teachings of great spiritual leaders like Buddha, Jesus, and Mohammed and renowned Rabbi Abraham Joshua Heschel. I found that their messages of love, compassion, and service resonated deeply with me, inspiring me to further embrace my own spiritual path.

Through my studies, I discovered the power of meditation and mindfulness. I learned how to quiet my mind and connect with the present moment. These practices brought me a sense of peace and calm that I had never experienced before.

As I look back on my mother's life and the impact that she had on so many people, I am filled with gratitude and awe. I am grateful for the example she set for me and the lessons she taught me. And, I am in awe of the power of faith and the incredible potential that lies within each and every one of us.

As the quiet room once again enveloped me, I felt the echoes of that moment reverberate through my being, when I thought I was letting my mother go. Yet, in the silence, I discovered that I wasn't truly letting her go, for the profound beauty of her spirit cascaded around me, ushering in a vibrant tapestry of life's wonders. As I held her hand, I felt the warmth of her love, the faith she had in me, and the hope that was born within my soul. In that instant, our connection transcended the boundaries of the physical world, and I realized that she would forever be a part of the person I am and the one I am yet to become. Her legacy, etched in love, faith, and kindness, now serves as a guiding light for my life's journey, as I strive to walk with the same grace and dignity that she embodied. Her memory ignites my faith, allowing me to embrace the boundless possibilities that life has to offer.

Rest in peace, Mom.

These four simple words hold so much meaning and emotion, yet they still fail to convey the depth of my love and admiration for you. You were more than just a mother to me; you were my guiding light, rock, and best friend.

You were a mother who loved her child with every fiber of her being. You instilled in me the values of kindness, compassion, and selflessness and taught me to always put others before myself. You were my biggest cheerleader, my confidante, and my hero.

And now, as I say goodbye, I take comfort in knowing that you will always be with me. Your legacy of love, faith, and kindness lives on in each of us, and I will honor your memory by continuing to live my life with the same grace and dignity that you exemplified.

Mom, you will be deeply missed, but your spirit will live on forever.

As you traverse the pages of your story, may it serve as a gentle reminder that our connections with loved ones have the power to endure, even beyond the boundaries of time and space. In moments of doubt or uncertainty, look within yourself and remember to believe in your own strength, resilience, and capacity for growth.

Draw inspiration from the lessons woven throughout your life, as they reveal the power of love, faith, and hope to light our paths and Ignite our spirits. By embracing the wisdom shared in this tale, you too can harness the potential for transformation, cherishing the beautiful connections in your own life and allowing them to guide you in your journey toward self-discovery and boundless possibilities.

IGNITE ACTION STEPS

- **Have faith** in yourself and in the potential within. *Believe that anything is possible if you have the courage to pursue it.*

- **Discover and nurture** your unique talents and abilities. *Learn to hone your skills and use them to help others.*

- **Be persistent and resilient** in the face of challenges and obstacles. *Keep sight of your dreams and goals.*

- **Embrace a life of purpose and passion.** *Aim to make a positive impact on those around you.*

- **Learn from the wisdom and experiences of others**, *such as mentors, spiritual leaders, or family members.*

- **Explore your spirituality.** *Seek a deeper connection with your Higher Power.*

- **Practice mindfulness and meditation** *to bring peace, calm, and focus to your life.*

- **Give back to your community** through *acts of kindness, service, and volunteering.*

- **Foster loving and supportive relationships** *with family and friends.*

- **Honor and cherish** the legacy of those who have inspired and guided you in your life journey, and *aim to be a positive role model for others.*

Becca Rae Eagle
M.S.Ed.

BECCA RAE EAGLE,

M.S.ED.

*"The Nativity Star anchors my Faith; my courage
to shine brightly in all seasons of life."*

**It is my intention that this story ignites your own Nativity Star, your own
Light of Faith within you, to anchor you here in the present, in the Presence
of All, that is beyond explanation but experienced best by *wonder* and by
heart. In seeking with a sense of awe and curiosity into even the tiniest of
miracles in life, we connect to the Divine within our own precious being,
the true embodiment of joy.**

ANCHORED BY A STAR

What use is an anchor if you don't have a boat? I wondered. You can use it as a
landmark, a dedication ceremony destination, or as a giant, intriguing paperweight.
If you don't put the anchor to its intended use, it is merely ornamental. This is

how many people perceive *faith* in their lives—ornamental yet non-functional, of no use or service.

This past Christmas season, I felt like an empty boat, compromising the integrity of its anchor, making a fool of myself in the abandoned, lonely harbor. Then, I saw the origin of my faith holding me seaworthy. I was anchored by a star I recall from my youth.

When I was a little girl, my favorite Christmas decorations centered around the Nativity Star. To me, it was Christmas itself. The Star and the Creche, the little Holy Family in the stable: Mary with an infant child, open hands with receiving posture, father Joseph, standing in awe over her, Baby Jesus lying asleep on the hay. Some Creche mangers come with small animals, some shepherds, some with wise men and camels, and some with angels. I was always mesmerized by it as it pulled me in, rapture in my small soul.

Yet, to me, the Angel that kept her watch was always missing something above her, something the crafters could not manufacture—the Nativity Star. It was the anchor to the miracle, the light that poured over the Light of the World, pointing the way to the One I held faith in since a small child. In pictures on prayer cards, my grandmothers, aunts, and grandfather kept close in their homes, there they were, the angels. Their wings wide and magical, part human, part bird, to my child's eyes. The allure of flight, aligning closer to the *heavens* than pulled down to earth.

As a little girl, I wanted to be closer to God. I wanted that possibility of flight, to be an important messenger. I wanted the glow around me, pouring translucently within the Light shining down upon me, airy, weightlessness, and anointing. The wanting I felt at these images almost made me weep, even as a young child. The Creche Angel was nothing without the Nativity Star. She had no halo and no light below. I wanted so much to fix this and see the Angel as she was in prayer cards, fully illuminated to bring good tidings to the world of the baby in the manger below. Later, I'd learn these were tidings of comfort and tidings of joy. Songs swirled in my ears from an early age at the touch of a needle to a record player and the choir loft above at Mass. The songs reflected those of the angels and their Nativity Star.

When I was little, the Creche held a special space on my grandparents' large stereo system and record player. It was a looming wooden box centered in the back of their living room. Growing up, we gathered In front of it every Christmas Eve: my immediate family, my grandparents from both sides, usually an aunt and uncle, sometimes cousins and godparents, and always someone who couldn't travel for Christmas but was adopted as our own to celebrate. The presents reached from the picture window with the tinseled artificial tree almost to the couch across the room. In a tiny three-bedroom ranch home, there was barely room to walk to grab a seat—a sea of gifts among the working-class folks who made the children feel like the richest children in the world.

The adults surrounding us were the matriarchs and patriarchs of our family, Polish and Ukrainian immigrants to this nation still celebrating a meal and a gathering in the old ways. With similar cultures, they revered Christmas Eve the same way—a sacred night to put all differences aside and focus on the miracle of love among us. Anyone was welcome at their table and in this living room. All dressed up from Mass if you cooked, you had an apron. If you helped clear the table and wash dishes before opening presents, you rolled up your sleeves. Dessert was served as children emptied their stockings. If a guest was with us, an extra stocking was hung with a last-minute gift. No one was left out. A secretary, a food distributor, a nurse, a homemaker, a top international executive, guests with various professions, from real estate agents to priests, and us, the children, from birth to college age, all gathered there. We were all equally loved, among the *presents*—the *presence* of what we knew as a family—the *presence* of us.

One of the most important guests, another miracle in the living room carefully tended by the Creche, was my father. The economy gave my father a tough choice when I was six years old: take a similar job in Mexico with the company or be left with no job at all. Then, the job took him to Singapore, Korea, China, Japan, and Singapore again. He would show up jet-lagged, in fancy suits and shoes with an ornate gold cross around his neck and *Rolex*™ watch on his wrist. His cologne left its scent on me when he hugged me, a smell that meant my Dad was home. To have his attention this one night of the year, at the table where the rest of us sat every Sunday, in the living room where we normally spent time watching football games with my grandfather and his friends. To have Dad home made my family complete. It made Christmas all the more special as he flew in just for this simple gathering in these humble surroundings. To me, he was a wise man at the stable among us. Though a high-level executive all my life, he took a holiday once a year to be a normal dad. And over us, the Creche watched, the Holy Family uniting us all.

The Nativity Star remained my anchor, and when I thought about every December 25th, I could appreciate Christmas as more than merely Santa Claus. The Star was what provided me comfort year after year, after year. My ornamental token, the symbol over humanity's darkest calendar day of the year in the Northern Hemisphere, is the representation of Love waiting to Ignite the hearts of humankind. That Light is the same, yesterday, today, forever.

Unfortunately, only some things from those days remain the same. The house is gone, as are the people and the laughter that filled it. Relationships became strained, and we stopped talking to one another. Time and illness took so many of them, and the loss hit each of us who remained so differently, creating rifts we couldn't mend. There is no more football or dinner on Sunday or getting together for Christmas. Where the idea of family was once an anchor, the term is now ornamental. My holidays have felt more like a horror flick than a *Hallmark*™ special the past few years. The light, once bright, felt dimmed in the testing circumstances, and I often felt alone.

I found a man who I thought perhaps could be a new anchor. He was my partner in so many senses, dancing with me, hiking with me, and helping me raise my son from a previous marriage. He has been many things to me, but in time would prove to set me adrift again. Years of broken dreams followed as my world was rocked by the loss of three of my parents: my mom, my mom-in-law, and my birth father. My mom's illness and decline had sparked us to leave our home in Colorado and return to New York, where I could scrape together substitute teaching jobs until a full-time job came along. Meanwhile, my husband worked various restaurant jobs, but COVID-19 would derail our plans. He was laid off not once, not twice, but three times because restaurants could not handle business as usual during the pandemic.

I loved my job and thought I could hold us afloat with my full-time teaching hours. I worked in a community that was a meld of Native American traditions and old-fashioned agricultural practices, a multicultural mix of children seeking their own shot at what was left of the American Dream in confounded COVID-19 times. We navigated online, in-person, and creatively learning together. Our happiest and most comfortable days were in the outdoor classroom space where we practiced expressive writing and mindfulness, free to breathe with one another until the weight of regulations brought us indoors under heavy lock and key. Together we explored relationships in a time when all were socially distanced but as close as we could be in heart.

I'll never forget the day I saw one of my students' smiles for the first time, masks off, safely distanced outside. I started to cry as the beauty I knew of her substance reflected in the corners of her lips, tilting upward toward her carefree cheeks. My students milked cows, worked with heavy farm equipment, chopped wood for the seniors in their community, attended Longhouse, beaded, and created captivating earrings and dreamcatchers. My adopted, creative children felt safe to explore while in my care. I held my students to higher standards than usual, as times were highly unusual. They never ceased to delight me, rising to the challenges of the times.

Eventually, though, it became nearly impossible for me to physically, no less mentally, cope under the weight of all the stress. My birth father's illness with COVID-19 was the last strike to my thinning shell. I became ill and was medically mandated not to wear a mask in order to heal my consistently infected sinuses. I was facing an expensive and painful surgery if I didn't clear up the infection on my own. That, coupled with the pressure of a marriage in strain and financial duress, clouded my outlook and my ability to teach. My doctor pulled me to rest and follow his care plan. By the time I had fully healed, my family medical leave had expired, and New York State still had a mask mandate in place for public schools. I could not return to my students, my beloved teens, even if I had wanted to. Politics had choked out my career and sense of immediate possibilities, yet they could not suffocate my *faith*.

We experienced poverty, food insecurity, and possible eviction due to all the health and employment shifts, and I wrote among it all. I journaled to save my own life and talk to God in the process. Meanwhile, unable to cope, alcohol tightened its grip over my husband, my best friend, and I found myself in its shadow. Chip by chip, wave by wave, the empty shell of my vessel remained tethered to the anchor, the anchor of my Star, the anchor of my faith. Yet, the anchor was not serving its purpose as it always had. Was it worth tying this debilitated, life-worn, rickety boat—myself, splintering in the shadows—to what started to feel like a glorified paperweight? No light seemed to break through, no less a Nativity Star, to spotlight any hope of our 2022 Holidays. I questioned, *Was it worth keeping the boat from splaying from the anchor when the outside world saw it as wasting away upon its heavy grounding point?*

After our simple Christmas breakfast, I took a moment to look over the blanketed white hill of our backyard, seeking Him in its purity: "Jesus, are you mine?"

I had offered my faith, full, true, and unwavering since I was around four years old. Staring out that window, I was forty-seven. In middle school, I had been taught to relax, to let go and let God as they say, in a simple breathing practice taught to me by a newly ordained Catholic priest, "Abba (breathe in); I am yours (breathe out). Abba, I am Yours." I have practiced this my entire life, and every morning, I wake up saying, "Abba, I am Yours. Thank you for this day. May I serve you in *joy* today."

This Christmas, though, it was time to reverse the question. "Abba, are you Mine?" I asked within my aching heart. I had never needed to know God's personal and healing love more than this Christmas. A turkey from the food pantry highlighted our meal; no Christmas tree, no presents. What we did have, though, was each other, a day off from work and the Christmas Creche of my youth (incomplete as before, with no Star). I remember when my maternal grandparents purchased it at Cosentino's Florist in 1983. They never bought any artificial lighting to highlight the manger scene, trusting it to shine on its own.

This Christmas Day we had the Creche, Morning Mass, Christmas movies, and each other. A massive snowstorm hit Christmas Eve night, and our mountain town roads were nearly impassible by morning. We braved the ice-laden, salty pavement, hidden lanes, all to arrive at a tiny, wooden Church. We said our prayers with hugs and tears, and each attending was left with a scrumptious orange-cranberry scone. We arrived home to a second breakfast and settled into cozy areas in our living room. No presents. No tree. Yet, on my mother's old wooden hope chest, there it was, the Creche, observing our holiday much juxtaposed with the holidays of my youth.

We tried to make the best of it. My son and I had a deal—I choose a movie, you choose a movie, and see if stepfather approves. We went with *The Polar Express* and *It's a Wonderful Life*. My son grew up boarding the train with Tom Hanks' characters to The North Pole while I grew up lassoing the moon and welcoming the bell ringing as an angel earns its wings in the Jimmy Stewart classic. My husband approved both titles, so down we sank, under blankets, space heaters pumping, melting into comfortable positions, lured into nostalgic bliss, forgetting the lack of material Christmas around us.

In our movie time, something magical happened. As Tom Hanks stared down at the young man and punched his ticket, I knew what he would say. I had known since I first saw the movie with my then toddler son on my lap, he said, "Believe."

Leading up to that point, my family had laughed with me as I cried at the songs, the dialogue, and the story's climax. But what brought me full-on sobs during *The Polar Express* was… "Believe." Had I not believed the components of that story before? Yet sitting there with two grown men, one who grew inside of me, and one who stretched me to my limits, beyond, and then back, it all came together for me. I glanced over at the Creche, and remembered the magic of Santa when my son was young. I recalled the *wonder* of Christmas past.

There it was, "Believe" in it all, every scene, from my cradle to staring at the simple wooden cradle that held the figurine Savior in the hay. "Believe" reigned in my heart, faith proclaiming its *presence* within me. All that had been testing me, gently melted away. As the evening progressed and the cast of *It's a Wonderful Life* sang "Auld Lang Syne," I knew I, too, had punched my golden ticket this Christmas. I knew I had also earned my wings. I sang with the angels themselves as I sobbed the happiest tears of all, the tears of *presence* in every Christmas holiday I had ever experienced all at once. As I sat in simplicity with my family, I finally saw the light above the manger—the light within my heart that no tossing or turmoil could ever unsettle again. I felt the light I had known before, staring at the Creche as an innocent girl praying on her knees in a blue cotton nightgown. Now it was brightly shining, illuminating *everything* I needed to see.

There we were, three humans who had been through it all together, dodging the squalls, stuck here in the harbor, a storm raging for us since May 2017. Six years had worn on us, yet hope was still present. Faith was at least still welcome here: in our hearts, in our gathering, in our songs, in our quiet prayers.

As I looked over at the now glowing manger, I felt the answer to the question I had boldly proposed. I felt the heartbeat of the baby figurine lying in the manger, living and breathing in the very heart of me. There was love in the room amongst the grace and forgiveness, healing humanity through my own family: my son, my husband, and me. We were a holy trinity by the mercy of life's allowances to gather, to complete the ritual around the ornamental stage with no light but our own to shine down on it below.

This year, the Nativity Star rose in my heart as I stood over that manger before settling off to sleep; Faith embodied in my being, in my humanity, the brightest light in the world, the *love* that I not only knew of but finally felt. I embraced the treasures I knew I still possessed: my mental health, identity, humanity, and love, the love that washed over it all. I was again safe, this humble vessel restored, and my question of faith replied to. Faith answered, "Becca, I am Yours." The Nativity Star anchors my Faith, and my courage to shine brightly in all seasons of life. May it shine within you also.

IGNITE ACTION STEPS

- **Give yourself Grace**—as you rest in your Light. Be gentle and forgiving to yourself, grace is a moment-by-moment process; forgiveness warms the way.
- **Truly feel to heal**—be patient with your emotions, and allow them to ebb and flow, for your Nativity Star will hold you gently if you don't rush the experiences.
- **Connect**—you're never alone along the journey. For any suffering you hold unique to yourself, trust that others have experienced it also. We are ONE and meant to be here for one another, walking closer toward our Light.
- **Rise up**—above your circumstances and shine brightly. Your faith is anchoring you. The view is always better from this vantage point, for remember, hope rises, just as an air balloon. Open your hands to receive the miraculous thread of Light, forever guiding you to the Source of all *love*. We are no different, you and I; we are each Anchored by a Star.

Karen Rudolf

Karen Rudolf

"Faith is awakening one's inner Self."

My intention is to open you to the possibility that *faith* is an activation, one that blossoms as an awakening of the wisdom within our *Selves*, reminding us the difference between flowers and weeds is within our own perceptions. The journey to self-mastery is a never-ending process of observing oneself without judgment, resulting in pure joy, beauty, and personal freedom. It is a journey that is still unfolding for me as I put this story to paper, one I know I'm not traveling alone. When we surrender control and release the false beliefs which we have carried over the years, faith becomes purely about believing there is something more, something bigger. We are truly greater than we believe ourselves to be, especially when we listen to our inner wisdom. When we lean into the *'BE-comingness'* of *Trust, Faith, Love, Peace,* and *Gratitude,* we get to see who we truly are.

Moving a Mountain Through Pain and Tears

I was never one to be as full of faith or mindful of faith to this degree, up until now. What is *faith* anyway? If I ask Siri what the definition of faith is, she responds with "1. A complete trust or confidence in someone or something. 2. Strong belief in God or in the doctrines of a religion based on spiritual apprehension rather than proof." I had no reason to question these dictionary definitions since God wasn't a noun used often in our household when I was young. Then faith was redefined for me when I was nine years old. My parents divorced, and my siblings, my mother, and I moved into my grandparents' home. There, a religious tradition that was foreign to me was strictly adhered to. It felt like the idea of faith was forced down my throat, and resentment began to build.

Yet, I tried in desperation to tap into faith, as I had been taught to define it, when I went through my own divorce. Within my mind lived a world of wonder, and I began to ask more *"why"* and *"how"* questions. Why had this happened "to me," looking at and blaming things outside myself, not realizing a whole wonderland was bubbling up within that I'd yet to explore. There was a moment when I was in the midst of my full-out pity party, feeling extremely sorry for myself, convinced the sky was falling. I recall dropping to my knees and praying of my own volition for the first time, which was very foreign to me. I begged God to save my marriage, save our family and make it all better. I trusted somehow, I'd land on my feet, which I did. That was the beginning of my own personal faith journey.

My first steps in trying to understand Faith led me to study world religions. I was looking outside of myself for support, encouragement, and guidance. I *knew* there was something more. *What was it about religion that flocked people together?* I discovered that no matter who we were, compassion seemed to be the common thread. Love was the driving force! As I noticed everything was interconnected, I devoured more quantum physics and neuroscience. My mind became a sieve with information overload. The world became my oyster; *Google*™ became my best friend! I became my own superhero and began the hero's journey of self-discovery and mastery.

I explored and attended many personal growth and development programs. In one particular business course, I'd learned team management and leadership skill sets, along with other masterful, life-expanding concepts. The course promised that I'd be able to be dropped anywhere in the world and land on my feet, to get through any situation. That training, and my personal faith, were about to be put to the test.

In January 2023, I headed down to beautiful Costa Rica for a group retreat. On the second day after my arrival, we were scheduled to go horseback riding on an amazing beach in Marbella. Having horses of my own, I was no stranger to the practice. On that glorious day, I mounted and hacked through the marshy tall grasses, which led to a beautiful expanse of open beach; rocky lined shores with waves splashing high. The group took off at a gallop, but my horse trotted a bit and stopped. I found it curious and edged him on. He had been avoiding the water, and the beach was quite rock laden. His feet were sore. So, I let him find his own way and just enjoyed the moment. As we eventually caught up to the rest of the group, the horse became attentive to staying with the pack. He did not notice the incoming wave, which hit his back hoof, causing him to spin around and send me *flying*.

Life took on the hallucinatory quality of a dream-like state. On my butt, not moving, I stared out at my legs for what seemed like an eternity as they were pounded by the ocean waves. First thought: *Oh shit, I can't move or feel my legs!* I was in shock and feeling numb. In the distance, I saw one of the participants come hauling butt down the beach. It felt surreal, like everything was in slow motion, until suddenly, poof! She was there, putting my arms around her neck as she and the guide attempted to lift me. It took all their strength to carry me and get me into a car.

No one knew what to do with me, frozen and numb. "Hospital," I said, trusting I had broken my hip. Not feeling my lower legs, the breathwork I use daily as a practice became my strongest tool. It supported me through the excruciating pain of going over rocky, bumpy country roads during the two-hour journey to the hospital. Getting pulled out of a small car and onto a gurney wasn't the easiest or most pleasant experience. I saw stars! Once in the emergency room, they told me that they would have to *cut* my pants off. In the midst of all the pain and agony, I remember telling them, "These are my only pair of jeans that fit really well. You've gotta peel them off of me." Although wet, they managed to roll them off and into a ball which is how they stayed for weeks till I got home. Go figure. So much for my good jeans.

Being in a developing country alone, having surgery while not speaking Spanish, was quite the adventure. Yet, I do not recall feeling fear at all. I believed I was in good hands. I chose to believe in something bigger than myself. I surrendered control, trusting and knowing I was going to be fine. I stopped and counted my blessings—It could've been so much worse.

After waking, the pain was incredible as the anesthesia started to wear off. Being a side sleeper and having to be on my back just created a whole other level of angst. I couldn't move; forced to wear a diaper which I could not change myself. When I asked for assistance, a nurse told me I could choose my wet diaper or intense pain, then walked away without waiting for my response, assuming I'd rather avoid the agony. I was humiliated, uncomfortable, feeling totally unheard and unseen. I would've chosen the diaper change because I knew the pain was temporary; it would subside. As long as I stayed still and used breathwork, I could keep myself calm.

That nurse wasn't allowed near me again. Thankfully my surgeon was amazing, getting me up and walking, and having me weight-bearing immediately. I was caught off guard learning the protocol for hip surgery was to get up right away and start moving, which proved *quite* intense. In the States, the protocol for a fractured pelvis was three weeks of flat bed rest. My mind became confused; stand or lay down? Painful either way! I had to trust my surgeon, which wasn't difficult. He took me to the solarium for some fresh air and vitamin D, with a huge dash of compassion, leaving me feeling looked after.

Privacy and modesty went out the window! Nothing like being further humbled as I learned to surrender, release control and let go of doing things myself. I was in excruciating pain. Having a broken hip, fractured pelvis, as well as a compound compression of the lower spine, it was a lot of pressure sitting, and it was a lot of pressure standing. Something that sounded as simple as getting onto the commode was unbearably painful. It put a lot of strain on my pelvis when I reached for the paper, which was just out of my reach, as was the call bell. I shed tears. I allowed the release to come. I questioned whether the physical pain or the emotional pain was more severe. Did it matter? *Pain is pain; I'm trusting the process.* I got to appreciate the little things in life, like being able to reach my toilet paper or wiping myself. These moments kept adding up, bringing me gratitude for what I had, not what I had lost. I never once thought in those terms because I believed this was only temporary.

I reflected back on quantum physics and neuroscience, how everything is energy, vibration, and frequency. I got grounded in the importance of mindset. Rehabilitation, whether medical or through my personal traumas, is having the grace and wisdom to discern when to release, surrender and trust the process while allowing myself to ask for support when needed. So many well-wishers' comments were, "Oh my God, how are you managing? You're in a foreign country, you don't speak the language, and you're all by yourself. How horrible it must be!" The truth was, it wasn't horrible at all. Ideal? No. I might've felt lonely from time to time, but *never* alone, and I knew I was expanding. Attitude is everything, and it seemed to me to support my best healing journey to make my choices count. I couldn't change what was, so I used translator apps, and somehow managed to communicate, making the best of the moment. The upside was I was learning a whole different culture and language. Every day was a new beginning filled with *gratitude*!

I recall looking out the hospital window at Costa Rica's volcanic mountains as I was reminded of a passage from the Bible about having the faith of a mustard seed. What the heck did that mean anyway? I pondered… *everything is work-out-able!* As I looked at the mountain from a distance, I realized how big it must be and how small in comparison I am. How might one move a mountain? Do we push it? Do we blow on it? I've come to realize the mountain is within. It's not looking at how big the mountain is, or how hard it would be to climb it, for me it was about looking more at my feet before me and taking one baby step in front of the other. Eventually, I get to see and experience not only getting to the peak but also moving down the other side. If we're brought to it with the right attitude and frame of mind, we *will* get through it. In the past, I would look up at the mountain and become overwhelmed by its height and breadth and think it was insurmountable, creating more anxiety. It's not a race; it's the forward momentum that carries us up to the other side. As with life, breathing deeply, one moment at a time, gives us the strength we need.

I set my intention before I left the hospital, I would walk out the door, which I did, however, struggling. This is when all the work, all the effort, and all the training actually came into play. I used all that I had learned to keep moving and make the journey home.

I would never be where I am now without learning how to open my mouth and ask for support. It's taken time, patience, education, and mastering myself, which meant leaning in, investing in, and recognizing I am worth it. Being my own advocate, I began creating support teams all around me. I found so many people who connected me to one person who connected me to the next person who could help me. I felt very blessed. I believe I am not meant to be doing life alone, and truth be told, it's taken me years to get to where I'm at. I am convinced it was me stepping up to be my advocate that moved me through this journey more easily.

As a child, I'd always loved and played with manipulative puzzles. I'd attempt to figure out the next best, quickest, easiest way to solve a puzzle, to fast forward through a problem or challenge. I love finding solutions to my own opportunities and the opportunities for others. The question then became, how to get myself home in my current state of being. *Universe, if I'm to make it home, I will be requiring some assistance and alignment!* That business course I had taken so many years ago paid off tangibly in this life-changing instance. After making numerous calls and educating myself on ways to get home safely, it wasn't an easy feat, however, supported by a team made all the difference. Thank goodness for friends and family showing up in support and good cheer on social media; it kept me connected. Once home, I spent my birthday in rehab and made the most of it. I chose to concentrate on my recovery and delegated as much as possible. *Thank you so much!* I asked, and the Universe aligned what I needed, showing me believing in a Higher Source comes from the inside out.

Has it always been easy? HECK no! Have I grown from each experience? HECK yeah! As I continue this journey, I realize I would never change the ups and downs of who I have become in the process. Shifting my stories, attitude and belief systems is creating lasting change. Life expanded for me by learning patience, believing in myself, and truly loving me first. Ultimately, reminding myself *faith* is awakening one's inner *Self.*

My inner *Self* visualizes my physical self walking and dancing again, and even getting back up on my horse. I'm seeing it happen; I'm feeling it. I'm experiencing it in my mind and breathing through it all. As the pain comes in waves, it's a reminder to slow down and breathe. By keeping a positive attitude and in the present moment, I will never lose *hope* or *faith, believing* or *knowing* there is something more, something bigger than myself. I am committed to believing in the power of prayer for myself and for those who have touched my life; they will never be forgotten.

To add to my walk in faith, I received a call while still in Costa Rica. I realized those who were going to inspire me most were not just two-legged but four-legged. That scared, sore horse who first sent me flying into this new journey was not the only one to bring me clarity. As fate would have it, Apache, my own rescue horse, went down and couldn't get up while I was away. "He couldn't use his legs" rang in my ears, 'I' couldn't use my legs either, no coincidence, we were that connected. "It's his time," came across the phone lines as I spoke to the vet. That day I cried uncontrollably. I cried for Apache, I cried for the guilt of not being there with him and cried for myself. I released, I forgave, I mourned. The release was cathartic despite the mirroring similarities.

That experience has impacted me mentally, emotionally, physically and spiritually. It seems to me that nothing happens by coincidence; it's now up to me to go deeper and continue to master myself. William Shakespeare said it so eloquently in his famous play, Hamlet, "To thine own self be true!" I live by that. My experience was merely an experience that needed to happen, to further define who I am. This is the only moment we will ever have; who might we choose to become in the process?

Life isn't always a bed of roses! One must allow oneself the grace to mourn and allow for a momentary pity party. One of the things I now declare is to be the leader of my own life, and what that means is learning *humility, surrender, releasing, patience,* and *trusting* the process. I am able to choose moment to moment who I am being, responding rather than reacting. I accept being in the moment and going with the flow with the things I have no control over, all while being grateful, and trusting everything is in perfect order. What we resist, persists. I stopped resisting, realizing what I embrace, I manifest. I look for the silver lining. Intuitively, I know I'm supposed to let go and let be.

Having faith is part of the journey. Without the challenges, there would be no contrast in life. Believing in yourself and your capabilities awakens you to your own inner beauty and have *faith* in yourself to see the unique potential within you.

Ignite Action Steps

- **Trust the God within.** Be your own superhero! Allow yourself to shine, granting yourself grace and ease. Spirit can only do *for you* what Spirit can do *through* you, and trials will only strengthen you.

- **Choosing to Trust** is a courageous act in and of itself, turning fears into love and hope. Allow yourself to be in the flow, making each moment count, because you never know when or what may happen.

- **Self-mastery** requires being in the present moment. Choosing faith as it calls us into action to build our personal power allows us to take the next best steps towards our desires, trusting we are safe.

- **Keep your thoughts**, emotions, and intentions aligned with a good attitude and sense of humor. Remember, laughter is the best medicine, and joy lifts your frequencies. It's the alignment that allows for quantum opportunities and synchronicities to show up.

- **Moving a mountain** begins with accepting, surrendering, forgiving oneself, and allowing. Believe in the impossible. Faith is the evolution, transmutation, and transformation of self-mastery, allowing for a new perspective without judgment. Bring forth your love and light as *love,* which is the strongest force in the Universe, and never take *anything* for granted!

- **Release the urge or tendency** to make excuses, as the power is within us all, which can heal Oneself and the World.

Cheryl Viczko

CHERYL VICZKO

"When your heart smiles, so does your face."

Trust that you are reading this story at the perfect moment. Allow the words to transform you. Fill your being with love and peace, free of judgment and self-criticism. Realize that opportunities for your own evolution present themselves through conscious awareness of unintegrated moments. Allow your emotions to rise to the surface to be acknowledged and witnessed, then, like the wind takes a leaf up and away, swirls through the body as if free for the first time. Together let's venture into the playground of curiosity, becoming inquisitive about all that you've experienced and that which has influenced your beliefs. May 'The Winds of Change' bring with them expansive questions aimed towards all you've been taught, told, or led to surmise.

ONE RED CARNATION

I have always been very inquisitive. Since a young age, I've constantly asked questions to gain clarity, and if the person I am asking can not supply an answer that resonates with me, I will keep asking questions or create an experience to better comprehend. This day's question in my curious six-year-old mind was, "Mom, why can't I crawl down the stairs going head first?" Her quick response was, "Because I said so." It was a phrase that was all too common to my young ears; it felt like an invitation to experiment and figure it out for myself. Ignoring my mother's comment, I headed to the top of the creaky wooden "L-shaped" staircase. Eleven stairs, a landing, and two more totaled the thirteen stairs in our farmhouse. Positioning myself at the top of the staircase, facing downward, curly hair and head leading the way, I cautiously placed my right hand onto the first stair in front of me, and my left hand went onto the next stair. I managed to get down maybe two stairs before the thumps began.

THUMP, THUMP, THUMP. I toppled head over heels down the stairs until I hit the landing with a loud crash. Mom came running in a panic to investigate the noise, and examined my little body for signs of blood or broken bones as she helped me stand up. Ensuring I was okay, she asked if I was 'satisfied.' Frustrated by my failure and stomping my right foot down, "But Mom, why can't I crawl down the stairs going head first?" I asked again. "You just can't do that, Cheryl." Not a sufficient response for me. If I could crawl *up* the stairs, I should be able to crawl *down* the stairs. Up to the top, I went again, positioning myself and sweeping the curls from in front of my eyes. I put my left hand on the first step, my other hand on the second step, and sure enough, went somersaulting down the eleven stairs hitting the outside wall on the landing. This time, there was no visit from Mom. She knew her little 'Curious George' (as she called me) was still not satisfied. *Yes*, I did it a third time. Same result. Shaking off the pain and confusion, I reluctantly admitted, "Well, I guess you can't crawl down the stairs forward." Mom smiled, shook her head, and continued preparing dinner. I went outside to play.

Growing up on a small farm with a large family, the church was a weekly scheduled outing. Sunday meant dressing up in our "best clothing" to attend church. Outside, people were talking and smiling, inside, they went solemnly. We recited the same mantras over and over and over again, becoming ingrained in our belief system. Every week, it was the same, so much so that I would kneel before being told to. I could predict who would be first in line and who would hide in the back pews because they were hungover. The older I got, the more I questioned this weekly facade.

My young inquiring mind had *oh so many questions*; if we live in integrity, with love and compassion, then what was the purpose of church? Was it simply a place to gather to hear about the escapades and gossip of the previous week? Or, was it to be given a clean slate of consciousness by confessing our sins to a complete stranger? How was that even possible? Who was he to wave a magic wand? Why on earth would we want to eat the body and drink the blood of

Jesus? Why were there only altar boys and no altar girls? What about the people that did not have transportation to go to church - could they communicate with God in their own homes? Why did people put their gum under the pews? Why was church only on Sunday? Why did we give money, was that what was meant by paying for your sins? Why did people go inside when they seemed so much happier outdoors? The questions were endless.

Outside was a sanctuary. Many carefree hours were spent in the fresh, clean air, playing amidst the poplar and willow trees, or running in the open landscape flying kites. The discovery of the first prairie crocus about to flower in the field was inconceivable. How could snow be on the frozen ground, and this tiny purple flower emerge to signal spring? The river would thaw, swell, and overtake its banks as the snow melted and the runoff added excess moisture. The current of the river would accelerate, shifting the sandbars to new locations. Debris would easily be swept downstream in the raging movement of the river. On rare occasions, the torrential river would swell to such a height it would encompass the bridge. Barricading the only access to town for our neighbors and farms to the south. Mother nature could be so powerful and yet so gentle in the summer rains that quenched the dry soil with much-needed moisture.

A favorite part of summer was swimming in the river, perfectly situated at the bottom of our farmhouse hill. One sunny afternoon, two of my siblings and I begged mom to let us go swimming. She finally agreed with the promise that we would be careful and play only where the sandbars were. Typically my older brothers would investigate and locate the safest places to swim. The three of us headed down the hill toward the water. I don't recall what my siblings were doing, but I do remember jumping off the sandbar. I went down, down, down into the blackness of the water. It seemed like there was no bottom as I kept sinking. Just before panic started, I could hear a gentle voice calmly saying, "We are here; just move your arms up and down." I followed the instructions, and when I broke the surface of the fast-moving river, gasping for air, I was about one-quarter mile downstream from where I had jumped in. My siblings hadn't noticed I was missing, but our golden retriever was there waiting for me as I clambered my way to the shoreline. Together we walked back to where the other two had been and joined in the fun.

Despite the power of having communed with my angels for the first time, I dared not speak about what had transpired for fear we would never be allowed to swim by ourselves again. Pierce Lake was at the center of our summer's entertainment. We spent sunlit days in the water by our cabin until we'd hear the haunting wail of the loons call in the evening, signaling quiet time as the sun set. All around the lake, campers knew it was around midnight when Tony (my dad) did his distinctive undulating "Tarzan jungle call," beating on his chest followed by a moonlight dive into the lake.

Frequently in the fall, we would take a drive up to Cold River for a picnic, skipping stones and scouring the water's edge for items that we could later turn into treasured gifts. I'd collect driftwood and share with Mom what I could see in each piece. She was very talented and creative, and she often commented that I had quite the imagination. Those one-on-one times with Mom created very special and treasured moments for me.

During the winter, dressed in our snowsuits, we would make snow angels while staring up at the northern lights. The crisp air filled our lungs as we laid in awe of the dancing colors' majesty across the night sky's deep blackness. At the time, I believed the lights were created by starlight reflecting off the glaciers. That inquisitive imagination of mine led me to experience many more adventures throughout my life.

It seemed the more questions I asked, the more questions arose. Like, why was our big yellow school bus called a "Bluebird" bus? That question would be replaced by a more profound one part way through the ninth grade. Sitting towards the back of the dusty, noisy bus, an image of my mom came across my mind. It was out of the ordinary for me to receive such a vision. I knew mid-afternoon she would lay down on the couch and often doze off while we were at school, awakening as we came home. She was the first to rise, making dad's breakfast and lunch and kissing him goodbye as he left to go to work, calling us when it was time to get ready for school. Her days were always filled with housework, baking, sewing, and laundry. You name it, my mother did it. There was no doubt in my mind that she relished her afternoon nap time before the chaos she called her children came in the door.

As the flash of her sleeping on the couch came to my consciousness, I instantly understood that she was ill. That she was dying. It startled and scared me to know such a thing. Shortly after that experience, she entered the hospital, never to return home. My vision had come to fruition. There I was, feeling abandoned without feminine leadership at fifteen. Thrust into a motherly role with a younger brother and my dad, on a farm, with no mom. My world came crashing down.

After Mom's funeral, the community gathered in support around us. They brought food, desserts, and condolences. People would apologize and say, "I'm sorry," a phrase that was confusing to me. I was angry. "Why are you sorry? You didn't kill her," was my usual response, fueled with sarcasm. I'd reach for chocolate or sugar as a source of comfort as new questions erupted in my mind. *How could GOD take my mom away from us?*

I hoped a conversation with our local parish priest might provide some insight. He agreed to listen to my questions and answer the best he could. I asked, "If God is everywhere, and God knows everything I do, and God knows if I am truly apologetic for what I did or said, then why do I have to tell you during confession?" He diplomatically started to answer, but the barrage of questions ended with one response that stunned me: "If you don't believe, you don't belong."

Those words created a ripple throughout my body. This was all the confirmation I needed. The church was not a place of safety or answers, it was a place of rules that were to be followed without question. That did not resonate with me and my innate curiosity. The end result of that conversation was realizing that my faith was not contained within four walls, a roof, and pews.

After graduating at eighteen I moved away from my hometown, and the random visions of death became more frequent. They would be coupled with a bottomless breath, like taking a deep inhale and not stopping the inhalation. Often I would see tragedy involved, like vehicle accidents. I never shared those images with others, concerned those around me would think I was lying or needed psychiatric help. The final straw was *seeing* and having a *knowing* that my oldest brother was about to die. Unlike the past instances, I disclosed it to a friend, hoping that would 'break the spell.' I prayed. I was wrong. The phone call came within hours of me voicing the vision.

Struggling to understand what was happening to me, I went for a long walk. I couldn't take it anymore and screamed up to the heavens that I did not want to see the future events. If all I would see was death and loss, I wanted nothing to do with it. The visions stopped, the knowingness stopped, and finally, I could breathe a deep sigh of relief and carry on with my life.

For my dad, however, carrying on was much tougher. I could see how my mom's passing broke him. He suffered multiple little heart attacks that weakened his heart. In my early thirties, I had an unexpected and strong urge to see him. I told my boss, "I'm going fishing with my dad." He could tell by the look on my face this was something I needed to do, but he didn't question me. It had been a while since Dad and I were together; by this time he had remarried and was living close to where I grew up. He loved to spend time fishing, and with his weakened heart he'd created an ingenious way to load and unload the boat from his truck without physically stressing his body.

When I got to Dad's we went fishing and spent the entire weekend talking, reminiscing, laughing, and having a great time. It was the last time I saw him alive. Within weeks of my visit, I received two simultaneous phone calls, from my brother and sister, informing me that Dad had suffered a fatal heart attack. My world came crashing down again.

The service for Dad had to be held at the community hall, as the church wasn't large enough. Many followed the slow procession to the gravesite. We watched as the people from the funeral home pulled the casket out of the hearse and placed it above the opening in the ground. Looking at the faces of everyone shrouded in the heaviness of loss I could feel the overwhelming grief of those in attendance. The questions came. Where was Dad? Was he okay? Here we were, standing at his grave; his body was about to be buried... where was *he*?

Searching for answers, I looked up at the cloudy, dreary sky, perfectly timed to witness the clouds part. I felt a ray of sunshine on my face. On that cold October afternoon, as if by magic, one red carnation was picked up by the wind and landed at my feet. Instantly I knew Dad, God, was there with all of us. There was no separation. If my dad could part the clouds and have the wind pull one carnation off his casket, he was with me; he knew my thoughts and how alone I was feeling. He knew his inquisitive daughter was wondering where he was, and now I knew that although his physical body was no longer functioning on this earth, his spirit was and always would be with me.

I've come to understand that I am an empath, meaning I sense and feel other people's emotions and energy. As a child, I did not realize my guides and angels were always with me. That is where the premonitions would come from. They were giving me signs, images or visions. I now accept, appreciate and continue to strengthen these talents, having created an agreement with Spirit that I willingly channel information for the highest good of all. I've established my own definition of GOD: **G**rand **O**verall **D**esigner. My faith lies within my heart, my mind, and my soul where I choose at any given moment to acknowledge and appreciate it or not. My faith is within my connection to Mother Gaia, my guides, and my angels.

I remain inquisitive; eager to ask and eager to understand. In my study of the Universal Laws I have thought, *Oh, if only my mom could have explained gravity to me, I would not have had to experience tumbling down the stairs multiple times to understand it.* Through my quest for knowledge, I now appreciate my early connections and encounters with wind; *Feng* means wind and reflects the unseen energy and my multiple connections with *Shui*, defined as water pertaining to the seen energy. The ancient principles of *Feng Shui*. The unseen, in my opinion, is more powerful than the seen. The wind has the strength to bring in a powerful storm, shifting the barometric pressure and affecting the physical human body. The wind can carve majestic sculptures into mountains, and move the oceans creating waves that destroy everything in their path. Wind can allow a child to understand the aerodynamics created in flying a kite. But can the wind alone pick up a carnation from a casket and gently lay it at the feet of a mourning child, or is there a greater law that explains and governs?

The answer lies within The Law of Divine Oneness: "Everyone and everything is connected in the world we live in." I believe in a **Grand Overall Designer** that is all-knowing, all-loving, all-encompassing; taking into account every tiny blade of grass on this earthly planet, every animal, large or microscopic. Everything, including our physical body, is made up of energy, and energy has no boundaries. My faith lies within me, for I am contained in the multiverse, and the multiverse is contained within me. I see its connection everywhere, in the star-filled skies and the dew on the petals of a red carnation.

Often things happen that we overlook, not realizing their significance. But if we take the time to acknowledge and witness them, we can find the connection, the importance, and the relevance. Those seemingly unintegrated moments are like priceless treasures. Invite them to tell their story and reveal their precious gifts. Be curious, be willing to listen, trust, and connect with *your* faith.

Ignite Action Steps

I leave you with this question: What connects us to each other, every star, planet, and galaxy? Become curious, and question everything. When a child asks questions, take the time to listen, and if you can't explain it, discover the answer together. Encourage everyone to be inquisitive; it is our questions and curiosity that will shape the future of this planet.

VANESSA CIANO SARACINO

"Walk in your power and let God lead the way!"

It is my intention that by reading my story, you will stand tall and trust in the Divine plan set out for your life. I want to encourage you *to walk by faith* even though you cannot see where your journey leads and embrace it. I hope that you can trust in and believe that *all things are working together for your highest good.* Surrender and trust in the process; God is at the wheel.

GOD IS BIG

Dad; it is you we are most proud of. We love, honor, respect, and commend you. You came to this country with nothing and built a life that some could only dream of. Your presence made every day a little brighter. You created the blank canvas in which for us to paint our masterpieces and gave us a better life that I personally will never take for granted. Your level of sacrifice is one we will never forget. We will always hold you in the highest regard and are so proud of what you accomplished. As we mourn our loss, we celebrate you for a life well lived. One full of honor, dignity, and respect. The masterpiece of your life will forever live inside our hearts, and I vow to always showcase it in mine and carry on your legacy. I thank you from the bottom of my heart for being the best dad a girl could have asked for. Thank you for being you and for all the laughter and love. I hope you realize now that the Holy Spirit that you were searching for lived in you all along. What I would not do to watch one more princess movie with you and be your remote control!

I said my final goodbye and stepped away from the podium in the church I grew up in. I was exhausted from waking up at 3:30 AM to put the finishing touches on my father's heartfelt eulogy. It took everything I had to choke back the tears and return to my seat. I thought of all the good times my father and I shared, and I was so grateful to God for having been able to spend the last seven years so close to him. I reflected on all the outpouring of love we received from everyone we knew during the many years battling his health challenges. My buddy was gone… this time for good. Or, *was he*?

Ever since I was a little girl, I have believed in God. My aunt was a nun, and I am named after my uncle who was a priest. I attended a catholic school and would pray for everyone in my family before going to sleep. Every Sunday, I watched my parents sing in the choir and forge meaningful friendships. My father went to church every morning and served communion. The love of God surrounded me via the example set by the congregation for the life I wanted to create for myself—I would sit in church and cry at the magnitude of it all. All I ever aspired to was to create my own family, and I dreamt of what love and happiness would be like.

After twenty years of independence, I packed up my belongings, left the amazing life I had built, and headed home to start from ground zero. Up until that point, my life had been a dream. I had *everything* I ever wanted: two houses, cars, money, a husband, a rewarding career, and an amazingly beautiful daughter. Everything I ever wanted, I received. Doors seemed to open with little to no effort; although I worked incredibly hard for everything I attained, there was no shortage of good fortune and wonderful favor in my life. I worked for successful companies in an industry I loved and traveled the world multiple times over, achieving financial independence. Even my daughter was contracted with the biggest modeling agency in New York City at just four years old.

Now my life had come to a screeching halt. I lost my husband to infidelity, lost my number one client in NYC, my daughter's modeling agency closed their kid's division, and I had to move and sell my houses. I didn't understand any of it. I had done everything right, followed all the rules, and yet I watched the empire that took me thirty years to build crumble right in front of my eyes. Nothing made sense.

My daughter and I moved back in with my parents while I picked up the pieces. We adjusted the best we could, and I tried to rebuild the life I knew to no avail. Soon after, I found out my father was once again diagnosed with cancer. After being in remission from prostate cancer for over a year, he now had esophageal cancer, and it was completely overwhelming.

It was starting to become apparent that God was orchestrating my life around my father's needs. Every time he had a debilitating illness, my work schedule changed accordingly. As if things could not get any worse, my mother got into a car accident, and my daughter and I took care of both of them, alone!

One day my dad told my mother, "Questa Vanessa e una cosa speciale," (meaning, *this Vanessa is something special*) and that was the first time I had ever heard him say something so endearing.

On the way home from visiting my mother in the hospital, my friend called me and asked me to pray with her for her daughter's father because she thought my prayers were powerful. And, so I did. Her prayer was answered, and that is when it struck me. *What is going on?* The power of prayer is incredible. Every time I prayed, things seemed to improve. I was in awe of how much prayer was impacting myself and those around me positively.

Six months later, my family and I received the biggest blow yet. The cancer had metastasized into my father's brain. Within four days of receiving that devastating news, I met a man who wrote a book about how he cured his brain cancer with organic vegetables. *What are the chances?* There are millions of people in the world, and I don't think connecting with him was a chance encounter. I knew for sure that meeting him was a Divine gift from Heaven. I felt *strongly* that it was the answer to my desperate prayers. I wanted to try the methods he outlined but no one in my family, nor the doctors believed that it was possible to overcome this, so they continued treating him with radiation. That course of treatment did not sit well with me, so I took matters into my own hands.

The urge came over me to pray over my father, so I did. My mother and daughter had no idea what was going on. I placed one hand on the top of his head and my other up in the air, and I commanded the cancer to be gone in Jesus' almighty name. That was not unusual because I grew up in the church and had witnessed people using the power of Jesus to cure one another all the time. I had no idea if it would work, but for me it was worth the try. This was not the first time I had experienced the Holy Spirit speaking to me, so I knew enough that when the Holy Spirit spoke, it was time for me to move.

The following day, my father fell and cut his hand, causing him to go to the hospital. Two days later, after having not spoken with the doctors, the hospital called me to discuss his discharge plans. I inquired about his brain activity and how it was functioning and the nurse said it was great. My first instinct was to ask if they did a CAT Scan, and she confirmed they had. I quickly asked how the tumor in his brain was, and her response was:

"What tumor, there is no tumor."

I wanted to jump out of my skin! "What do you mean there is no tumor? You do know he has brain cancer, right?"

The nurse fumbled with her words and said, "Um, um, I will have the doctor call you," and proceeded to arrange discharge plans to a rehabilitation center with no further explanation.

I begged them to do another scan and they refused. Within six days, they arranged six rounds of radiation even though they could not prove that the tumor was still there. I was livid. My father had signed a letter giving me power of attorney, yet they still did not listen and proceeded without either of our consent.

When he returned home, a Do Not Resuscitate (DNR) order was signed, which sadly put him in hospice. I was feeling powerless, angry, and distraught. I had always been at the forefront of my father's care since he had become ill. I was not ready to say goodbye, but I felt I had to concede and regretfully go along with it.

During his final days, my daughter and I were so grateful that we could make memories that we will cherish for a lifetime. We gathered in his room daily, sang his favorite songs with his guitar, sang to him, held his hand, and shared our love and gratitude for everything he had done. I will never forget him taking us in when we had nowhere else to go and providing a safe haven. It was the saddest time of my life and tore me up inside. Within a couple of days… he was gone.

Or, so I thought.

Three months later, I was driving home when suddenly I felt something strange come over me, which I could not shake. I started praying incessantly. I looked up in front of me, and I saw a white Cadillac—my father's favorite car. What was unexplainable was the license plate that said *TOTO*—my father's personal nickname. I could not believe it! I frantically searched for my phone to capture a picture knowing that if I hadn't that no one would believe me. It was as if the Angels orchestrated that encounter to let me know my father was indeed watching over me. I knew that car meant he was guiding, protecting, and leading the way. It confirmed for me my faith. Without a shadow of a doubt, I felt that it was my father communicating with me in a way only I would understand. It was like an Angel before me—a white car. I lost my breath when I saw the license plate—his nickname! I raced home and could not wait to recount the story and show my family the photo. For all those circumstances, indicators, and personal references to all come together right before me, I believe that was a sign from my father that he is always with me.

On that day, it totally clicked; I knew for certain that I had been handpicked and brought back home to be my father's support and be there when he transitioned into the afterlife. I can't say ending my marriage and coming home was easy, but I can say that through that process I was able to find the Divine gifts of who I was created to be. All those situations ignited my faith and awakened my ability to see that everything that happens—happens perfectly, and that I was being divinely guided.

Most people would say my story compares to that of Job in the Bible. I lost it all! Stripped of everything. I often wondered why God would do this to me. I thought I was being punished for something I did wrong, which could not have been further from the truth. God saw the things I did not see at first and heard what I did not hear. All the struggles that I have been through were working together for my greatest good, and what I gained is absolutely priceless. I learned that faith is not what you are told or shown; it is what lives inside of you, in your heart, spirit, and soul. There is a Divine master plan, and Jesus is at the helm.

I now know that I am right where I need to be and finally understand why God took me out of a situation that was not meant for me and positioned me where I would be celebrated. He bestowed upon me good friends, genuine care, and loving relationships. The kind that I saw growing up and learned to value and trust. The job I lost was replaced by one that only I could do, a daughter loving her father, and with much greater purpose, meaning, and gratitude.

What happened *to* me happened *for* me.

I am finally free to follow my calling and where it leads. Nothing is tying me down or holding me back. I feel fortunate that I have been so blessed in this life. Most people would have caved, but by the grace of God, I did not. I am whole, healed, restored, and loved more than I could have ever imagined. The love I experienced during this journey is one I would never change for a moment. It was an honor to be a part of my father's path and experience all the faith that got me through it.

I truly believe that God is at the forefront, pulling the strings and orchestrating your life the way He leads you. It is never how you plan and is a true test of character as to what you decide and what you will do. If this was a test, I know that I passed and am being celebrated in heaven. I am confident that God will bless my life with abundance, good health, and a future that I can devote to me. I know I have been a good steward and served my family well. I am confident God has seen it all and will promote me accordingly.

My hope for you is that you lean into your faith and follow the signs presented to you. Open your heart to helping wherever you can because God, or the Power you believe in sees it all. Stay faithful and be receptive to the Holy Spirit that guides you to follow faith and listen to your intuition. No one really knows what life has in store, so surrender and know it is exactly how it is meant to be. Remain positive in all that unfolds because whatever happened is divinely designed and will make sense one day.

In the words of my father, "GOD IS BIG!"

And, my response to that has always been… "You don't have to tell me, Dad… I know!"

Ignite Action Steps

- **Use your gifts, talents, and experience** to create the legacy you want to leave for your kids and future generations.

- **Practice gratitude:** Start a gratitude journal and list all the things you are thankful for in your life. This practice will enable you to acknowledge all the small things God has enriched you with. Thank Him for the unpleasant moments—in hindsight, they always prepare you for something greater.

- **Pay close attention to your intuition.** Your intuition sends you Divine Messages that give you ideas to lead to your greatness. What the enemy steals, God always restores in one way or another. Give your battles to Him, and He will provide. Remember that He always prevails.

- **Pray.** Ask God to open the door and show you the way. Ask Him to guide you to that which is best for you. Stay in peace, and have faith. Surrender your life in God's hands, and trust that He will protect you.

Jeanne Bundy

Jeanne Bundy

"Faith is having a belief to trust in a Higher Power greater than myself."

My hope is for you to find the resources within yourself that allow you to access the knowledge you hold deep within the recesses of your soul. The light inside us sometimes gets hidden under layers of emotion as we navigate some of our darker challenges, trusting that our inner guidance system will lead us to higher ground. Having faith in a Power greater than ourselves also ensures we stand tall once again as the vibrant colors of Creation emerge from our very Being.

Trusting My Faith

As the bird soars to the top of a tree, never doubting he will land on a branch that will support him, is it faith in his inner guidance system or trust that the branch will be there exactly where he needs to land? Both are equally important. *Faith and trust go together.* Faith is that trust within the deeper layers of my being. It's silent, never carrying a banner to proclaim its existence to the world, as it dwells deep within the confines of my soul, nourished by divine love. Faith is always present.

Faith has always carried me through many chaotic moments in my life. At sixty-one, my best friend, my mom, with whom I did everything—shopping, lunch, even gambling once in a while at the casino together—exited my life. After dropping her off from our shopping excursion, the very next day, she became ill and was put into hospice at the hospital. *A week later, she was gone.* That was just the beginning of my life that got upended. Eight months later, my husband, with whom I shared forty-three beautiful years of marriage, the love of my life, as we sat having our coffee discussing our plans for the day, clutched his chest, had a massive heart attack, and died in front of me. *There were no signs.* He was a soulmate to the core; we did everything together, we traveled the world while he was in the military for over thirty years, and we raised our two sons together. Our adventurous whirlwind of a life came to an abrupt end that morning as we were preparing for our grandchildren to visit for the holidays. *Nothing was ever the same.* Two months after his death, the world declared a pandemic, leaving me in a place so dark I wasn't sure I could ever crawl out. Every day was a question of whether I would make it to the next day. The bigger question for me was, *Did I really want to?*

Each day as the world closed up more and more, I myself became more con-tained within, so much that my world reduced itself to just me and my trusted cat, Chloe. As faith revealed the understanding that I had animals to feed. My daily routine of caring for something other than myself helped me realize how getting up and moving around was an important part of surviving. I would sit and talk to Chloe for hours. Eventually, even the cat got tired of hearing me sob, so she sent me out to talk to the birds! When the birds got tired of my sobbing, I acknowledged the lesson. *I was learning to find humor as a healing tool in my recovery.* Maybe it was time to slow the tears, take a breath, and chuckle over how even the animals knew I was depressed.

During lockdown, faith and humor went hand in hand for me since both bring clarity over things that may be devastating, helping us to cope with such things. When everyone in the world was looking for toilet paper, I was searching for boxes of tissues to cry into. That's what was important to me; what part of my body to wipe. I found the entire situation kind of hilarious. Humor was partly how my faith showed up for me, exposing how vulnerable I was. *Despite my loss and grief.*

The day I could not get my printer to work (technology was never my strong suit, to begin with) was another example. I had important documents to copy and send within a time frame, so my frustration was mounting. My husband was the person that I went to for help with technology. So, there I was, sitting in front of the printer, totally overwhelmed, tears dripping all over the documents that needed to be printed, I was screaming at the top of my lungs at my husband that it was all his fault! If he hadn't died, he could have fixed my printer for me. Think about what he must have been saying on the other side; "Like, really, Jeanne, get a grip." At that point, I just started laughing thinking about how I was blaming my husband. *It is not his fault he died.* That's when it hit me, to have faith in my God-given talents of having a brain and google to learn how to fix a printer. Interestingly enough, I was able to complete my mission and print out the documents, all by myself.

As the days passed, the darkness had a way of consuming me as it enveloped every thought and emotion. The loss of the two people closest to me was huge; it was like no other. To experience it during complete isolation was almost unbearable. I felt like I was sitting at the bottom of a pressure cooker, ready to explode. Sitting there in the dark, I knew there was only one way to go: up and out. The big question was: *How? What did I need to do?* Faith brought me to seek out a way to quiet my mind. I had always been a hit-or-miss meditator. I was familiar with the peace it could bring to my mind. Meditation became my best friend during that time—connecting to a Higher Power was the key for me to change how I needed to live, not just exist. I started to make new choices for myself, brought on during a meditation on how to coexist in a new world, without my closest companions at my side.

One interesting choice I made was realizing the very simple shift of finding out who I truly was since I was no longer the wife, the party planner, or the daughter. That simple act of seeing my life and I differently would open up a whole new world to me. My faith led me to believe there was another life to lead. It taught me that life would be different for I would be different. And, that was the first glimmer of light I needed to guide me back up from my well of despair.

I started first by making choices for myself, because faith brought me the knowledge that as we move through life, we make decisions that accommodate many others. Sometimes those choices are not actually what we like, so seeing what I liked and what I did not like was the first step in my liberation. For instance, one day I went to the grocery store, robotically putting in all the food items I would normally buy. I looked at my cart; tears started to flow. I noticed the items were all things my husband would have consumed. He was the meat eater, and I was the vegetarian. What on earth was I going to do with steaks in my basket? Faith was helping me to acknowledge the choices I was making from an old program that I lived, not who I truly was or who I had been. I recognized that my programming had to change; the puzzle picture that was once my life had been rearranged. Some of the pieces of the picture were the same, but the shape of the puzzle pieces had been altered. My life had changed; I had changed. *Who was this new person?* I felt I had to find out how to put the puzzle of my life back together, as all the pieces were fitting together quite differently now.

When I got home, I started to look around my house, finding the things I always wanted to change. The first thing that I changed was my bathroom rugs. Always being in a dominant male household—two sons and one husband—everything was in very neutral colors. The first choice was pink rugs and pink towels. I felt exuberated!!

Faith brought me the ability to make choices to inspire me. Knowing I had more to do, to inspire people to never give up, to reach into themselves, finding the bootstraps that they are grounded to. I felt pulled to share that faith is a greater Power and ensures we can stand taller in a better version of ourselves. As a result of listening to that inner voice that aligns my faith with my guidance system, my creativity sprang to life. It felt like it came out of nowhere, but it was only hidden under my many layers of emotion.

I knew it would take time for my light to shine again. Even after liberation with the bathroom rug and my printer fix, my depression grew. I was constantly deprived of sleep. I would long for the days to end so I could justify settling in for the night, lock the door, and crawl into my pajamas. Those were very long nights because in Rhode Island, where I live, sunset in the winter is around 4 PM. Those long nights were more of an endurance race than a rest for me.

On one of the long evenings, TV being my constant companion, a commercial came on advertising some type of clay to create with, the kind that you could bake in the oven or air dry. As I sat there watching the demonstration, a spark of life came slowly seeping back into my being. A realization of "I could do that," and I have done that! As I watched the commercial, a memory of my mom making roses out of bread dough when I was a small child came into my mind. Beautiful memories of those times flooded my awareness. I'm sure faith guided me to a path of healing that I was totally unaware of. As I visualized the happiness those memories brought me, my heart slowly started to feel life again. The shift in my physical body was almost tangible. Quickly, I ordered the clay online. Once the clay arrived, inspiration struck. The faith I had in myself, being creative, gave me a way to slowly find meaning in my life.

I had a purpose for getting up every morning. Beautiful pieces of art started to emerge from me out of the clay. Roses, like my mom used to create, blossomed. I couldn't help but order different colors to explore with, shaping a new kind of enjoyment in my soul. I had faith in my Higher Power, and that faith showed me how to heal. Finding an outlet in which my heart could slowly open, like a flower, was how my faith revealed the avenue I needed to begin my healing process. My creativity had meaning, a purpose; it brought me bliss and wonder after so many losses, so many dark corners. *Faith brought my spark back to my soul!* This was a great Ignite Moment in my life: the spark of creation was born from the simple act of being willing to find pure enjoyment in creativity. Painting then became my new passion. My artistry flourished through many new roads of exploring various art forms, learning, researching, and taking online classes. A whole new world opened up for me. That is when my faith in something greater than myself led me to know everything would be okay.

The light of faith pointed me in a new direction. I trusted my instincts and was guided to heal through the arts. I trusted in a life force far greater than myself to lead me out of the dark that had almost consumed me and guide me into a world rich with color. *I felt joy again deep in my soul.*

I progressed and learned new creative ideas, along with many new modalities of the art world. My whole universe expanded into something I would have never dreamed of. I became a multi-dimensional artist. Interestingly, it was faith that showed me how to trust in myself again by following my inner guidance system. *Guidance was always available to me.* The more I trusted in my faith, I was capable of escaping out of the darkness into the colorful paths of hope. I had the capabilities, by having the faith, to see a new perspective of how I could bring purpose to my life once more. I knew I could do this, and felt I was being guided to know how to do it well.

I started to rediscover how capable I truly was. I became a different version of who I was before the passing of the two most important people in my life. Fate had brought me unbearable circumstances, yet, I found that choosing to grab onto my faith in a Higher Power, whom I call God meant the unfolding of my true destiny, helping me discover how I move through things when challenges come. *I found gratitude.* I felt grateful that faith brought forth new perspectives and a sense of compassion, an understanding of the choices available to me based on my values in life. Being grateful for the gift of faith will forever inspire me to never give up. Knowing God has my back, I can trust in that Divine, Universal Power of Love.

I look back and ask myself, when did my faith kick in? My answer always seems to be the same. Faith was always there within the deepest parts of my soul. I used it daily without even recognizing it. *I know that now.* Faith stepped up to lead my way so many times in my life. My core values, the non-negotiable part of my very existence, are based on faith. They are the part of me that stands up for the rights of others, champions the underdogs, and supports people's ability to live freely with whomever they choose. All of those non-negotiables come from my faith that all people are worthy. My faith is based on the greatest principles of all, which for me is the Power of Divine Love that comes from what I call God.

198 / Jeanne Bundy

That love and faith sit deep in the core of my Being, which radiates outward.

I am deeply grateful that I have learned to fully trust *Faith*, the unseen essence of what we believe, that deep inner guidance system we all have in a Power greater than ourselves. Trusting in a Higher Power, which we believe exists, is like trusting the sun will rise in the morning and set in the evening; it's infinite. *We need to have faith that the simple things we overlook will happen.* Accepting life will always bring challenges, and trust the answers are there when we look inside ourselves. Faith walks the path alongside us, as a familiar friend, a trusted companion that will always lead to higher ground. Learning from our experience brings what's called a *Talisman*, it's learned wisdom that we integrate into our life, teaching the gifts we revised from the journey itself.

People are always looking for faith and act like it will fall from the sky and land before them. How do you know faith is there? How do you tap into your inner faith? Many people seem to find faith when they least expect it. Faith is so integrated into all of us that many of us feel lost without the inner trust we desire and need. If you are searching for your faith, find out where you come from, and discover your authenticity, the essence of your soul. Faith is your inner guidance system, the core of you, that connects you with the Divine and reminds you; you are worthy of ALL.

Ignite Action Steps

Creating faith and finding your faith is an inside job. Here are a few ideas of what you do to incorporate it into your daily routine. Faith is not going to drop out of the sky before you; you have to search for it, look for it, and most importantly be open to it. Try one or many of the suggestions I have shared to inspire and awaken you.

Meditate!
- Try it. Start simple. Do meditations that are a few short minutes to start.

See the world through the eyes of a child.
- Let life's wonders expand your world from being limited to unlimited possibilities.

Open up to your curiosity.
- Find things to experience the joy and discover the creativity within you.

Listen to your heart.
- When you listen to your heart, you can find peace within yourself.

Allow new discoveries.
- Make time and effort for personal growth.

Educate, be mindful of your thoughts.
- Think positive despite the challenges you face.

Trust your inner knowing.
- Listen to your instincts, and pay attention to your inner voice.

Take a walk in nature.
- Let the outdoors clear the 'stuff' of the day. Smell the roses, and take a breath.

Be willing to take a leap.
- Have the faith you need to Ignite the spark in yourself.

See endless possibilities.
- *Enjoy* the simplicity of life and never cease to believe.

Pray.
- Prayer is gratitude. Be grateful for even the smallest things.

Just BE.
- To be is just to observe, to be aware, and in the moment. To be *present* is a present you give yourself.

Create by writing your story.
- Be authentic, as it allows you to find different avenues to share.

Bobbie Kowalski

(removed)

BOBBIE KOWALSKI

"Death is Where Life Begins."

My personal desire, in the humble words I share, is for you to find courage and strength even when you feel lost in life, because that is, paradoxically, when we truly find ourselves. Through our pain, we discover our strength deep within us. This is where we learn we exist not only for ourselves; we exist for each other. The inner light inside of us is not meant to remain hidden but to help illuminate someone else's path when they find themselves in the dark.

THIS LITTLE LIGHT OF MINE

Death is where my life began. That is where the pages turned, and a new chapter started. Fearing death is something we all experience as we go through life. We all are fated to face our mortality, asking ourselves questions such as, *Why are we here? What did we accomplish?* and *What was the meaning of it all?* I never had to confront all those questions until the ground beneath me began to shake. That was the turning point of my life. It was not me who died, it was my father, but he took a part of me with him… or did he leave a part of him with me? His death was my gift.

I'm sure you're wondering, *How can death be a gift?* Yes, it brings so much sorrow and pain, filled with an unspeakable loss, but it also brought upon what I call The Gift, one that transformed me from who I was then to the woman I am today. I first took the time I needed to process his loss with anger, followed by sadness, and grief, and from that point looked deep within to find the meaning in all of it. Yet, I only found a spark of light hiding there. That little light wanted to shine, but needed courage. I looked everywhere in search of finding my own faith.

My upbringing was filled with faith. Faith-filled Sunday morning church services followed by afternoon brunch at Grandma's house full of down-home southern cooking and many times followed by Sunday evening church services. I honored my Christian upbringing, but started to feel there had to be more to the story. I began the journey of trying to understand the faith I had been taught for so many years. I started by asking really hard questions and stepping outside the box of belief as I had known so far. I learned the story was grander than I ever thought. I had to break down the walls of everything I was taught and my old belief systems so that I could begin rebuilding who I thought I was, and who I was going to become. That is where transformation unfolded.

The first big lesson came in the form of gratitude. Watching the spiritual teacher, Deepak Chopra, on TV, I was confronted with the task of finding the worst thing that had ever happened in my life. Obviously, with the recent loss of my father, I could not help but think there was nothing worse than that. I was then asked to think about that difficult scenario and come up with something I could be grateful for within it. For a few minutes, I thought, "You must be kidding," but I chose to do it. Then, it hit me; I found the gratitude and became lost in my tears. You see, as my father was in his last few months of life, he changed completely. I saw a love in his eyes that was unexplainable, I could not understand it, but I knew it was profound. Everything shifted; everything changed. I went from being disconnected to my faith to seeing and feeling it all. I was touched by him immensely and ignited by *his* faith. He showed me a love I had never felt as I looked into his eyes, and he shared he was ready to go. That peace and tranquility was so filled with grace and became a powerful example of Love. He showed me, love is intertwined with faith. I cherished the love he emanated; it brought a peace I had not known.

That was the beginning of my transformation, and it was not easy by any means. Think of a caterpillar morphing into a butterfly; it must go through a tremendous change. Change can shake one to its core while bringing out fear and being uncomfortable. As I have learned over time, nothing is permanent, and everything evolves. As I began to change, all I wanted to do was study, study, study! I started watching documentaries on world religions, trying to learn other

Holy scriptures than the Bible and other Eastern and Western philosophies. I wanted to make sense of why humanity felt so separated from one another and the division amongst so many religions.

What I began to learn was that separation came from our human self, not God. I learned we are all derived from Love, whom some choose to call God, some Universe, some even call it Source. God has many names, but truly there is only *One,* and that essence is deep inside every one of us. It knocks on our hearts each day, wanting to be heard, but so many of us don't hear the knock or even understand our soul is trying to communicate with us.

That knocking in my life came from many directions I did not understand. If I could break it down to the simplest form, it would be my intuition trying to break through, and I sensed there was more to me than just the physical body. That intuition would give me the feeling of things that did not feel right or where I found joy; it was my road map, and I was unsure how to follow it. Have you ever walked into a room to feel a tense energy, and realized something did not feel right? That's a part of your innate communication. I learned to look at my intuition not just as a word, but as a Being, my Spirit. I could feel that little light inside me beginning to Ignite and flicker.

Think about planning a trip. You are going to visit a country that speaks a foreign language. You cannot read the road signs to drive or even a dinner menu to eat. It becomes a challenge to navigate this trip. Most people will bring in what they call a guide to get them through. My intuition became my guide.

We are all on this trip, we call this trip *life,* and that intuition I speak of comes from your Spirit to guide you through this life. The thing we need to do is learn to listen. Sometimes we don't understand the language. It would be so much easier if our Spirit spoke in linear sentences as opposed to our body. It does try very hard with small whispers to get your attention, but if we do not begin to listen to that whisper, it will become louder until it is shouting. Usually, we call this a "Dis-Ease", and when we ignore the problem over time, it will manifest into a *disease.*

Change was not happening easily for me. It was as if my Spirit was giving me breadcrumbs to start walking down a new path. My first set of crumbs came in the form of numbers. Everywhere I looked, all I saw were patterns of them. Each night as I would go to bed, I would get into a nice deep sleep and feel a tugging at me, almost as if someone was standing next to my bed trying to wake me up. I would then wake up and see no one but my clock on the dresser. One night the clock would read 11:11. The next night, it would be 11:11, and then I'd wake up again at 12:12. This continued till it became all hours of the night. For a month straight, this kept happening to me. The pattern continued from 11:11 to 12:12, 1:11, 2:22, 3:33, 4:44, and 5:55 until I was utterly sleep deprived. I was not receiving any messages, explanations, or clarity, just numbers! I became frustrated and decided to scream out, "If you're trying to get my attention, you need to do better than this!"

The next night I was able to get more rest, but the spirit world had a sense of humor as the patterns of matching numbers changed after my outburst to waking me up at 12:34 (get it...1.2.3.4.) This time I giggled and went back to sleep. The night number game stopped, and I decided there was more to it, as the spirit world had achieved what it wanted; they now had my full-blown attention. Something most definitely was saying, "Hey, we're here; you can't see us, but we're trying to talk to you." I asked myself, "Where does this lead?" Once again, it led to my search for Faith; for Faith is something we cannot see, that is not explainable, yet it takes courage and connection with our innermost being.

There were so many breadcrumbs and paths that I was becoming lost and scared in the journey of finding myself. I thought I was losing my mind. I headed straight for the nearest psychologist. I needed someone to talk to and help me. That began weekly sessions on grief. Of course, in the back of my mind, I knew grief hurt, but these phenomenons had turned up the dial another whole notch! Over many months the fear began to dwindle as I started to accept my new normal in life. My senses sharpened, and I began to see *and feel things;* over time, I was growing a stronger awareness of *something* I never realized was standing by me my whole life.

When something goes wrong in my life, my gut is the first thing to talk to me. So naturally, when my father passed, my gut decided to bring it to my attention. Not long after his passing, I was going through some serious "gut-wrenching" issues. I ended up in the hospital, undergoing gallbladder surgery. Just as though there are times our digestive tract cannot process certain foods properly on the inside, my illness was a mirror of my exterior not processing my father's death on the outside. That lesson alone was getting my attention. The metamorphosis I was in at that time, peeled away things that no longer served me, and apparently, that included my gallbladder.

The next lesson that came, was with my hands. I began experiencing painful tingling sensations in my palms. I decided to visit the nearest University hospital to seek help. After many consultations I was diagnosed with nerve damage. I was given prescription painkillers and a cream to use. I remember feeling in a state of shock—*I am only in my mid-forties, how can I have nerve damage in my hands?* I was truly saddened by this diagnosis, yet I see now in hindsight, that these health issues were Spirit trying to get my attention, and were fundamental in my path to discovering my faith and healing.

Spirit had tried to talk to me through many people, but I had not given the words much attention. About a year later, I eventually began to listen. I was standing at work, wearing a business suit with my colleague, when a stranger, who looked like the lead singer of a rock band, wildly cool, big black curly hair, high heels, strutting a punk attitude, walked right up to me and told me, "You're not sick." She boldly shared with me that I could use my hands to help heal others. She discussed a form of healing that I was unaware of, called Reiki. With so much pain in my hands, I gave in and decided I would search for a metaphysical form of help since I had tried Western medicine. That is where my inner healing began. That stranger's words, completely and oddly unexpected, pushed me out of my comfort zone and into the realm of a teacher who would guide me through the process of understanding energy work. Once again, I discovered another area of faith. I could not see energy, but it was right there. I was made of it! It is woven into my biological human self, and I had never even realized it. My life was dramatically moving from a place of fear into a place of magic and love. My faith was accelerating.

My whole essence was changing, and I could feel it. I began looking at everything in the world differently. Things that would normally upset me in the past, were now the things I looked at and realized I was being taught something new. I became a very neutral person, finding that it is my way of contributing to uniting, as opposed to dividing. I learned to drop any judgments I carried and look through a different lens when trying to understand situations.

As I was morphing into what I felt had become a sweeter spirit, I also grew a connection to the animal world. This was unique for me. I began to attract wild animals and feel a strong connection to them. Of course, I cannot understand them or their language, but I can understand their energy and vice versa. I started as the woman who never wanted to get up before 9:00 AM and became the person who now gets up early to feed blue jays peanuts. There is a connection between humanity and nature. As I have grown, I have allowed nature to reflect on me what I need to learn. The birds alone have taught me a piece of faith I hold tight to every day.

"A bird sitting on a tree is never afraid of the branch breaking, because its trust is not on the branch but on its wings." ~ Unknown

That quote helped me start to fly. I opened my heart up to others about my journey and allowed them to see my flaws. I welcomed my vulnerability and was willing to be transparent, with the hopes of helping others who may also share the same experience. I leaned into my father's love, loss, departure, and deep impact on what faith meant to me. His love helped me decide one of the best ways to share my love was to be by the side of families as a hospice volunteer. I realized it was not about the person lying in that bed, but about the family that stood beside them, walking them home, helping each one of them keep their faith alive.

We all ask ourselves at different times in our lives, *How do we all see the world with our perception? Why do certain things happen to us? Why am I here? What is my purpose?*

The transformation in my cocoon of life came from death. It took years of unpeeling layers and finding that little light inside me to realize that we are just shedding our physical bodies even in death. Our Spirit's journey does not end, it transforms. Life is a circle. We begin with life, and when this life is over, we begin another. Our Spirit is ever-evolving. From life to death.

As my transformation continues, I realize I am blessed each day to walk this earth and be given a chance to make the best of what is set before me. The deeper I dive into faith, I no longer ask myself what my purpose is, and I know my purpose is to be full of peace and joy. When I found that little light inside of me and the flicker became brighter, I truly began to shine. When that light came on, so did life itself. This is where compassionate action came alive. When I looked inside myself, I was able to forgive myself for the past and look toward the future.

Today I stand in honor of all the challenges that were put before me. I may not fully understand how deep my roots are dug, but I know I am surrounded by love. I have love from above that will never leave my side, even when I am not aware it is there. I have also been given the gift of parental love. Being a woman and realizing the wonderment of carrying a child and bringing forth life, I think of my son. I think back to the days of holding his little body in mine. I feel blessed to have had that life in my arms, knowing I was given a child who now houses his own little light. It is a joy to witness his growth, and observe him with others as they discover their unique spark.

This is how I was able to Ignite my life, by finding that spark while searching for my faith. That search has brought me to a place of love and growth. I now work with energy in the form of healing. I see everyone as whole beings of physical, mental, emotional, and spiritual energy. I studied many forms of healing, from Reiki to tuning forks, and I discovered that *words* have a powerful and profound effect. The love we share with one another, just in encouragement, or to say *I love you*, is magnificent. To be an ear when someone needs to speak and express their pain and then be the arms to hold them while they are hurting is a precious gift I cherish.

Despite a tragic death, I found my little light. That light ignited something in me that now shines and will never dim. In a world that is shifting rapidly, being a force of love and helping others are my mission. To be a guide who helps the lost in life to find their place, in their perfect timing. I keep close to my heart this quote by Rumi, "Being a candle is not easy; in order to give light, one must burn first." I love that the Creator, who expresses through me, loves me. That faith has become my way of sharing deep, unconditional love for myself and those around me. And, faith has allowed me to see all the life there is in each and every one of us.

May your life be filled with faith, love, and a path of beautiful blessings.

Ignite Action Steps

- **I encourage you** to break down the walls of beliefs that no longer serve you. To look them in the face with bravery and step out of your comfort zone. This is where growth begins.

- **I challenge you** to learn other cultures' beliefs and open your hearts to the understanding we are one human race, and each and every one of us is on the same spiritual path trying to find our way home.

- **I invite you** to take compassionate action, first and foremost, to yourself. Once we begin to forgive ourselves we can then begin to heal one another. This is where we find that little spark in every one of us, that spark that is ready to Ignite.

Kathy Strauss

Kathy Strauss

"We are the artists of our lives—our thoughts, words, and actions create a better, more colorful, beautiful world each day."

When people go through challenges, they sometimes find themselves isolated and alone. What they have to remember is the universe will not give them more than they can handle. It encourages them to dig deep and learn who they truly are. It is my hope to teach others that by putting yourself out there, sharing your story, and exploring bits of creativity—you can find your faith, dig into your strength, gain clarity, and learn how to navigate the system.

Making an Impression

I was married to a man named GC who loved to impersonate Elvis. It wasn't the Elvis impersonation you're used to. My Elvis had a chipped tooth, soft brown eyes behind aviator glasses, a brown mullet above a salt and pepper goatee, and the biggest smile framed by huge dimples. He had the sharpest, most sarcastic sense of humor I have ever encountered. And, he took me on a journey that would test my faith and unlock my unknown creativity.

It was a month after my divorce that I met my second husband, GC. It was pure synchronicity and love at first sight. I was working as a senior graphic designer at the World Bank in Washington, DC. I had been asked to teach a workshop in San Diego, CA. The problem was I was also being invited to work in Hong Kong for three weeks and had a choice to make. Traveling the world was my dream, but being a woman of my word, I chose to teach at the conference instead.

That choice brought me to the love of my life. GC and I met in the conference hotel bar. He was sitting chatting with friends and he smiled—the first thing I noticed was his chipped front tooth. We chatted, and he started telling some of his stupid jokes—the tension in my muscles just melted away as I laughed. I was having so much fun that I didn't want to leave, but I had staff meetings to attend and preparation to do. Little did I know that GC would be sneaking into my class the next morning to watch me teach. We met up afterward, and what I learned gave me even stronger faith that it was fate. He told me he had been asking his boss for years to attend this annual conference but was always told, "No, it's not in the budget!" However, this year, his boss told him, "Whatever it costs, I want you to attend!" He never knew what changed his boss' mind, but the synchronicity was undeniable. We knew each other for five days, and even though our worlds were 3,000 miles apart, we sensed immediately that we would be married. The story GC would tell anyone who asked how we met: "She picked me up on the San Diego freeway when she saw me wearing short shorts and cowboy boots, and she liked the package."

We talked every day on the phone for six months, racking up a ridiculous long-distance phone bill. Finally, he told me that he had everything worked out and would be moving east to be with me! I pulled my daughter, Lynne, out of school, and we flew to Salt Lake City to meet GC. We were driving cross country back to Virginia! He greeted us at the airport holding a piece of paper with Chinese brush-painted letters that read, "Will work for food." I just smiled at the sight of GC and gave him a huge hug. Lynn wasn't as thrilled as I was for this new adventure, nagging us about having to ride in the back of the cab of his uncomfortable pickup truck.

Once we got to Virginia, our lives took on an air of excitement, learning how to live together in harmony. I was thrilled that GC didn't want to impose himself too much into my daughter's life, too soon. So out of respect, he told us he would sleep in a separate bedroom from me. He further melted my heart when he shared that he wanted us to learn about each other before he and I slept in the same bed. Eventually, Lynne told us that she gave us her permission to sleep together. GC and I started looking for a new house that would be better for our new melded family. It was during this time that I asked GC to marry me! We moved to a new house, got married, and started our business ImageWerks—all that same year! For over a decade, we loved deeply, laughed, learned whatever we could, explored our world, created amazing art, experienced loss, and grew together as a family and a couple.

Like in any marriage, I experienced it all—ups, downs, sideways, and feeling like I was going in circles. I got my first peek into the healthcare system and testing of my faith and prayers about eight years into our marriage. GC was told he had prostate cancer. I broke down in tears when he told me. That C *word* brought up all sorts of fear and the great unknown. I had dealt with my own suspected cancer diagnoses years before and with that, I knew deep down there was nothing wrong. But with the tables turned, I experienced emotions from fear to loneliness. Yet, with his usual dimple-filled smile, GC assured us there was nothing wrong, and together we could beat anything!

Much to my relief, he made it through the cancer surgery initially, only to have to visit the ER the following summer. GC didn't heed my warnings to hydrate while working in the heat. Mr. Stubborn only wanted to drink beer. That night, our friends asked us out to dinner. After we were seated, GC told me he needed some air, and I sensed something was off. Shortly after he left the table, we heard a scream, "someone has fallen outside!" Running, I found GC passed out on the pavement. He was taken to the local ER wearing the only clothes he had on... soiled and all. I pulled myself together and asked our friends to get a clean set of clothing. I got a full dose of laughter in the hospital when our friend walked into GC's room holding a pair of white briefs and shouting at the top of his lungs, "Tighty Whities!?" We all burst out laughing, holding our stomachs while wiping the tears from our eyes. It felt like GC had gotten a taste of his own playful sarcasm despite how seriously his health had been compromised.

Two years later, our lives took a turn where I learned to dig into creativity and most of all, tap into my faith. On the fourth of July, GC created fireworks of his own when he was rushed to Potomac Hospital. The ER diagnosed him with a case of gastroenteritis. They gave him meds, but he was still feeling nauseous and in pain, so they kept him overnight. After the meds took effect, his sense of humor kicked in. "Wanna see my Elvis impression?" he would say with a smirk. Then he would lay backward, folding his arms across his chest with his feet in the air. He loved doing that dead Elvis bit at parties, so it was no surprise he used it to liven things up in that hospital room.

In between his jokes and moaning in pain, the doctors ran tests, giving us enough diagnoses to make our heads spin. They said it was gastroenteritis, gall-bladder, diverticulitis, etc. I was confused and my head felt like a ping-pong ball. I knew GC was a private person. He told me, "Do not tell anyone what's going on; I don't want them to know or feel sorry for me." On the other hand, I am a social person, and I was feeling alone. Something told me I needed to share our situation with the world. I didn't know where to turn, so I did the opposite of his request and shared what was happening via Facebook™ . I listened to my gut and brought my laptop with me to the hospital, which assured me I could communicate with the world. It also gave me a creative outlet; artistic creativity was how I kept my head clear amid the beeping machines and rotating cast of nurses. With the graphic design work I was doing and the Facebook™ posts I shared, that laptop was my lifeline.

Believe me, I needed a lifeline. The doctors continued running tests, with many of them coming back as "unremarkable." Go figure! They decided to send him home with a vague diagnosis of "a virus." A doctor friend recommended that I arrange for a gastroenterologist to check GC out. I took him to see this new doctor, who immediately asked, "Are you always this yellow?" He couldn't move and just shook his head "no," then glanced at me and the nurses, collapsing on the floor. He was admitted instantly to the Prince William Hospital ER. The doctors took one look at him, knew what was going on, and they confirmed his gallbladder needed to come out! Looking at my poor husband, I just thought, "Why couldn't this have been diagnosed at the other hospital?!"

I was relieved that GC was getting the treatment he deserved, happy knowing that we could put this nightmare behind us. What I didn't see coming was another series of health issues. It began when he started complaining about severe neck pain. I felt like we were on a crazy rollercoaster ride. Normally I am the glass half full type of person, but seeing my husband suffering tested my patience and faith. I was angry that he was in such pain, and I told anyone who would listen to me what I thought. Doctor after doctor, tests, treatments, and more diagnoses, it was off to the "medical races." I was exhausted. To cope with the stress, I buried myself in my work. I kept my daytime free to accompany GC to the doctor. He liked having me there as a sounding board, and I could take mental notes on what they would tell him. As I worked, I watched GC pace around the house in agony. He even tried to sit and focus on doing some of his artwork, but it didn't help. I felt lonely, helpless, and unable to fix his pain.

One night I noticed the side of his face drooping. Calling *another* doctor, I was told, "Sounds like a stroke!" Off we went to the ER, but they didn't want to treat him there and transported him to Fairfax Hospital! As I followed the ambulance down the highway, I called my family to let them know what was happening. In my head, I felt alone and was screaming for help! The next morning, we were told the facial paralysis was Bell's Palsy plus another diagnosis, cervical stenosis. He needed surgery to correct it! I was scared as I watched a parade of doctors coming through his room. I got on my laptop asking Facebook™ friends, "Please send goofy get-well cards, I want to 'cheer the sick out of GC'!" There were so many funny conversations—I felt the support, which gave me strength, courage, and faith. One friend told me her husband was on "tighty whitey patrol," and another claimed my husband was a Secret Shopper investigating area hospitals and ERs. Each time I laughed, I felt better. And, as I felt better, GC did also.

Feeling better meant GC was released, but we were told to also seek a second opinion. After weeks of waiting, the conclusion was he needed surgery, for which we would have to wait another four weeks. I watched helplessly as he complained of increasing pain and paced the house like a caged animal. I noticed physical changes in his arms and his losing control of his hand grip. I knew something had to be done soon, so I screamed at the doctor to schedule the surgery now! Back to the hospital we went, with GC's mother and brother flying out to support us. Having help around the house and someone else to talk to besides the dogs or my Facebook™ friends was wonderful.

I found myself burning out and wanting to tap more into my creativity as I was forced to learn how to handle and work with the hospitals. After his neck surgery, I saw him writhing in pain and getting nauseous. Despite his history of ulcers, GC's neurosurgeon neglected to prescribe stomach medicine, so I had to advocate for him. Without the doctor's order, the nurses refused to help, but I refused to back down. Showing them his medication list, I finally got them to take action. I built a reputation for demanding quick action, and at discharge time his nurse walked in and just tossed the papers at me with no explanation about his release, follow-up, or home medications. When I got GC home, I discovered she forgot to give me the prescription for pain medicine! If you thought I was frustrated before, you didn't want to see me then. Shaking, I did everything to keep myself from crying before calling the floor nurse to let her know what had happened. Because the pain meds were narcotic, she couldn't fax the order to the pharmacy. Two medication mistakes in one day was just too much to take. "Do you know how upset I am?" I snarled into the phone through gritted teeth. Snapping back, she said, "Yup, even madder than you were at the hospital!" before promising to meet me at the hospital's front entrance. As I drove back to the hospital, I screamed to the universe, "Enough!"

As the stress mounted, I sought new creative outlets. I couldn't quiet my mind and was playing on the computer one night when I stumbled upon a Facebook™ page entitled "The Artist Within." Piquing my interest, I saw it led to online training to become a *Creatively Fit*™ coach. I was so intrigued I stayed up late and read the entire site. I finally found something that sparked my creative soul and signed up immediately.

Unfortunately, my new creative adventure got detoured when the hospital called to say GC tested Lyme positive. In shock, I listened as she asked if he had been bitten by a tick. I never saw the telltale bullseye rash, but it dawned on me that GC's love of camping and history could be to blame. I had been a reluctant follower when he got us involved in Civil War reenactment, preferring the comfort of a camper over a hard cot, and being in full costume in the heat. But he loved playing soldier, marching, and crawling around on the ground in the woods; a scene that played like a movie in my head as all of his health issues began to make sense.

The bad horror movie in which I was being asked to play the heroine led us to an infectious disease doctor, whose treatment our insurance refused to approve until we provided proof GC had Lyme disease! Time to advocate again! When I heard they thought the claim was fake, I dug down deep, called them up, and pleaded my husband's case. The doctor finally called and said, "I don't know what you did, but everything is approved!" I smiled and assumed that everything was finally on track for healing, though perhaps I should have known better. Each time GC landed in the hospital, we got additional answers while uncovering more issues. I don't know what kept me strong, but I *can* say my new creative activities kept me sane.

At long last, my advocacy took me somewhere new. I was invited to a community meeting to meet the new presidents of two of the hospitals that treated him. I was asked to share GC's story to make his healthcare nightmare public. GC smiled at me and whispered, "Go get'em, tiger." I took a deep breath, stood up, and started with, "I have a story." As I read my journal, the room became silent, and the faces of both presidents became sullen as they said, "Can we talk afterward?" I finally had their attention!

One hospital sent me an apology letter, and the other hospital called me. "We heard about your story and are pulling GC's records. We want to investigate! I felt heard as they promised they would use his case as a teaching tool and then appointed me to their patient/family advisory board. While becoming a strong patient advocate, I remained my husband's personal advocate. I learned how to use my intuition to pinpoint his pain or what part of his body was failing. In a short time, I became a forensics investigator, record keeper, medical student, and chief cheerleader. All the while, I took the time to tap deep into my faith in "knowing" and used creativity as a tool to destress and heal. I had to dig in and make my life flow. I had a business to run and was excited about my new adventure as I expanded my creative practice. I relished in the feeling of peace as I did each art project; it was in those moments of peace I was able to focus on everything that truly mattered.

I am grateful for the journey I took with the man I loved; a man who remained focused on the positive, created art, and was my biggest supporter. He knew I always had his back; whether it was one of his health issues, critiquing his latest painting, or laughing at one of his stupid jokes didn't matter. He was my greatest teacher; helping me learn my own life lessons: to be confident in myself, my talents as an artist, my voice as an advocate, and especially my faith and intuition. Though he's not physically with me anymore, I know he's still with me. It was evident as he went into hospice he would continue to joke and share his opinion on everything and do his best to create art. On the day he passed, he didn't let anyone cry—only laugh. Using Elvis as his conduit, GC kept letting us know he was with us, folded arms and all.

It was a long road, but one I was willing to travel. My faith and conviction helped me stay strong, knowing when I needed to seek support. I had to listen and trust that inner knowing to keep me going forward. GC always said, "trust yourself; you always know the answer."

IGNITE ACTION STEPS

- **Believe in something bigger than yourself.** When you are going through a stressful time, meditate, call on whomever you wish, and scream it at the top of your lungs, but most of all, know that the Universe will not give you more than you can handle.

- **Tap into your innate creativity.** The simple act of creating quiets the left-brain voices of logic, judgment, and analyzing everything. Color, meditate, watch a silly movie, slap paint on a canvas, take a walk out in nature, or even take a nap.

- **Don't be afraid to share your story.** Don't stay quiet. If you need help—ask for it: in a journal, in conversations with people, on social media and support sites. Accept people's prayers for you, and find a tribe of support who can step up and be there for you in the most stressful times.

- **Be grateful for everything you have in your life.** Write a gratitude list every day, or pick a word a week that prompts you through your journey. Make a list of people you appreciate, and don't be afraid to share it. And, most of all, remember to say "thank you" when you wake up and as you go to sleep, to start and end each day with gratitude.

Caroline Oettlin

CAROLINE OETTLIN

"Faith is not the absence of struggle; it is the strength to go through it."

By sharing the journey of how I ignited my faith during the most challenging time of my life, I hope to provide inspiration to others who may be going through similar struggles. Obstacles are inevitable, but even then, we cannot let our faith dim in the storm of life. Life is precious, and though it isn`t free from suffering, we can find a way to live gracefully with it. Faith is the courage to live life as though everything that happens does so for your highest good and learning. And it's because of faith, that deep trust is reborn and you are guided to take the first step, even when you don't see exactly where it is going or the outcome yet. The following pages give you an insight into my spiritual reconstruction and my personal growth. From worship to embodiment. As much as I wanted to hide in my little cave, I decided to enter the spotlight and hope that my story would be a light to others, maybe to you.

RISING FROM THE ASHES

Life can be unpredictable, and sometimes it feels like the Universe is conspiring against us, challenging our faith. Even if we have a plan in our mind, so many things can change within moments. For me, the past two years have been a rollercoaster ride that I could never have anticipated. My husband and I married, welcomed a newborn into the world, changed continents three times, moved houses fifteen times, and finally ended up back where we started, with nothing but the clothes on our backs.

In general, during my life, I was most likely designed to **change the outside**. And as I felt, from 2019 on, I was given this huge gift, where my outside became no longer manageable. Then, I felt a shift coming through; I knew that the energy would flow in another direction, and everything was swept away, all which didn't feel authentic anymore and did not serve a higher meaning of truth and alignment.

Let's go back a bit further. It was in 2019 when I met my husband. We shared the dream of bringing peace and harmony on Earth by offering Akashic Records Readings, Cacao Ceremonies, and Healing Vortex Circles. The Akashic Records are said to be a cosmic library that contains the past, present, and future of all souls. After being initiated, I worked closely with my guides to strengthen my connection. I received certain revelations that helped me make decisions and prepare for the challenges that later arose. It was the perfect opportunity to clear a lot of karma, so I quit my job in the pharmaceutical industry in Switzerland and moved to Argentina. I broke the chains and freed myself from what felt cramped and inappropriate, and by that, a combination of new possibilities and unpredicted situations opened up before my eyes. Glimpsing into a higher vibration, I knew that I was ready to become an Akashic Records Consultant, and yoga instructor and travel the world, bringing inspiration to others.

What attracted me to my husband was the same interest in having adventures and enjoying the freedom of a nomadic lifestyle. We traveled the Inka Path with five friends of ours, where I was shown in a shamanic journey how we raised our child in the future, surrounded by the jungle. After returning home, the world changed significantly within one day—the pandemic lockdown hit Argentina. From the globetrotter feeling to our relationship having the first real "test" to see if we were compatible with each other. Chaos, health issues, losing friends, and having discussions with family members about values, narratives, and upcoming decisions were constant. As it got louder on the outside, I went inside and meditated more.

Then, something happened that shook my feeling of control. I remember one day, my breathwork practice didn't work out anymore. I stopped and tried the next day again. No change. The only reason could've been... *Uhh*. So, I went to the pharmacy and bought a pregnancy test. Positive. I was a little shocked because I wasn't prepared to receive a child. Not in these crazy times, not with my goals in my mind, structured and envisioned for the next three years. Not while I was still in the process of actually knowing my partner; I had been living with this man for only four months! I took a deep breath, leaned into my faith, and the voice of my heart whispered, "If that's the man you want to create a family with, you are going to have an incredibly transformative experience." How vital those words later became…

As I connected to my guides and asked for direction, my Records told me frequently to be close to my mum for the first months after birth. We took the message seriously and went to Germany, where we found a midwife angel, preparing us to give a conscious lotus birth at home.

Without reading any sort of books, and avoiding hearing any story, I trusted and stayed close to my intuition, treasuring my own unique experience. I focused only on the strength of my body and the wisdom of my ancestral lineage to receive my baby in the most natural way, giving up any kind of drug or medicine, letting myself feel what had to be felt. During my labor it felt as though I was being torn apart. I told my baby energetically, "We are one team." Luckily, everything worked out amazingly. We left the umbilical cord for five days on the placenta until all the nutrients flowed back into our son. I immersed myself in the feeding experience and blessed the baby's food so that my child's soul was fed in the most extraordinary and motherly of ways.

With a newly expanded family, my husband and I drifted away a little because of me putting all my love and energy towards this little being and him feeling not included. We considered a change in the face of so many pandemic restrictions. We directed our main focus to finding the perfect place to live—with the best conditions to raise a child into a self-determined life out of the matrix: good water, fresh air, healthy food, and a conscious community. The chosen destination was Costa Rica. Newlyweds, we arrived in the jungle with our toddler six months later. With the green, lush nature, blue ocean, and an outstanding spot for unique channeling experiences, all seemed to be in alignment. I was moved to tears when I walked barefoot to the beach for the first time and smelled the salty air of the Pacific. For many years my deepest desire was to live close to the ocean, and it became reality. Fresh tropical fruits every day, coconuts, and like-minded people seemed like the perfect lifestyle.

The limited choices we were facing since the beginning of 2020 were mirrored in our living space and the confined areas we had to work in. The many hours of heat and sweat for our copper golden-haired child and lots of rain became an absolute challenge. The reduced sleep that comes with breastfeeding and all kinds of jungle noises increased my stress level immensely. As if that wasn't enough, the many scorpions, mold, and a gas smell in the house prompted us to move twice. But what really became the final straw was the rising addiction of my husband to plant medicine and gambling, which he used to escape from his responsibilities as a father and as a partner. He would stay away from home for several nights, neglecting my desperate need for support. Consequently, due to his lack of energy and some other factors, financial problems appeared.

Everything seemed to fall apart. I was worried by our life state of insecurity, instability, and disharmony, about the turbulence of parenthood and its devastating impact on my marriage. I was at my lowest point, feeling the warning signs of, "Watch out, you've reached the limits."

In those moments of conflict with my husband, overcoming the daily struggles and not being able to see a light at the end of the tunnel, I was desperate for relief. *Hope* kept me going, the possibility of improving my situation. But why did I focus on *hope*? Hope is future confidence, always steering somewhere else. The rejection of the present moment kept my unhappiness alive. The chronic emotional distress had a destructive impact on my health, career, finances, and relationships. Everything I was holding onto or felt a connection to fell away. My faith was at an all-time low.

It felt like I was suspended in the unknown. Being absorbed in motherhood and difficulties made it hard for me to appreciate life's many marvelous gifts. By being frustrated with my life situation and the constricted time for self-healing and meditation, I fell back into my old habits of compulsions for control, need for security, and addiction to criticism. There were few times when my husband could do something right, and I was often craving for more things to fill the void. By not being able to put the mirror in front of me, I projected onto the outside. However the situation was, it taught me patience to trust in the process of life. I still had a glimmer of faith that we would be able to create a loving, harmonious family with contentment and joy.

Easier said than done. We had to break down our tents in Costa Rica and move to Argentina to take a break. Somehow, I held the hope that by settling down, we would gain our stability, and our love would get a new chance. Of course, that didn't happen and that triggered an aggressive and angry reaction from me. The constant need to protect my child from an inadequate environment added to the lack of touch and emotional support I profoundly craved; it created aversion, doubts, and apathy inside of me. The affection and welfare my husband needed so desperately, I was not even able to provide for myself—how could I be able to give or sustain it to someone else if my cup was empty? In that pervasive lack of clarity, piggybacking on timid inertia, I began to lose my resolve.

Through the increasing seclusion of my heart, I offered to get support. But all attempts for coupling counseling had failed. So I took time for my own process of healing. I decided to go to Germany with my son to retreat, to be nourished by the support of my parents, friends, and my own language. It took me almost two months to get back in alignment because I could sleep in and had more time to reflect on our situation. My recovery brought love to the past story of the hard times in my marriage, where my partner and I became more and more distant and hurtful to each other. I found peace in accepting and honoring his wounds by not sprinkling more toxic emotions or wanting to change him. Instead of finger-pointing, I returned to my values and cleared my lenses, which had been blurry and intoxicated from my wounded patterns. I identified all the barriers that I had built against love, faith, trust, and hope.

When the time came, and I was able to open up my heart again to talk things out, my husband dropped a bombshell on me. He had met someone else and had been unfaithful. I was devastated, heartbroken, and utterly lost. I could no longer trust the man with whom I shared my life. I knew then, in that moment, that I would be finding the courage to divorce him. The vision of a harmonic family, a spiritual partner sharing our main mission, and a father who accompanies our son's path to prepare him best for life, was gone.

Yet amid my pain and confusion, I remembered a moment when my husband and I met for the first time, and I opened his Akashic Records. During that session, it was revealed that a third person was going to be involved. Though it was difficult to hear and see, I believed we were going to be capable of overcoming such destiny and staying together. Things turned out to be very different from what I'd pictured. It felt like the Universe tested my capacity to embody my spiritual practices in daily life. And when those challenges arrived, I found that I had a newfound faith in the Universe's plan for me.

Even though everything around me seemed to be falling apart, I believed that there was a greater purpose at work and a reason for everything that was happening. This belief and faith gave me the strength and capability to keep going. Of course, it wasn't easy. I struggled to make ends meet, to find a stable place to live, and come to terms with the end of my marriage. But slowly, over time, I began to realize that I was stronger than I ever thought possible. Life still crumbled around me, but I could no longer ignore my dreams and aspirations. I had been too afraid to take risks, too afraid to put myself out there, and too afraid to fail. Not anymore; it was time for transformation. The phoenix within my soul reborn from the ashes. I started my own business to support my son and me, made new friendships, and began to rebuild my life one small step at a time.

My son was a constant source of inspiration and renewed my faith. Watching him grow, learn and explore the world around him reminded me that life is full of wonder and possibility, even in the midst of pain and hardship. It was him, who taught me that nothing lasts forever and how valuable every single moment is. He gave me the love and strength to keep trying and to keep believing that things would get better. As a single mother, I had nothing left to lose. I started to carve out time for myself, waking up early in the morning to do yoga and meditate. New forms of movement and expression, like ecstatic dance, freed me. The healing arc that had been calling me for so long started to shape. I filmed yoga videos in my living room; I hosted small gatherings in my home, where I offered breathwork and meditation practices. And I created a new website and became present on social media to share my offerings with the world.

There were many times when I wanted to give up. I struggled with insecurities, wondering if anyone would be interested in what I had to offer. Then I reminded myself of my Ignite Moment—of the knowledge that had come to me through the Akashic Records. I knew there was a reason for each chapter in my life story, including my dreams and aspirations. The end of my marriage and the disappointment of the life I had envisioned became a turning point for me. I realized that reclaiming my power to govern my own life was a critical component of my inner peace and mental harmony. I was not alone, and something greater than me was at work.

As I look back to those challenging years, I am filled with gratitude for my journey. It hasn't been smooth, and precisely because of that it meant a deep catharsis and rebirth of my own growth and evolution. By taking responsibility for the reality I chose to live in, I found the most loving treasure because my experience taught me that faith is not the absence of struggle; on the contrary, it is the courage inside ourselves to overcome it.

Through it all, I remained connected to the Universe, thanks to my experience with Akashic Records. Even when things were at their darkest, I could make it way easier and lighter, forgive faster, and love myself and my situation with more ease and gentleness. My faith was truly ignited during those dark times, and it kept me going.

If you're going through a tough time right now, I encourage you to hold on to your faith. Trust that there is a greater plan in the process. Know that, like a phoenix rising from the ashes, you too can Ignite your faith and ascend your spirit to new heights. I want you to remember that you have the ability to navigate through this life. You`re part of a team with all the resources you need to get in touch with your guidance, soul, and faith.

IGNITE ACTION STEPS

- **Keep your faith**, even during extreme challenges, and ask yourself what your **soul** wants to learn from each difficult situation. Every challenge holds lessons and gifts; dare to discover them.

- **Contemplate the wonders** with **faith**, visit painful places to come out stronger, and remember to take baby steps. Repeat these words daily, "Right now, on this day, in this place, in this moment, right now," to stay present and calm.

- **Obstacles are inevitable**, and your conscious mind cannot navigate them alone. Surrender them to **grace**, and use them for your growth and upliftment. The Universe is there to help you expand your consciousness.

- **Remember your unique gifts** and move towards joy, not suffering. When you fully embrace your gifts and shine courageously, others will respect and love you for them.

- **Take responsibility** for your spiritual **mastery**, protect your energy, and keep your body and mind healthy. This will allow you to ground, manifest, and be open to receiving.

- **Exercise your freedom** to choose what you want to do with your life, and have control over your valuable time. If you're not satisfied where you are, *move*, you're not rooted like a tree!

- **Practice gratitude** before sleep. You will cultivate a positive mindset by reflecting on what you're grateful for, proud of, and what you've done for others.

Xila C. Hope

MS, MBATM, DCPM

Xila C. Hope,

MS, MBATM, DCPM

"Reach Beyond Your Limits!"

When you pray in faith, you will come to know that Jesus doesn't want us to reject one another; rather, reach our hands to bridge the gap when someone is experiencing a deficit in their life. I hope you are inspired by my courage to make positive change and greater influence by showing how God is our vindicator to our adversaries.

Bullies, Broken Wings, and a Bullhorn

I remember as a six-year-old girl that I was shocked by the floor's shininess and thought in amazement, *"Wow, where are we today?"* When I left, the cleanliness of the floor was less important than understanding why I could only hear silence around me.

Someone called my older brother and me into a back room with big chairs. There, this lady asked, "Who do you want to live with?" Without hesitation, we both said, "Grandma." Sadly, our mother had no words for us when we departed. l wondered what could have gone wrong; I just wanted to eat food at Grandma's house! I recalled the times of having to share mustard packets with my brother late into the evenings or even on weekends when there was no food in the house and no meals from school to eat. I also knew that I wouldn't get in trouble at Grandma's house for telling someone we needed food.

My parents suffered through the crack era, affecting how we were cared for. It wasn't until drugs were detected in my baby sister's system that my siblings and I were finally going to Grandma's house. This was where everyone ate good meals, like dressing that was made with the drippings from a roasted turkey. Or, where little girls learned to pick fresh greens by flickering off little bugs with the stems. And, roux that was made for baked macaroni and cheese! With this good eating, everyone felt safe and was accepted with a seat at Grandma's table.

It was also at Grandma's house where I had to quickly grow up in order to take care of the household; this included being able to pray over the family. I learned how to pray at her bedside, which prepared me for my prayer life in the future. At that time, most of my prayers were centered around the safety of my older brother and my mother to get the help that she needed.

In the 80s and 90s, minority communities like mine required resources to keep our families together and functional. But, there wasn't enough financial and social capital to assist inner-city black families with healthy living. Most families were torn apart without healing our broken wings that resulted from incarcerations, addictions, and even deaths from gun violence. Consequently, school-aged children suffered the largest impact from these broken families.

Back then, my middle brother and I were bussed to an elementary school over an hour away from our grandma's house. We were not allowed to attend school with our other siblings due to overcrowding at our grade levels. We stood out like a sore thumb at the new school and were constantly in trouble. Unfortunately, there was no recourse because there was no one advocating on our behalf. Furthermore, we could never speak about how we were wronged. While our voices were silenced, the other children would tell blatant lies and have their words taken as truths. Such injustice was indeed frustrating, especially for vulnerable kids who needed to feel heard and protected.

There was a moment when I was called to an administrator's office. I stood there, barely at the height of the table, trying to speak up to defend myself. Then came this woman's voice, in a demanding tone, stating, "No one asked you a question!" She scolded me further, and I stood there wondering, what am I supposed to do? With tears rolling down my face, all I wanted was someone to call my grandma so she could come and be my voice. I'm sure my brother had the same experience, added to the fact that the school constantly opted to deny him access to his education through the suspension process. These tactics ultimately led him to fail his grade. And, unfortunately, not one single person in the school—not the pupil personnel worker, or even our case manager, found it advantageous to place the proper academic and behavioral supports in place for him.

After experiencing those circumstances, I only hoped for change and aspired to begin again. As I got older, the time came for me to be as resourceful as possible before the next battle. I knew my grandma gave me the basic tools to pray. It was time to use them effectively. As an adult, I began using prayers like a bullhorn over my children and their academic and athletic journeys. Those prayers were strong and had the ability to carry volume into multiple environments.

My *loudmouth* became the tool to expose the action and inaction of others. A soft awareness came upon me when I was a young girl that sparked the desire to Ignite those who had the power to help. Eventually, I flew alongside children who encountered abandonment from bullies, and I was able to show up in their time of need.

Years passed, and I started walking on shiny floors again, but now as a mother. This time the silence was so loud that I could feel it. Instead of being escorted to a judge's chamber, I entered educational institutions, advocating for students with disabilities. I quickly realized that children who experience deficits with their cognitive functioning are rejected. Their conditions are regularly not seen by the naked eye. People who lack awareness misconstrue and form opinions about their true God-given purposes. Meanwhile, the students are alone, simply trying to reach beyond their limitations because they lost their voices while in the battle. Guess what? I didn't even need to hear their voice to recognize when they exhibited non-verbal pain. Due to my childhood, I could mirror their situation and feel their hurt and anguish.

At a *micro* level, these children are often bullied by their peers for appearing to be different, resulting in isolation from social engagements. At a *macro* level, sometimes the adults who operate in the systems designed to equip these students continue this cycle of abandonment. In some cases, they abuse their authority and project themselves as bullies, causing more broken wings. For most, the wings were not fully developed from the start or had been injured during life's journey.

When an air current impacts the wings of a bird to take flight, the bird cannot move forward and may lose its ability to soar among the flock. In the same way, the uninformed individual may mistreat, adversely judge, cause injury, or even catastrophic events that lead to exclusion for people who have limitations. But, when the wings catch the air, it glides them through their flight. A person with a limitation who gravitates toward a culture of inclusion will soar just like a free bird in the air.

Unfortunately, this expansion rarely occurs in the traditional educational system. Students can fall victim to the inadequacies of the professionals governing their education and amateurism in their extracurricular activities. As a ward of the system *and* a praying mother, I managed to overcome some of the challenges. Since I was a child, I knew that God expects us to be one with Him and one another. I also understood that creating division and rejection pulls us from being considerate of someone's needs. To achieve this union and harmony requires additional efforts to make connections. I want us to get closer to God. The totality of everything demands prayer for conviction and understanding, coupled with believing faith will bring change.

Prayer and faith were resources I had for the journey. However, it wasn't until I became a mother that I knew how to apply them. Grandma taught the family how to pray, but the word "faith" was never explicitly explained or how it could be powerful toward what was being desired. I gained insight from my church and studying the Word. And, when God blessed me with maternity, He wasted no time in putting my faith to the test. He also reminded me that circumstances may feel like I'm flying alone in this battle, but it was faith that I needed to reach victory. Like many mothers, I was going to be tested and needed to stand on my faith.

For me, it began when I sat in front of a second-grade teacher who told me that the data from my son's reading scores were being used to build his future jail cell. My body was quick to react as I suddenly felt warm, just as if my blood was boiling. Hmm, I wondered, were these the same jail cells that were built as a result of those who sold drugs that led to the destruction of my first family? I lost my father, mother, and older brother to this statistical basis. This was a pivotal moment for me because either I accepted the story she was painting for me, or I had to grab hold of my faith and be the one to change it.

Based on her assessment, my family was going to be ripped apart unless I stood on faith. That statistic died as I got up and left the discussion. I then became known as the "bag lady" while advocating for my son as a student-athlete. As I walked on the shiny floors with my red bag, I requested a seat at tables where decisions were being made about his education and amateurism plans. Having records readily available to validate or correct what was being verbalized was important. But, it was clear that the institutions didn't care and shifted us back and forth as we navigated on his path. Therefore, receiving the seat also brought a high cost to my emotional state, injuring my wings.

I would leave the meetings with bloodshot eyes and a pounding headache. My mission was to ensure that we discussed the plan as a team in order to help my son perform at a level of proficiency and have the tools to be a productive citizen. That didn't happen! Instead, meetings tore his character apart. Each word spoken moved like a sound wave, dancing off-beat. Every beat appeared to be an accusation, failure, or some form of wrong about his ability to progress. At times, the meetings were perceived as hostile because the staff took offense to the questions I asked instead of being taken as a tool to obtain clarity. I recall a meeting at the secondary level, where I had just heard the word "combative" for the first time. I couldn't even actively continue in the discussion because I tried to comprehend what was being said and whether it was a tactic used to deflect the issues being discussed. If that wasn't bad enough, there was a time when a staff member stood up, exerting her voice to bully *me*, while everyone sat there and watched. It illustrates how the system broke my wings and tried to silence my voice.

It became clear that as a sole soldier with my red bag, I wasn't equipped for those battles. I continued to struggle to find a culture of genuine care and a desire to work as a team at various institutions. I also had my younger children, who were just learning how to use their wings to soar into success. Unfortunately, they also faced challenges within the educational system involving their limitations. It became clear that praying in faith and using my voice needed to be a must. Otherwise, we all would have been defeated.

Therefore, I determined that I needed a BULLHORN! My bullhorn would help me to deliver my message more powerfully and leave an everlasting sound mark, rather than being remembered as the bag lady. It would be laughable to my family if I told them no one heard me when I spoke. They know my voice is carried a mile away. The lack of audibility, in certain environments, impacted the important facts that I wanted to relay. Such as when I needed to tell the judge why I wanted to live with my grandma. I was brought into her chambers, where my voice didn't compete with the noises from the courtroom floor. As a mother, I ended up competing with people who chose to talk over and above me. Using my *bullhorn* approach resonated when other mothers simply wanted people to hear them out so that they could explain *who* their child is as an individual. These discussions required the listeners to be receptive to what was being spoken and actively listen for understanding. I was pushed to pray with certainty because being heard and being an advocate is what I knew would influence those around me.

God heard my plea! He connected me with subject matter experts who shared their knowledge and would intercede in prayer on my behalf. These individuals represented my *bullhorn*. They ensured the appropriate strategies were executed, showing me how to be effectively heard during the discussions. And, they encouraged me to endure the trials in order to help other children who lost their voices. The Holy Spirit even led me to a favorite prayer from the book, *Prayers that Avail Much.* Using my *loudmouth* during the school year, I read this prayer: *"Father, in the name of Jesus, I pray and confess Your Word over my children and surround them with my faith—faith in Your Word that You watch over it to perform it! Great is the peace and undisturbed composure of my children, because You God, contend with that which contends with my children, and You give them safety and ease them."* I then watched God move on our behalf.

I realized taking flight against exclusion meant to impact a culture. My mission became *one*, to be heard; *two*, to be understood; and *lastly*, cause enough pause where we all analyzed the dominating standard. As I continue this pursuit, I hope to connect with individuals who will have the courage to question the action or inaction of people who, directly or indirectly, engage with youth who need support.

God has already demonstrated how He has the power to advance each of us. By faith, my son soared into his greatness by entering his tertiary educational level to study zoology and compete athletically in basketball. He has also become a published author. He doesn't even realize the impact that he has made, motivating other youth to spread their wings and soar! Knowing that families are still faced with opposition with their children in the educational settings, both his and my mission shall continue.

As a mother, my heart expanded, seeing my own mother via a new lens. Through faith she eventually won her children back. She may have lost her voice in the process, but she *never lost* her faith. She regained her identity of motherhood and re-established relationships with her adult children. This encouraged me, as a mother, to persevere through it all and fly high in the process.

When we face the challenge of supporting our children, we must remain faithful believing the will of God shall be done. My inclination is to give you more of the facts to surmise my educational battle: *1. Staff will subconsciously ensure children are protected in their educational settings; they will also shift their mindset to focus on the potential rather than the shortcomings of a student or athlete with a cognitive deficit; 2. Student-athletes will come across programs that are inclusive on and off the court; and 3. You may be the catalyst to ultimately revise rules that prevent children from having access to their rights.* Yet, my personal desire and the mother in me would like for you to know, the journey may seem never ending, but with faith in God, know that He creates cultures where His children are gladly accepted despite any limitations. Through His love, and faith in Him, we shall live in harmony with one another.

Ignite Action Steps

- **Journalize your discussions with God.** This will help you to know what to pray and it will bring things to your remembrance. There may be times when God wants to speak to you about navigating the advocacy journey; you will need to take notes and begin to walk in faith.

- **Amplify your voice and be the bullhorn.** Individuals may not want you to be a contributor because of your level of experience. But, have the courage to know that your input is necessary; question the acceptance of common actions. Let your voice leave an everlasting sound for continuous results.

- **Embrace what some may see as flaws** and utilize it to empower the youth so that they can employ their true God-given gifts. Encourage youngsters to reach beyond their limits.

- **Create a soundboard** where you and your support system will strategize action plans to ensure you have laughable and joyful moments during challenging times. You will need a reboot when faced with life's circumstances and also need the courage to keep going, persevere, and even begin again. Use your circle of support for a sounding board of clarity and next steps.

DR. JO DEE BAER

"Have Faith, Live Faith, Do Faith."

Your faith breathes; it's you with every breath, and it's always there. Ready to support you in your life, and when you activate it like a muscle, it will perform its task. We all have spiritual muscles, and like your inner child, when called upon in your time of greatest need, will always hear you and grant you the desires of your heart.

MESSENGERS ON THE SHOULDER

HAVE FAITH:

"Away in a manger, no crib for His bed…" I recall the soulful singing of the big brown-eyed, brown-haired, pony-tailed little five-year-old Jo Dee filling the rafters of our hometown church, adorned with a white cherub-like cascading choir robe. All the while singing and believing in my heart that this baby in the manger was born on earth to save my soul and me. From that time forward, my childhood Pastor, Giles, delivered his Sunday sermons, and I felt and understood his message as it pierced my soul and formed my spiritual destiny forever.

SHARE FAITH:

While other teenagers were rebelling, at age thirteen, I was studious, focused, and totally cognizant of who I was and my purpose in life. I nearly lost my widowed mother and became orphaned as I entered my teen years. Traumatized by seeing her collapse on the living room floor, I disobeyed her instructions to leave her alone and called 911 instead. A few hours later, as my sister and I waited in the seemingly endless sterile confines of the surgical waiting room, the surgeons finally announced and encouraged us that our mother would live and that she had suffered a perforated ulcer. Her life was teetering on a precipice, and had I not called for the ambulance, my sister and I would have experienced our second loss of a parent in a decade. My heart throbbed. My sister and I sobbed and hugged each other for what seemed like an eternity to never let go.

Years later, in adulthood, we laughed because we believed my faith in action at that intuitive moment saved our mother and saved us both from living and being raised by our 'obsessive-compulsive' Aunt Ida.

DO FAITH:

Amid the economic downturn that hit my industry of Holistic Health during the Great Recession of 2008, I temporarily redirected my personal, corporate health and wellness consulting business and took a position with a Fortune 100 Business brokerage firm. I was thrust into the stress and weekly corporate commuting life of being out on Monday and back home on Friday. My new high-paced, high-stress executive corporate life and Sunday corporate flight assignment schedule was filled with cumulative frequent-flyer logistics and Hotels.com™ rewards. These became my daily social interactive companions. While flying out from the customary weekly closing of a funeral home in North Georgia to potentially listing another funeral home in Southwest Florida, I was exhausted and overwhelmed, projecting on all the work I still had to do.

That was the day of the 'Perfect Storm' back-to-back funeral home week—closing one and listing another. I was panicked and racing to catch a flight at one of the most trafficked airports, Atlanta Hartsfield-Jackson Airport, widely renowned that if one were transported from heaven to hell, they'd have a stop-over in Atlanta! I arrived, shoes in hand, sprinting to the gate, only to find out my flight had been canceled. I would now be flying into Orlando rather than Tampa. *Noooo!* Another two hours became an amplified crescendo into my marathon of a day.

Looking at a sixteen-hour day, which was customary for my career workload that year, I flew into Orlando with every child adorned with Mickey Mouse™ ears singing, "It's a small world after all" and exuberant for Disney World™, so I was unable even to catch a 'cat nap.' But soldier on, I did, through my rudimentary checklist. The rental car was the next checkpoint. With the GPS plugged in, I realized my ETA to Naples was 1 AM the next morning.

Always one to lay my clothes out the night before and get the lists made in pre-prep for the next morning, I made the executive decision for Me, INC. I would forego a hotel in Tampa, drive the two hours to Sarasota, and be prepared for my Potential Client Evaluation and listing in the morning. Driving and dialing was my preoccupation to stimulate my adrenaline and keep my tired eyes peeled on the road before me. With my hand on the steering wheel and my right arm nested onto the car console, I made my merry way, focused on the destination ahead. Immediately after hanging up my cell phone to book my usual Hampton Inn, a meteor-like bolt of light attacked my car.

An enormous mass of metal careened into me and thrust me down the road's left shoulder—leaving me juxtaposed 180 degrees backward on Interstate 75 South.

FEEL FAITH:

The blinding flash of light and piercing decibel noise that had the magnitude of an atomic bomb accompanied by sirens, similar to that of the emergency broadcasting system, shot into my ears. The other car engulfed mine and fishtailed into my left lane. The portable GPS bolted with accelerated spiral force from the opposite car window, around, around, and AROUND. I concurrently somersaulted! My head and shoulders were impacted with such centrifugal force that the seat belts and shoulder harnesses could not support or contain me.

Around, and Around, and AROUND… The car somersaulted and lifted, similar to an airplane taking off. Blood everywhere... I belted my primal cry from the depths of my soul, "Heavenly Father, SAVE ME!" The driver's side door smashed into the ravine between opposite ends of the Interstate. Smoke coming from the car engine… Again, I screamed, "Yahuah, help me!"

In the blink of an eye, like a flash of lightning from heaven, two men with crowbars in hand frantically pried me out of this ticking time bomb of an automobile. So captivatingly handsome were they! One resembled Owen Wilson, and the other a twin of Prince Harry. They immediately engaged in conversation. "Can you move your feet?"

"Yes!" I said.

"We've got to pull you out of this window quickly!" Proverbially organized, I, of course, replied, "Wait a minute… I need my cell phone and day planner for tomorrow's meeting."

Quintessentially conversant and referred to by my family as a "Professional Talker," the two handsome hunks and I were talking the whole way through. Once I was freed, we walked down the Interstate divider ravine. The ambiance was one of a luscious scent and grassy meadow filling the night air rather than the reality of smoke and disintegrating rubber. I asked, "Where are we walking to?"

They replied, "We need to get you up on the back of this Ford™ pickup truck." They hoisted me up at the back door of the truck cabin. I asked them for a towel for my bleeding wrist—I remarked that the luxury of the towel was of a quality only recognized at a Ritz Carlton™. Their reply? "Only the best for you."

My ritualistic nourishment routine for these long trips was always a bag of mini carrots, mandible mouth activity, and natural sugar for the road. However, those little orange bits were not destined to be digested tonight. Struggling with the impending involuntary urge, I pleaded for a bedpan… And, instantaneously, one appeared. Sirens and lights flashed, and I sighed deeply with relief for the third time and said, "Thank you."

Two EMT officers and multiple Florida State Troopers had arrived and asked various unanswered questions… "Who were you talking to?" I looked to my left, and no one was there. "Where did you get the towel? The bed pan?" (now occupied with carrot remnants) "How did you get on the back of this truck? Who pulled you out of your car?" Looking over my shoulder, Owen and Harry were no longer there. Shortly after that, they reappeared one final time as I saw them ascend above in the explosion and flames of smoke—which was my demolished rental car. My handsome messengers had vanished.

The next things I saw were strobe lights, and then I felt the tubes painstakingly forced into me everywhere! From the ER to Intensive Care… I saw the image of one of those two men that were my messengers, but their faces merged into one I now recognized. It was the face of my youngest son, who had flown from Nashville to Tampa General Hospital to be by my side.

As the days painstakingly moved into weeks, my then 'companion,' although a medical professional himself—a dentist, his narcissistic persona was void of any bedside manner, only speaking of himself rather than supporting my recovery. My son gave me my next sequence of goals for my life, "Get away from your catheter. Get out of this hospital. Get a dental cleaning and move ON!"

But move on, HOW?

LIVE FAITH:

My injuries were as vast as a holiday dinner grocery list—broken wrist, ribs, head, shoulder, and a frayed spinal cord. Level 10 pain! With profuse short-term memory loss, my only predominant memory was that every breath created a ripple effect of excruciating pain. The vertigo was so intense that I spent my waking hours spinning around as though I was still in that car with every step. My big world of flying around all over the U.S. evaluating and brokering health companies became a nine-by-twelve-foot room.

Once discharged from the hospital, I was unable to fend for myself. I needed a caretaker. My girlfriend, Christine, gave me respite in a spare bedroom upstairs in her home. It was a triathlon just moving from the bedroom to the bathroom. It was at that time that I decided to "Do Faith" and make each day, as Les Brown says, "The most amazing adventure that today can hold."

During those eighteen months when I couldn't and didn't drive a car, I lived a faith-filled attitude of gratitude. Although I had just competed in IRONMAN 70.3™ two short months prior, I was reduced to pranayama breath and hatha-yoga breathing. My only transportation was worker's comp chauffeurs to take me to rehab. They became my new friends. Not to mention that I attracted a beast of a physical therapist who was also a fellow triathlete! My entire daily life became a focused bubble as an exercise in gratitude. My life's greatest realization during this time of transition was that *the journey itself is a gift*. Gratitude activated from faith unlocked the fullness of that gift.

As my then three-decade-long health coaching expertise slowly came back to me, I knew to shut down my digestive system so that the energy that my body expended could focus on my energy and frequency on healing. My weight had ballooned from one hundred and twenty pounds to over one hundred and sixty within a few weeks. Although I didn't consciously remember, I instinctively knew what to do—lemon juice and coconut water for forty-two days straight. Halfway through that protocol, my short-term memory started to improve. I recalled all my professional experience and the tenacity of dedicated physical work, knowing my faith would bring me back to the fullness of health and vitality of life.

I carried my 'Messengers' on my shoulder each time I entered the rehab unit. I did yoga, prayed, and developed my signature green 'Miracle' drink. I called it a miracle because I was a walking miracle myself. My weight stabilized, and my spleen was energetically restored. Parallel to one's Spirit, the body is a miracle-making machine and can heal itself. And in my eighteen months of building, reclaiming, and restoring myself back in body and mind, my Spirit confirms the answer to this question:

Who were those messengers?

My plaintive cry of Faith called out in a time of need. Those Messengers were there from my "Away in a Manger" singing and resided on my shoulder every day till today. Pastor Giles, my mother, and my soul's inner children, both male and female, all concur: *"Have Faith, Live Faith, Do Faith."*

The good book says in Hebrews 11:1, *"Now faith is the substance of things hoped for, the evidence of things not seen."*

It was then that I realized I embodied the invisible made visible with my Messengers, what I needed to survive and thrive. I now live a testimony of healing of hope, and those Messengers abide in my residence—ON my shoulder to this day.

For me, FAITH was formed in my song as a little pony-tailed girl, my heart-rending cry in the spinning automobile, my spontaneous and intentional healing, and my abundant living of today. Faith is an ACTION word from your inner self, displayed in a flowing cherub's robe, no matter how old you are. It is the essence of your eternal soul. The Messengers and I proved it. *I am living proof.*

You may have had Messengers in your life, faces and hands that reached in a moment of need. You may not have had faith that they were there for you. But when you look inward, you are directed upward, discovering the faith and belief that they are all around you, eternally.

IGNITE ACTION STEPS

The quintessential thought leader and philosophical author, Wallace D. Wattles, voices these three mantras in his 1912 classic, *The Science of Getting Rich:*

"There is a thinking stuff from which all things are made, and which, in its original state, permeates, penetrates, and fills the interspaces of the Universe."

"A thought in this Substance produces the thing that is imagined by the thought."

"A person can form things in their thoughts, and, by impressing their thoughts on Formless Substance, can cause the things they think about to be created."

What *if* the interspaces of the Universe are filled with power smoldering inside of you and me like your own Messengers? Like the wind, that inner Universe is eternally there, filled with positive, consecutive, sustained thoughts.

Like body, mind, and spirit, this is the trifecta. *Relax, Reset, and Restore.*

Relax—Slow down to speed up. Believe that all is well right here, right now. Be at peace, beginning with the earthly vessels we've been given. "Una Cuerpo. Una Vida": One body. One life. Live and be the Law of Attraction in the immediate mindfulness of the moment to fulfill your future.

Reset—A conscious part of daily gratitude. The only thing constant is change. Live life from the present and be grateful for the moment so your future can build upon the success ladder in knowledge, beauty, and grace.

Restore—You can achieve anything you desire. Daily meditation is life's reclamation. Our bodies are either degenerating or regenerating; you decide. It takes ninety days for a new blood supply and six months for completely rejuvenated new cells. Commit to those ninety days and become fully charged, one hundred percent energetic beings, living fully in this life until we are called to the next.

These three **Rs** can and will be yours with these daily acts of self-love. Commit to loving each part of your body as you meditate from your toes to your brain. Repeat: *I love each part of my body* as you move upward from your toes to your brain. Feel the healing, feel the love, feel the faith.

Christine Ebeltoft-Bancalari

Christine
Ebeltoft-Bancalari

*"You don't have to go far, have an extravagant story,
or experience a miracle to impact the world."*

Everyone has a story of faith designed to impact others. Each of us is an integral part of the human tapestry of life intended to create something spectacular when interwoven with the lives of others. I encourage you to look for God in your daily details because the most precious gifts and opulent opportunities are often overlooked as unimportant occurrences. Paying attention and reflecting on the simple things will unveil God's plan and purpose in your life. Faith often resides in seemingly insignificant details, like individual threads obscured in an exquisite tapestry. It is when overlooked segments of our lives intertwine that *faith ignites*.

No Passport Required

As a longtime Central Florida resident, visions of rocket boosters preparing for blast-off are the first thing I picture when I consider the force behind the powerful words: *Ignite Faith!* I think most people expect their encounter with God or faith to be one of such magnitude that they will never forget precisely when or where it happened. For much of my younger life, I believed that to come to *know* God and solidify my faith, I would be in a distant land, on my last breath, or at a critical crossroads. I envisioned it to be like the awe a person experiences at a rocket launch on the Florida coast.

I watched my grandparents travel to Mexico on missionary trips. We prayed for families who relocated to African nations and South America, demonstrating their unwavering faith. So, from a very young age, I began to write in my prayer journal, "I will Go, Lord!" expecting to meet God on my road to Damascus while serving in the mission field or living in a foreign land. I was confident that developing a deep, meaningful faith would require a passport and a life-altering adventure accentuated by a milestone experience. I am not a product of privilege, but as a citizen of the United States, I simply could not conceive how it was possible to experience God or find the extraordinary faith that moves mountains without a tremendous experience in a far-off land. Different, difficult, demanding, deprived, or nearly dead. I expected that tribulations and toil, struggle and surrender, or the ultimate sacrifice would be what it would take to solidify my faith to articulate it tangibly to others. And, to find an experience like that, I always felt I needed (or wanted) a passport.

When I was fifteen, my mother sensed I needed an attitude adjustment. She sent me to the Boundary Waters on a two-week canoe trip where we had to carry all our food and supplies through the Minnesota wilderness—this seemed a relatively simple assignment. Once there, I feared nothingness and the vast open space between where we were and civilization. I embraced "I will Go, Lord!" as my resolve: paddling across endless waters, carrying our canoes and belongings over portages, sleeping with bears, bathing with snakes, pulling dirty water from the lake for our instant dinners, and cooking over an open fire, rain or shine. The pilgrimage was formidable. The journey almost met my preconceived *Go* criteria. I was deprived of basic comforts. I was in a remote place. I was out of my comfort zone and witnessed God's power in nature all around me. I was even dipping my toes in a foreign country, Canada. I felt closer to God and relied on my faith throughout the expedition. I constantly thought, *Is this my Go experience?* Ultimately, I was not convinced it was my pivotal faith moment.

Still pursuing my powerful faith story, I used journaling to sort out my prayers, dreams, and ideas as I transitioned to collegiate life and beyond. I wrote in and amassed dozens and dozens of prayer journals spanning decades of my life. At some point along the way, writing "I will *Go*, Lord!" became a repetitive practice until it evolved into my daily mantra. When I was hopeful, "I will *Go*,

Lord!" When I was desperate, "I will *Go*, Lord!" When I was alone, afraid, or anticipating something extraordinary, "I will *Go*, Lord!"

I was so convinced I must *Go* but needed to figure out *where*. I attempted to give my discovery of faith some momentum by planning to study abroad or on a ship for Semester at Sea, but *my* plans never actualized. I went on domestic missionary trips and singing tours around the midwest with my church choir and often wondered, *Is this it? Is this where you are calling me to Go, Lord? Is this my consequential faith moment?* Little sparks of faith shone on my path, but I wasn't stretched or tested as expected; the big bright faith eruption never occurred.

I faced numerous circumstances where my faith would grow and blossom. Like any teenager, I made my way through my fair share of bad choices and periodically felt alone, forsaken, and unsteady. There were the familiar heartbreaks and disappointments: a break-up with my first love, falling short of making the cheerleading team, and typical teenage angst of wondering where I belonged. More significant moments like my parents' divorce shook me profoundly, leading me to wrestle with God and question my faith. While my faith grew and sustained me, these junctures were not equivalent to what I expected to encounter in my "I will *Go*, Lord!" moment.

I recorded so many glimmers of faith at work in my journals. Nevertheless, I still felt an expectation to *Go* somewhere. I expected an adventure, something uncertain, unfamiliar, and uncomfortable. I didn't realize how God uses each seemingly inconsequential affair to build a formidable foundation of trust in Him. Every encounter gradually assembled an extravagant arrangement that evaded me because my attention was diverted; I was foraging for something else.

I graduated college and prayed that God would use my education to send me into the world as an international reporter or US Ambassador. I was sure I could share His love and story in a position of power and authority. Neither happened. Eventually, I was blessed to become a Rotary Ambassadorial Scholar in Chile. I encountered answers to my prayers without fully recognizing them at the time. In high school, I planned to go on a ship as my way to *Go* and put my passport to use. As a scholar in Chile, I sailed on a Chilean naval vessel to Easter Island. In college, I prayed for positions of influence. In Chile, I traveled with officers in the Navy, business leaders, and professionals from around the world, working on research and launching the internet in the Southern Cone. I didn't realize it, but my earlier ideas were whispers of how God would use me to share His love and story. I just didn't know it yet. God used many unrelated experiences to build my ability to connect with people, bridge cultures, and understand how to communicate well. While living in Chile, I started to feel like my Go moment was happening, though it wasn't as rocket-fueled as I had been picturing for so long.

When it came time to leave Chile, I prayed that God would continue to send me to foreign lands to do His work. I was hired as an international marketing manager for a Fortune 500 company. My professional and philanthropic roles allowed me to raise money for charities and impact lives around the globe. My passport was now getting a lot of use as I jetted to Mexico, Aruba, Thailand, and all over Europe and South America. I continued to be involved with Rotary, and I knew I was doing *some* good in the world. But I wasn't entirely convinced that I was doing God's work. I began to take some pressure off myself as I pieced together the blessings and saw how incredibly fortunate I was at such a young age. I started to see how God had been working behind the scenes, recognizing these opportunities as answered prayers from years prior. While my faith was maturing, I sensed that God was ready to use me to do more. There was still more *going* to be done. I was simultaneously accomplished and unfinished.

As I wrestled with how God chose to use me, I lost some of my connectedness to Him. My prayers fell flat. My little moments of awe were dimming and spread farther apart. Life threw me curveballs, and my clarity slipped further and further away. I was dealing with infertility, my marriage's stress, and an undercurrent of fear and frustration about choosing between a highly successful profession where I was making a difference and becoming a mom. I was caught between guilt and restlessness, success and submission. The pressure of wanting children when my biological clock was ticking and maintaining a career I worked hard to achieve were opposing forces straining my heart and mind. Journaling prayers of desperation and even deal-making were once again my morning and nighttime routine. There were days that all I could write was, "I will *Go*, Lord!" with the hope that the agony of my struggles would end by being dispatched on my *Go* journey. God's promises and purposeful formation of my faith were evident but only slightly discernible.

I felt especially broken one night as a friend inquired about my faith. I struggled to explain why I was sure God heard and answered my prayers. I remember thinking, *Just say it! Of course, He does!* But then she asked, "How do you really know this to be true?" I was silent because it was the first time in my life that I felt like I couldn't just say, "Because, I know." I didn't. I had prayed and prayed to God, yet there I was.

I needed to understand why my call to *Go* still felt unanswered, so I searched for clues. I had never done this before, but I decided to go back and read my prayer journals. I read dozens of them and systematically began highlighting and putting tabs on pages that connected the prayers to the answers. As my highlighter joined my prayers and their answers pages apart or even journals later, my faith exploded. There were so many answered prayers throughout the volumes; the requests to God were fulfilled in ways I didn't recognize at the time. I uncovered how obstacles were stepping stones, and the roadblocks were barricades of protection. Separately, mere everyday experiences and observations were nothing, but once connected, my pleas to God had been covertly answered.

Deep inside, I still believed that "I will *Go*, Lord!" meant that I would be sent to distant lands for remote missionary work. I wasn't sure if I'd live in a tent or without running water, relying on God's word and promises to stay strong in desperate conditions while giving hope to those less fortunate. But my faith was firm, and my resolve even more robust. I was ready. *Now, it must be time.*

It took me another six years to learn that "I will Go, Lord!" sometimes means "Do His work right where you are standing!" That realization came once I finally made it through my journey of infertility, conceived and had my son, and then my daughter, just sixteen months later. I was a mom of two who walked away from an international career toward the most important demonstration and use of faith possible. I received a much more unique and uncommon appointment than living in a foreign land. Presented with what most people around the world plead with God to save them from, I became the mother to a child with Down syndrome. I was not expecting this kind of *Go* assignment. I was both excited and terrified but committed because I *knew* God was using all the encounters and experiences up to that point to ensure my faith was strong enough to Go where *He* had planned.

Amazingly, my faith moment wasn't as tremendous to me as it may sound. It was a profound yet simple, "Yes, Lord! Yes! I am ready, and I WILL GO!" I was all in! 1000 percent *game on* from the first minute I heard, "It looks like Adriana has Down syndrome." In a split-second, the highlighted pages of my journals filled with answered prayers and thousands of committed statements, "I will *Go*, Lord!" flooded my mind. I felt all the preparation put into place long before my commissioning washed over me as doctors and nurses hurried into the operating room, saying things like, "Why didn't we know? Who didn't do the testing on this baby?"

When I finally put a voicc to my thoughts, I said, "I knew. It is okay. She is perfect. I am ready! I will Go, Lord!"

It's a humbling and gratifying experience to stop and think about WWJD (what would Jesus do) every minute of my day. It's an incredible responsibility and gift to be authorized to raise someone that whole countries would erase before ever giving them a chance at life. God heard my prayers. I read in my journal how He answered them, so many of them, not too long before she was born. Countless experiences highlighted in my journals show how God had this perfect plan for me to *Go* into uncharted waters from the very beginning. My

Ignite Faith moment was not one big moment. It wasn't even a moment, it was many small ones spread over time that prepared me to go into the world every day as the best mother and advocate possible.

Adriana is now a brilliant young woman answering the call to be a light in the world and make inclusion a way of life. I love that my dream assignment, which I once titled "Always an Adventure," is "Adriana." God gave me far more than a *Go*; He gave me a *why*. We still go to distant lands, and there are sacrifices and challenges along the way. There are days I still cry out, "I will *Go*, Lord!" Only now, I know where. I will *Go* where there is intolerance for inclusion. I will *Go* where parents are met with devastating news to shine a light of hope. I will Go to the steps of Capitol Hill to advocate for laws that improve the lives of people with unique abilities. I will *Go* to the halls of Corporate America, school board meetings, and medical conventions to change perceptions and open doors of opportunity. In 2010, I watched God move around me as I joined three other families to form the *Down Syndrome Foundation of Florida*. My *Go* became a catalyst that gives people the *Down Syndrome Experience*. Our tagline is "When *POTENTIAL* is given *OPPORTUNITY*, the outcome is *SUCCESS*!" God saw my potential and is giving me a grand opportunity. He placed the desire in my heart long ago. My goal is to keep Christ's commands at the center of my life and help Adriana develop her gifts so she can do the same and grow into something even greater. God graciously expanded my circle of influence, and now over 2,500 families benefit from the years of preparation and prayer through the works of our non-profit. It is truly an amazing adventure!

My prayer now is, "We will *Go*, Lord!" Our family and The FOUNDATION move through the world with affirmation and conviction of the assignment given. I know our story of overcoming obstacles, finding the best in every situation, and trusting His word was a call to help others look for how God is using each one of our experiences to weave a story of hope and success. My "I will *Go*, Lord!" was about changing hearts and minds regarding the value of every life and person you meet. We all have beautiful stories and endless possibilities when we shift our perspective and *go* in faith.

What I realized is that God provided me with a simple path lit by exceptional events that, when added together, create a faith that is as purposeful and powerful as those blazing rocket boosters. It didn't require a long or distant journey. Although I have traveled to many far-off lands, it was not the remote places that forged my deep faith. My faith story feels more like the uncomplicated light strands that hang around beautiful backyard patios. Each bulb is bright enough to cast a little glow on its own. Still, when strung together and hung out on a summer evening, the collective warm brilliance transforms the otherwise void space into something captivating and inviting. When my individual God moments connected, obscure shadows no longer hid important faith features; the picture became so beautifully clear and more vibrant than I could ever picture in my dreams. *God is so big that He expresses himself through the tiny things.*

I have not consistently recognized Godly 'light bulb' encounters, and I am sure I miss many throughout my day. Nonetheless, I try to be intentional and look for God's hand in my everyday experiences. I do not consider myself extraordinary—actually, quite the opposite. I am merely a vessel who has wanted to be a conduit of God's love to others in the world for most of my life. I have learned to document and notice where God shows himself to me along the way, but that didn't happen overnight. Journaling and reflecting is how I continue to build my faith and define my *Go!*

Even when you become more intentional in pursuing your '*Go* moments,' you often won't realize them until long after they happen. This is by design. We are all a work in progress. Your insignificant encounters, when strung together, will cast light upon God's plan in the making. Take a seat and watch the landscape around you change as God uses the experiences and desires in your heart to fill your life with the necessary experiences to go into the world—no passport required.

IGNITE ACTION STEPS

- **Pay attention** to the little things in your life and write them down—they contain clues about how God wants to use you to create the most exquisite tapestry.
- **Start a journal** and record your prayers and petitions, they often become part of a bigger picture, but you cannot see this while it is happening.
- **Take time to go back** and read your journals every six months to see your answered prayers. Note where you may have seen obstacles and roadblocks and look for how they have guided, saved, or redirected your journey.
- **Intentionally highlight prayer** requests and answered prayers—connect the dots. God puts dreams in our hearts and will guide us to a place where our life has meaning and can serve others.
- **Tell your story** to Ignite Faith in yourself, others, and the world.

CANDICE CPOETICSTEW

"The storms of life rage, but an anchored soul will not sink."

I want the person who holds this book and reads my story to understand that during the darkest moments, we must hold onto faith and keep fighting until we conquer our destiny. You may be a person of faith, but sometimes circumstances, obstacles, family, or health can dampen your hope and spirit. In those times, you must focus and deepen your faith, trusting God is guiding your way.

STAGES OF GREAT FAITH

I remember the day my legs decided they were no longer my own. I was sitting at a restaurant after church. I had just relocated back to my home state and was catching up with old friends. We normally always laugh and talk about life. After enjoying our meal and fellowship, I proceeded to get up from the table to head to the restroom before leaving. Suddenly, my muscles went tight as a sharp pain shot through my legs and up and down my back. I was having difficulty walking and gripped the walls just to get where I needed to go. My thoughts were, *What is happening to me? I can barely walk.*

As I continued to wrap my head around what was happening, I reflected on signs that I might have been missing. I recalled having trouble sitting at church that morning and thinking it was due to the wooden pew with just a small padded cushion. Now I knew it wasn't the seats but something going on in my body. An elderly lady at the restaurant asked me, "Honey, do you need my cane?" I told her no, and that I was fine. When I got back to the table, I asked for my food to go, knowing I had to get out of the restaurant. I leaned against the walls and held my friend's arm to make it to my vehicle, then gasped for air as I drove home through the pain. I prayed, "Lord, please don't let me get in an accident."

There are moments when we are tested to fight for our dreams and destiny. It sometimes appears that the closer you get to your dreams, all opposition and obstacles keep you away from them. This health storm I was about to embark on was one of my biggest tests. Going through that storm felt like a tsunami with raging tidal waves coming unannounced into my life, leaving me no time to prepare. The floods of life were about to rage, and I was holding on by just a large branch.

Once I made it to my house and pulled into the driveway, I dragged myself out of the car, still in excruciating pain. I limped to the door and made my way to the sofa, once again using the walls for help. I yanked out my laptop and began researching my symptoms on the Internet, hoping to find a possible diagnosis.

I didn't find all the answers, but I learned what questions to ask my doctor.

I called the very next day to book an appointment but was told I would have to wait a few weeks before being seen.

I continued with work and life as I waited. I'm unsure if it was due to being in a highly stressful position that aggravated my condition, but my health worsened. The pain started increasing more, and my ability to walk decreased drastically. As I counted down the days until my medical appointment, I tried to fight through the agony I felt. Thoughts swirled in my mind as I attempted to get my work done, knowing I didn't have enough scheduled time off to take numerous medical appointments. As I walked my clients out of my office each day, the pain was so intense that my colleagues started to take notice.

I thought, *This is definitely a sciatic nerve issue.* I experienced shooting pain out of nowhere and could only lay on my side, not my back. When I finally was able to see the physician, I was put through numerous tests and procedures were performed, such as MRI, progression of pain, scheduling for physical therapy, and other treatments. The pain was so severe that the technician had to help take my shoes off, as they laid me on my back for a full body scan. At that moment, I felt like rescheduling the appointment but pressed my way through to see what was going on with my health. I was in so much pain tears rolled down my face. You know… the kind of pain that hurts so much it is like silent misery and leaves you speechless.

As the technician played classical music in the exam room, I entered the huge MRI machine, some sort of miniature cave, where I was having an X-ray to better understand what was happening inside me. I was on this silver flat plate bed, very small and narrow, similar to a side bench in a gym. As I lay on the table with such undesirable pain in my body, I yelled, "How much longer? I need to get up now!" With a vague answer of "Not too much longer," I felt like my pain wasn't important. I was so alone, and in the worst physical condition and all I could say was, "Lord help me!"

While I lay on the X-ray table, I didn't know I was about to receive a life-changing diagnosis. Of all the battles I have had to overcome, this tested my faith in God the most. But I would discover that when the storms of life rage, an anchored soul will not sink.

A week later, a young physician with red hair returned with the test findings. As he presented the results, I was shocked by what he reported. "We see some-thing on your MRI. We will have to send you to a specialist." His voice was stern and frank, but what I heard was shocking and explosive. My mind immediately began to worry. It took me a long moment to digest the news.

I was overwhelmed. "Wait, a specialist?" I asked with a loud voice.

He replied stoically, "Yes, so we can remove it."

I still couldn't quite understand what he was saying; "Okay, what?" I asked now, feeling numb all over. "This is happening so fast." I felt devastated and just wanted the pain to stop—now I have to see a specialist. He then provided a little comfort by saying, "It is a good thing we are acting quickly." He seemed positive, but I was crumbling. Between the lingering physical pain and the news he delivered, I had to sit down. I put my left hand on my forehead and leaned my head on the wall in his office, processing the information. "Lord, what is going on?" I found myself saying. I looked at the paperwork he gave with a business card to a specialist with their name, number, and next steps.

When I arrived at the specialist's office I was nervous and frantic, trying to anticipate what the surgeon would say. He reported even more bad news. He stated they would be unable to operate due to my issue being in a risky location. He wanted to observe my condition for a year. I didn't know how much more

I could take with the pain, not walking and using a cane for assistance. *Now I have to be observed for a year?* I asked the surgeon, "What if it grows?"

He declared, "You can die."

My immediate thought was, *Did he just say I can die? Where is his compassion for the patient?* However, he was a direct, forward doctor and was said to be the best in his profession. The thought of it growing and how I could die at any time made me lower my head in disbelief, thinking, *This means, I could be at the grocery store, on a family outing, or away on a trip and if this thing grows, I could drop dead without any notice.* It took me a while to accept this information as I realized I was in the fight of my life.

Battling that storm, my dreams appeared so out of reach. To be honest, I stopped dreaming and was ready to throw in the towel. I had no hope, was getting ready to die, and even accepting my death.

I found myself questioning:

Is all this opposition worth the fight?
Is it possible to reach my dreams?
Do I give in because the dream seems so far out of reach?

Beyond the mental exhaustion of confronting those questions, my health storm caused me to be physically drained and depleted with numerous medical appointments, countless medications, and constant physical limitations. I went from walking and having no leg pain to barely being able to sit down or stand up without the help of someone else. I began to run out of words to describe my pain and suffering. All I could say is, "Lord help me, *please.*"

One day on the sofa, agonizing over my condition, I decided to prepare my family for my passing and make funeral plans. I called my prayer team, asking them to pray for me through this test of affliction and continue my walk of faith, whatever that was going to be.

During that same time, my mother had been dealing with the loss of my sister, and I wanted to respect and honor her grief. I decided not to share the full extent of my pain with my mother to cherish her emotions as she was healing. I kept thinking my mother was not ready to hear about another family member's death after grieving the loss of someone so dear to her.

One day my mother called me on the phone, with so much joy in her voice, and asked, "How are you doing, daughter?" I could sense by her uplifted tone she was having a great day. I didn't want to take away from her joy, so I disguised my truth by saying, "I'm hanging in there, Mom. Can I call you back later?"

It was at that moment that I changed the narrative of my life. I was too young to die without my dreams and goals being fulfilled and manifested on earth. Being a woman of faith, I thought about a passage of the Bible scripture in Psalm 91:16; "With long life, I will satisfy you and show you my salvation."

I'd had enough!! I was not satisfied with my state of condition and circumstance! I yelled, "God, I'm not satisfied! Enough is enough!"

My strength, faith, and fight for my destiny started to Ignite, like a campfire created when the only tools given are a rock and tree branches. I chose to Ignite the fire of faith and spark into the life I was meant to lead.

At that moment, I was lying on my stomach in pain, when Les Brown's quote came to me; "If you can look up, you can get up." I knew I was able to look up just a little. Yet, I declared: "I will not die but live and declare the works of the Lord." I began to focus on that scripture in the Bible and God. I was confident and assured my trust in God would see me through this. I began to say these words daily until my health and faith strengthened. My faith began to grow stronger and deeper. I took my focus off my circumstance and put them on God. I believe God could heal me. I began to thank Him in advance as I walked in faith *with* Him.

I was using an assistive device cane to walk. I had to wear tennis shoes instead of the beautiful footwear I had collected over the years. But in that moment of faith, I looked at the cane and said, "Not so." I began to leave the cane in the vehicle during work. Many times, I had to grip the walls at work with my colleagues, supervisors, and directors looking at me, asking where my cane was, and having them offer to get it out of the car. I would politely say, "No, thank you." In my mind, I was thinking, "Okay, God, I'm trusting you for a miracle and healing. I took a leap of faith by leaving the cane in the car." It took a while—several months, in fact, but I permanently stopped using the cane and began to walk on my own.

After another six months, not only did I not need the cane, but I was also able to rock a variety of shoes.

I kept declaring and decreeing daily, "I will not die but live and declare the works of the Lord." After a year, I went back to get an MRI, and the result was shocking. Everything was normal! I gained my mobility, but they also could not find the original issue anywhere. That's right; it had dissolved! The female blonde technician, smiling, pulled me to the side and said, "Do you believe in miracles?"

I said, overjoyed, "Yes, I do! He is the same God."

She gave me the transcripts of the new MRI, and my eyes were astonished with a big candy apple smile on my face. I experienced a miracle and was completely healed. I was thankful for the miracle God made. My purpose was aligned with the direction God had planned for me.

I was so in awe and viewed the transcripts that were given from the MRI. I shared the news with my family, friends, colleagues, and strangers. I was reminded of the scripture in the Bible, King James Version in Hebrews 11:1, "Now Faith is the substance of things hoped for, the evidence of things not seen." I believe God was able to heal me. I didn't see it, but I believe it in my heart. My faith matured in the process by focusing on God. I knew God would heal, and the healing and pain would cease. My faith was ignited, and that was truly all I really needed.

New doors opened to be around a community of speakers, including the top motivational speaker on the planet, Mr. Les Brown. Imagine that! Les Brown came into my thoughts when I was agonizing in pain. Now, I was one of his speakers at an international summit and assisted with his international community. I had the opportunity to sit for hours a week, gleaming from his profoundly inspirational messages. Les Brown came to my thoughts when I needed him most, and now I spent time with him learning how to inspire others and hone my message.

My faith in God not only allowed healing and a miracle to manifest but also spoke to me in a time of need through the legendary Les Brown, and I heard the calling indeed.

My life today is void of physical pain. I can't remember what that pain felt like as I ran, jumped, leaped, and poured full force into life. I choose the emotions I feel now, and they are energetic, adventurous, and passionate about life. I also help others discover their destiny and dreams by reaching their maximum potential and embracing their walk through faith.

When you are overwhelmed in the face of great trials, find the faith that can hold you. The storms of life will continue to rage, but an anchored soul will not sink. Life can place so many obstacles that your confidence gets knocked down with your dreams. It is in those moments, when you feel alone, that you question your ability, skills, and dreams. In your darkest hour, you must keep the faith. You must remind yourself—*I know God did not bring me this far for this. It is a deepening within.* You realize what FAITH is all about. It's not about what your mother, father, or grandmother told you or what you learned in Sunday's church service. Faith in God gives you supernatural strength, not in your ability but in God's ability to conquer the unenviable. It's a conviction within you. God is who He says He is and does what He says He will do. Have faith that God *will* do exactly what he's promised you.

Ignite Action Steps

What obstacles are stopping you from reaching your maximum potential in life?

- **Write the vision of what you would like to see.** Many times a vision board helps you to focus on your goals and change your perspective on what you see. Your situation may be bad, such as loss of job or financial hardship—you may be at your wit's end. Create a vision board that will help you to focus on where you would like to be. You can put pictures from magazines, or articles of inspiration on your vision board. View this daily and watch your vision come to reality.

- **Speak affirmations and declarations.** Speak positive affirmations and declarations daily. Choose to say affirmations of what you *will* do and declare it *will* be done. If you desire to have a home, speak affirmations on when you will get your home and put a time frame around your desire. When you speak affirmations or declarations you are speaking life to your situation.

- **Keep a Faith Journal and write in it.** Keep a journal or notebook on faith journeys. You can write down what you are believing in and asking God for, and mark it off when it manifests. Journals also increase your faith. You can view your journal on your faith walk over the month, days, or years and see items that came to fruition. Writing your faith down strengthens your conviction and reminds you to trust God. If He did so in the past, He can do so in the future. If He provides graciously for others, He undoubtedly will provide graciously for you. Keep your faith constantly ignited within you.

Jammie M. Matheson

"Trust your inner voice."

More than anything, I want you to know to trust yourself. Trust your thoughts. When your inner voice speaks to you, follow it. Act immediately and with the intent to initiate a discovery period. Developing a relationship with your inner voice will strengthen your self-reliance. I would like to share a process I developed to do just this, to help you learn to trust yourself and your decisions. By doing this, I hope you may have the tools you need moving forward to trust your inner voice.

The Whisper

Is this what death looks like? Is this how it happens? How do you slip from the fingers of life into the grasp of nothingness? I never thought my journey through the valley of the shadows of death would take place as a short walk from the living room to the kitchen to get my sleepy little boy a bottle. Without warning, I collapsed to the floor before I could finish my first step. I lost all strength and no longer had the use of my limbs. I find my cries for help only echo off the canyon walls in a desolate valley; I must get to a phone. I don't remember taking a wrong turn between the living room and the kitchen, but somehow I ended up here, in the valley of the shadows of death!

The phone may as well be on the other side of the grand canyon. An hour ago, I was happily walking through the large 1940s farm-style kitchen. The warm honeydew green color of the cabinets draws you in like someone placing their arms around you to give you a big hug. I heard the birds chirping through the window as the scent of freshly plowed fields flowed in on the fall breeze. What a beautiful day to play with my sweet baby. Now, I was hoping that at such a young age, he would somehow retain a memory of me. What a difference an hour can make.

The room is spinning; I am desperate to maintain awareness of my surroundings. This quickly shifts into panic as I realize moments from now, my five-year-old will be bouncing in the door with excitement wanting to give me a gift. A treasure he finds for me each day, a beautiful white rock. We call them 'Hope Rocks.' When he proudly hands them to me with a smile, he says, "I hope you get better, Momma!" And gives me a loving squeeze. All I can think of is him charging through the door only to find his *person*, his momma, unresponsive, lying on the floor. The phone, the phone! I try to stand again to reach it but to no avail. It takes every bit of strength to crawl across the kitchen. The grains in the wood floor fade into each other as my consciousness drifts out. I try to focus on moving forward, one hand in front of the other, while listening for the kitchen door hinges to creak, expecting it to fly open.

This is not the experience I want my child to live through over and over in his mind for the rest of his life. Knowing that every time he reaches for a door knob his fingers will tremble and sweat, his heart will pound, his throat will close off; it will reignite every emotional response of finding his mother dead on the floor. I rebuke this, I can not live with this thought, and I am not willing to die knowing that could be his future. I understand full well I must protect my family from this terrifying journey through the darkness, as it is never a trip you take alone. To what extent will be the cost of this journey? Only time will tell.

Three weeks earlier, I received my diagnosis. At twenty-nine years old, maintaining the care of three busy children, and sharing my life with a charismatic husband with whom we are building a prospering future, I found out that I had aggressive Stage IV breast cancer, a type of cancer without specific treatments. I'm the first person being given an experimental chemo, willing to do anything to stay alive.

My husband and I worry about the price our oldest son is paying while I'm on this forsaken trip. Our oldest is seven. He has designated himself as my personal guardian. He is worried no one is home to take care of me. Even though he loves school, he comes up with every excuse to come back to the house when the bus arrives, thinking if he misses it, he will be able to stay home to watch over me. For several days, getting him on the bus has been a fight. The bus driver patiently waits as I try to convince my son that he must go. He is so physically strong and so strong-willed that I am no longer a match for him in this particular battle. He feels he has to step in and take the place of his dad, who is working out of town.

My husband, who is building our family business, has incredible strength, broad shoulders, and equally-matched devotion. This driven thirty-year-old man, an example to many, is being torn between the responsibility of maintaining our household, being out of town, and facing the reality of my prognosis. This balancing act takes strategy and character in a normal situation, but this is a heavy load to bear for any man.

If there were ever a child like his father, it would be this seven-year-old that I am continually dragging back out to the bus. His quick wit, skills on a motorcycle, and love for animals truly show the respect and love for life his dad has instilled in him. The other side of this headstrong little cowboy is that he dresses up for every occasion. He will only wear nicely kept jeans with a leather belt, cowboy boots, and a button-up dress shirt when going to school. He means "business" when he is ready for school; this is his "job." When getting ready for the day, his dress shirt is always buttoned clean to the top. He gets this from his grandpa. So, when I see the top button on his shirt isn't done up, I know exactly what his plans are; he has no intention of getting on that bus.

My husband asked me what my wishes were with the children while going through this illness. I wanted them to go to school every day and be able to spend time with friends and classmates. This would provide an escape where they could just be little boys. After school, I wished for them to have brownies, drink fresh cold milk, then sleep in their own beds at night. I desired for them to have as normal of a life as possible.

My husband supported me in this. I heard him defending my wishes to others several times, always honoring me. By following my wishes, he was risking that someday, the simple act of reaching for the kitchen doorknob could lead to the unpleasant scene of finding their mother had passed. He might have to live with that guilt, but it was my last wish, and he was trying to fulfill it.

Looking back, I realize the boys were triggered every day they left the house. While at school, the anxiety would set in, wondering what they would find when they arrived back home. The negative experience I was trying to protect them from was being played out every single day. I didn't know who was going to find me on this particular day, if it would be the five-year-old or, in several more hours, the seven-year-old. All of these thoughts were going through my mind as I continued to work toward the telephone. I finally reached the other end of the kitchen, where the phone was hanging high on the wall.

I must stand in order to reach the phone. I go a few feet further into the hallway to the little bathroom. I have never been so happy to have a tiny bathroom in my life! It's so small that when you open the two-foot wide door, it swings and stops against the tub. I will never complain about the size of that bathroom again! The space allows me to place one hand on the side of the heavy cast iron tub and the other on the sink. I lean into the old wooden door and use it as a ramp to slide myself into an upright position. As I stand and turn, the world seems to stop. The cries from my sleepy baby become silent as I catch a glimpse of something in the mirror, and it isn't me.

People say there *is* such a thing as deathbed repentance; I discovered those people are entirely wrong. I looked into the mirror and was so close to death that my physical reflection was no longer there; I was engaged eye to eye with my soul. I was not repenting. There is a time for repenting to be done, which had long passed. I was making deals and promises to whomever or whatever would listen as I begged for my life. I locked into a gaze with my soul. In that *moment,* the world changed.

It *could have* been that split second which ignited my faith. After all, I was in a staring contest with my soul and was waiting to find out who was going to blink first!

That flash of an exposed soul could have given me structure behind the belief system people had been spoon-feeding me since I was a child. Or, that moment could have reinforced my desire for life, striking that proverbial match to Ignite my faith. That moment could be the light to my path, the iron to the rod! For me, it was not. That moment was a time of clarity. It was very clear to me the full reality of my situation was dark and grim.

One month earlier, the moment that ignited my faith *did* occur. It was not an explosive moment, but a quiet whisper warning me of this unforeseen illness that had led me to the valley I now stood in. I prayed that the same whisper would act as a guide to lead me out of this situation. When I first heard it, I was taking our boys to my twin sister's house. She had agreed to tend them while I was working. I had only been back to work for a short time. I had been on bed rest for months before our baby arrived. He had been in the hospital constantly since then. Now, at ten months old, he was healthy enough that I could start working again.

During that drive to see her, something happened I will never forget. On the short drive to my sister's house, I noticed someone leaning against a tractor, wearing coveralls, and sipping from a cup. I knew this person wasn't alive. I am not one that "sees people," or so I thought. For three days, I saw this person. Driving past on the third day, I heard a whisper in my head, "You have cancer." Where did this come from? Am I seeing dead people AND hearing voices? If I tell anyone about this, I am going to be shipped directly to a mental hospital! The next day, on the same drive, I heard it again, "You have cancer." I knew I had two options; pretend I was not seeing dead people and hearing voices, or do something about it.

That is when I started putting together the building blocks of my belief system, and figuring out what next steps to take. *Can I trust this voice? Is this some sort of sick joke my mind is playing on me after months of trying to get our baby well? Is postpartum depression kicking in? If I really do have cancer, what will this do to us? If that whisper speaks the truth, what will come next?* I had to start looking inward. I had to ask, *Is the thing that lies ahead of me a belief or a fact?*

I needed to follow up on that whisper without telling anyone I was seeing the departed and hearing voices. If it's a medical diagnosis I was looking for, I would need to see a doctor. I cleared my throat and picked up the phone. I made an appointment at our local clinic for the next day. I told them something was wrong; I didn't know what it was, but for the last few days, I had not been feeling like myself, and I was having a hard time swallowing.

It seemed that the previous day my lymph nodes had started swelling up in my neck. The doctor felt my neck and said, "I think it's just allergies. We are starting harvest, and there is definitely a lot of grain dust in the air this year. Take these allergy tablets, and if you don't have an improvement in two weeks, come back, and we will look into it further, but I am sure this is all that it is."

Whew! I did my due diligence; I acted on the whisper. I have allergies. I can let this go and not say a word about this to anyone. I felt conflicted, however. I wanted to share my concerns with my husband. He had been working out of town, and in a few short hours, he would arrive home for a week. I didn't want my worries to overshadow our plans to leave the following morning for a family getaway, a surprise trip for the boys to Yellowstone National Park.

On the first night of our trip, we stayed in West Yellowstone. We followed the boardwalk from our hotel to a pizza place. Here, you give your order at the window and stand in a corridor while waiting for your pie. Suddenly my husband grabbed me and, with great concern, asked if I was okay. "Of course I'm fine; why are you asking?" I replied. "Because you looked like you were passing out," he said. I noticed everyone looking our way, then I distinctly heard the whisper again, but this time it was louder. "You have cancer."

"Oh," I replied to my husband, "I think I'm okay; thank you for catching me."

I knew immediately I needed to see a different doctor, someone more aware of my personal history who was invested in my care and had helped with my pregnancy and the illness with my son. I needed the doctor I had been going to for years, Dr. Carrigan.

As soon as we arrived home from our trip, my husband had to leave and go back to the job site, which gave me an opportunity to call and schedule the new doctor's appointment without anyone knowing. I tried to find a sitter, but no one was available. I had to put my "apprehension" to rest.

Arriving at his office, we repeated the same scenario as the week before. I told him I thought something was wrong, probably just allergies, and I was having difficulty swallowing. He felt my neck, did a quick exam, and said, "Wait here for a moment." He walked out of the room with some urgency in his step. Returning, he calmly stated, "You *will* be back here in three hours for an ultrasound."

"That isn't possible," I resisted. "I won't be able to find a sitter and come back."

"Your boys can stay with the nurses," he assured me, "I will see you in three hours."

I anxiously drove back home to wait there before the next appointment. My mind was racing the entire drive. How could this doctor have any indication of what I was experiencing, and why would he be intuitive enough to schedule an ultrasound? Maybe the 'whisper' had been speaking to me and putting ideas into my head as I felt like I had been directed to contact this particular physician.

I called the neighborhood girls again and was able to find a sitter. I was losing my nerve at this point; actually, I think I had lost it. What if there *was* something wrong? I wished I had told my husband what had been happening and asked him to stay home a day longer. If I had, I wouldn't be going to the ultrasound by myself. I wanted someone at the appointment with me, but who? Mustering my strength, I made some calls.

There I was, standing in front of the kitchen phone; it seemed to be taunting me as I didn't know who to call. I picked it up, I would start dialing a number, then hang it up before I was through, talking myself out of it. I did this over and over and was running out of time; I would need to be leaving soon. If I wanted someone to go with me they would need to live nearby. I picked up the phone to dial one last number. This is stupid, I thought to myself. As I went to slam down the phone, a voice answered and said in her grandmotherly tone, "How are those sweet grandsons of mine?"

After three pictures, the ultrasound technician directed my mother-in-law and me back to the doctor's office and exam room. Hanging his head in a manila patient chart, Dr. Carrigan approached the exam room, shut the door behind him, sat on a stool, and said, "However you find solace you need to do it; this is bad." He started to sob, to the point I didn't think he would be able to speak; he choked out the words, "You have cancer."

I would immediately have to start treatment and chemotherapy, which led to me eventually undergoing an experimental process that would give me a twelve percent chance of survival after all of the medical treatments. I had a type of cancer there was no specific treatment for. The news was devastating. All I could think of was how glad I was that I had listened to that voice because now I knew I had to exercise my faith and fight to save my life.

My Ignite Moment was that whisper in my ear, the voice I kept hearing in my head. Over and over again during my illness, I listened to that voice and acted. My only choice was to believe, discover, and hope. Yes, I could have given up at any point, and no one would have ever questioned or blamed me. But, instead, I chose to affirm my faith and *only* focus on my future.

That man leaning on the tractor? After one of my chemo treatments, I was at my mom's house sorting through a box of pictures. In the bottom of a box was a faded photo of a heavy-set man in coveralls, leaning against a tractor, sipping from a cup. I grabbed the photo waving it in the air, exclaiming, "Mom! Who is this man?!"

"That is my dad," she told me. "Your grandfather in his fifties." My grandma had always displayed the wedding picture of her and my grandfather on her bookshelf in a beautifully ornate golden frame. I had only ever known what my grandfather looked like as a young man, not as the middle-aged farmer he was at the time of his passing. I felt it was he who was watching over me, and I knew I was protected.

After being given a twelve percent chance of living, six months of chemo, weeks of radiation, and multiple surgeries, I knew I didn't have to worry; I would live through this experience. I don't think I would have been warned by the whisper if I wasn't meant to survive and share this important message of faith with others like you.

I am not a number, a percentage rate, or a statistic. I am one of the lucky ones. Often it is easy to feel guilty for being one that survives when many children are losing parents, and many families are losing loved ones. Did a voice speak to them? Many have stories of hope that deserve to be shared. We all experience faith in our own way. Mine showed up as a man leaning against a tractor, letting me know he was there, along with a whisper that spoke to me in a feminine nature, reassuring me that I was going to be okay. We all have an inner knowing, the gift of listening to that voice from within. I now recognize that exposed soul when I see my reflection in the mirror. She was there, with me, all of the time. When I finally trusted her, it was her whisper that guided me here.

When you are feeling you need a voice in your life to lead you through the struggles that show up in spirituality, in your physical body, or intellectually, following that voice, listen to what it has to say. Ultimately, we know what we need to do, and we just have to be strong enough to make the choice and do it. If you have not developed that trust in your inner voice, lean into your faith and listen! You already have a foundation and understanding of who you are. Look into the mirror, see that beautiful person, and know that reflection is the one guiding you and has guided you here today.

Ignite Action Steps

How do we take control of our lives once more after a tragedy? Where did we start? Below are the action steps we, as a family, followed.

- **Take back control over one part of your life.** You may not be able to control things happening around you, inside or outside of your home, but you do have control of your bedroom. Clean your bedroom, and create a sanctuary.

- **Work to regain balance in your life.** Start by lifting up one foot, inches from the ground. Balance on one foot, then switch to the other. Increase the length of time you do this each day. Creating balance in your body will translate to creating balance in your life.

- **Keep $100 in your wallet.** The confidence and security of having $100 in your wallet if you need it is life-changing. Start with a $5 bill. Next week, switch it for $10. $100 can change the life of someone in need. Be prepared to give that first $100 away. Knowing someone needs it more than you do helps us to understand that you are in a better spot today than you were yesterday.

- **Learn to cook.** You don't have to be a great cook; just learn to cook one thing great. I don't care if you start by taking a frozen lasagna out of the box and putting it in the pan. You are still cooking! Own one nice pan; you never know when someone is going to show up at your door more hungry than you are.

- **Give hope.** Hope is the one thing we can give others when we don't have hope ourselves. It took a five-year-old to teach that principle to me. Hope is not something you can go to the store and buy; it is a gift and must be given. Hope is an action. If you want a suggestion, share a white rock with someone you love.

AUTHOR CREDENTIALS

Ash Bhadani — United States of America & India
Certified Empowerment Life Coach, International Bestselling Author,
Extraordinary Wife, Supportive Mum and Friend.
ash@dreamrealitycreators.com
🅞 *dreamrealitycreators*

Ava V. Manuel — United States of America, born & raised in the Philippines
Newspaper Editor, Events Producer, Business Coach, Physical Therapist
FromShowtoBusiness.com
LATribuneSpecialEdition.com
🅕 *avaVillaManuel*
🅞 *avaVmanuel*

Bobbie Kowalski — United States of America
Reiki Master, Tuning Fork Practitioner, Author, Death Doula, Speaker
🅕 *Bobbie Kowalski*
🅞 *BobbieKowalski*

Becca Rae Eagle — United States of America
Wife, Mother, Author, Writing Doula, Podcast Host, Journaling Visionary
Linktr.ee: yourwritingdoula2day
🅕 *yourwritingdoula2day*
🅞 *yourwritingdoula2day*

Caroline Oettlin — Germany
carolline.oettlin@gmail.com
Akashic Records Consultant, Yoga Instructor, Intuitive
www.we-are-eternal.love
🅕 *Caroline Oettlin*
🅞 *caroline_go_beyond*

Cheryl Viczko — Canada
Speaker, Author, Essential Feng Shui® Practitioner, Intuitive Organizer, Channel
www.fengshuiwithcherylv.com
www.allinalignment.com
f fengshuiwithcherylv

Christine Ebeltoft-Bancalari — United States of America
Co-Founder, Down Syndrome Foundation of Florida
f Christie Ebeltoft-Bancalari
○ cebeltoftbancalari
in christineebeltoftbancalari

Dan Gilman — United States of America
Speaker, Author, Host of Discover Your Potential, Show Producer,
Design Director
○ dan_gilman_

Lady JB Owen — Canada
Founder and CEO of Ignite Publishing, Ignite Moments Media
JBO Global INC and Lotus Liners / Award Winning Humanitarian Winner /
Knighted Lady / 22x International Best Selling Author / Publisher / Speaker /
Philantropist / Executive Producer
www.jbowen.website / www.igniteyou.life / www.lotusliners.com
f thepinkbillionaire
f JB.Owen.herself
○ ThePinkBillionaire
○ JB_Owen

Jacki Semerau Tait — United States of America
Speaker, Author, Real Estate Success Coach, Lead Realtor® for Team Three 23
www.StepsToStrength.com
🅕 *StepsToStrength*
🅞 *Jacki.Semerau.Tait*

Jameece D. Pinckney — United States of America
President & CEO of HyQuest, Speaker, Author, Entrepreneur
www.hyquestconsulting.com
www.businessbosscollection.com
www.inspirationsbydarcelljai.com
🅕 *darcelljai*
🅞 *jaipinck*

Jammie Matheson — United States of America
Hopeolgist, Mother, Business Owner, Real Estate agent, RPSGT, CSE
Hopeologistnow.com
FLDIndustries.com
🅕 *Hopeful*
🅞 *mathesonjammie*

Jeanne Bundy — United States of America
Author; Beyond Goodbye: Living Through The Experience of Loss
🅞 *bundy.jeanne*

Dr. Jo Dee Baer PhD. — United States of America
Certified Health Coach/Holistic Nutritionist
www.DrJoDee.com
www.HealthAPedia.net
🅕 *DrJoDee*

Joanne Latimer — United States of America

Judy 'J' Winslow — United States of America
Speaker, Trainer, Coach/Consultant, Author, TEDx Speaker Coach, Designer
www.UnforgettableBrands.com
www.SugaPlumRebel.com
f *judywins*
◎ *JwinsCEOpro*
in *judywins*

K. R. Rosser LTC (R) — United States of America
f *krosser1*
◎ *notsoshy_town*

Karen Rudolf — United States of America
Life Stratigest, Consultant, Mentor, Teacher,
Presenter, Facilitator with Tranquil Soulutions, LLC
www.TranquilSOULutions.com
f *karen.rudolf.14*
◎ *tranquilsoulutions*

Kathy Strauss, CCFC — United States of America
Visual Storyteller, Creatively Fit™ Coach
www.imagewerks.net
f *kathy.strauss1*
◎ *imagewerks*

Lea Barber — Canada
Early Childhood Educator, Life Coach for Children Youth and Families,
Speaker/Workshop Facilitator,
Reiki Practitioner, and
Tao Healing Hands Practitioner
Lmbarber76@yahoo.ca
f *Lea.barber.79*

Makenzie Elliott — United States of America
Young Life Leader, Student, Jesus Lover
Millerkenzie28@icloud.com
f *Makenzie Elliott*
⊙ *Itskenzziee*

Mimi Safiyah — United Kingdom
Book Developmental Editor
f *mimisafiyaheditor*
mimisafiyaheditor@gmail.com

Natasha Rae — Canada
Health & Wellness Coach, Social Worker, Author, Speaker, Business Owner
Website: www.preciouspurityhealing.com
f *NatashaRae*
⊙ *preciouspurityhealing*

Nicole Shantel Freeman — United States of America
Christian Life Coach, Encouragement Speaker, Author
f *Nicole Shantel Freeman*
⊙ *nicoleshantelfreeman*

Nolan Pillay — South Africa
Mindset Specialist, Speaker, Coach, Mental Health Advocate, Author,
Philanthropist and CEO of StraightTalkWithNolan
www.straighttalkwithnolan.com
www.soulmindbodyinstitute.com
www.bethebestversionofyourself.co.za
f *nolan.pillay.37*
⊙ *straighttalkwithnolan*
in *straighttalkwithnolan*

SCAN The Goddess — United States of America
Music Artist, Humanitarian, Photographer
www.iamscan.org
www.scanthegoddess.com
🄵 *scanthegoddess*
🄾 *scanthegoddess*

Vanessa Ciano Saracino — United States of America
Speaker, Author, Founder of be•You•tiful, Mother
www.studiobeyoutiful.store/shop
🄵 *inspirationfashionfaith*
🄾 *inspiration.fashion.faith*

Xila C. Hope, MS, MBATM, DCPM — United States of America
Mother, Principal Designer, and Founder of: HIS Wingspan, HER Wingspan,
and the Dip Show, Author, Advocate, and a Loudmouth!
www.hiswingspan.com/theshop and *www.hiswingspan.com/thedipshow*
▶ *spreadthedip* and *thewingspans*
🄵 *spreadthedip* and *thewingspanshop*
🄾 *spreadthedip* and *thewingspans*
🄳 *spreadthedip* and *thewingspans*
TikTok: spreadthedip and *thewingspans*
🄸🄽 *hiswingspan*
🄸🄽 *spreadthedip*

RESOURCES OUR *IGNITE YOUR FAITH* AUTHORS RECOMMEND

Ava V. Manuel
- Free Leadership Publication: https://latribunespecialedition.com/Crash Course on Creativity. http://engineering.stanford.edu/profile/tseelig
- Whitney Freya www.whitneyfreya.com

Bobbie Kowalski
- Energy: The foreign language we all speak but don't understand https://a.co/d/2bRmbFx

Becca Rae Eagle, M.S.Ed.
- Linktree: https://linktr.ee/yourwritingdoula2day
- *The Joyful Journaling Podcast w/Becca Rae* @ https://thejoyfuljournalingpodcast.buzzsprout.com/
- *Embodying Joy: A Heart Journal, a Memoir with Journal Space for Body, Mind, & Spirit Health* @https://tinyurl.com/embodyingjoyaheartjournal

Cheryl Viczko
- https://westernschooloffengshui.com/
- https://firstmedia.edu.sg/self-development/12-universal-laws/

Candice CpoeticStew
- Bible- King James Version
- https://Daretodreamteam
- https://11pubhtml15.com/nplsp/mza5/Edition-19

Judy 'J' Winslow
- You 2 - Price Pritchett (You Squared) - https://www.pritchettnet.com/digitalbook/you2/samplebook.php
- Creative Problem Solving Institute

Jacki Semerau Tait
- THE HOLY BIBLE, NEW INTERNATIONAL VERSION®, NIV® Copyright © 1973, 1978, 1984, 2011 by Biblica, Inc.™ Used by permission. All rights reserved worldwide.

Joanne Latimer
- Gary - The Indiana City that has Become a Ghost Town (worldabandoned.com)
- Images for civil unrest in Gary indiana 1960s Guided Search Filters

Jammie Matheson
- Dynamicprincipalsofhope.org
- Hope-Rocks.com

Kathy Strauss
- Rhonda Byrne. The Magic. www.thesecret.tv/products/the-magic-book/
- Jill Bolte Taylor, Ph,D. My Stroke of Insight: A Brain Scientist's Personal Journey. www.drjilltaylor.com
- Ted Talk: Jill Bolte Taylor's "Stroke of Insight". https://bit.ly/3lxnU9G
- Tina Seelig. InGenius.

Nicole Shantel Freeman
- www.biblegateway.com

Natasha Rae
- Books: www.amazon.com/author/natasharae
- Podcast: https://open.spotify.com/show/701iJ7nr65oiWfCHOPUb3i

Dr. Jo Dee Baer
- www.TraverseTV.com LIVE TV Shows: "Life's Milkshake Moments" "Mindset Mondays" "Dr. Talk: Come Play in our Health Sandbox"
- YouTu.be: https://youtube.com/@DrJoDee
- Published Books: *Ignite the Hunger in You* and *Ignite your Wisdom*
- "21 Days to Your Best You: Keys to a Life of Excellence"

Xila C. Hope, MS, MBATM, DCPM
- Americans with Disability Act. Retrieved from: https://www.govinfo.gov/content/pkg/USCODE-2009-title42/html/USCODE-2009-title42-chap126.htm
- Copeland, Germaine. (1997). *Prayers that avail much.* Harrison House, Inc.
- Go here to see information about how the organization: HIS Wingspan, works with the youth through The Dip Show Project: www.hiswingspan.com/thedipshow
- Individuals with Disabilities Education Act. Retrieved from: https://www.govinfo.gov/content/pkg/USCODE-2010-title20/pdf/USCODE-2010-title20-chap33-subchapI.pdf
- Maxwell, C. John, & Elmore, Tim. (2002, 2007).*The Maxwell Leadership Bible*. Thomas Nelson, Inc.

PHOTO CREDITS

Ash Bhadani - *Nilesh Bhadani*
Bobbie Kowalski - *Jessie Coleman*
Becca Rae Eagle - *Shaun Ondak*
Candice CpoeticStew - *Felty Photography.com*
Cheryl Viczko - *Rachelle Scrase, Infinity Brand Photography*
Christine Ebeltoft-Bancalari - *Derrick Creative LLC*
Dan Gilman - *John Harmon*
Jameece Pinckney - *Luke Christopher*
Jammie Matheson - *Kyle Scott*
JB Owen - *Kyle Scott*
Jeanne Bundy - *Brittany Adams Photography*
Judy 'J' Winslow- *Jolanta Bremer*
Karen Rosser- *Анна Шушмаркина*
Karen L Rudolf - *Erica Rudolf*
Lea Barber - *Seydy Salinas*
Makenzie Elliott - *Herring Photography*
Nicole Chantel Freeman - *Leroy Sanders, Jr.*
Nolan Pillay - *Amy Leigh Morgan*
Mimi Safiyah - *Mohcine ait benmed*
Vanessa Saracino - *Alexa Saracino*
Xila C. Hope - *Isaiah Smith & Xzavaier Hawkins, HIS Wingspan*

THANK YOU

To all our readers, we thank you for reading and cherishing our stories; for opening your hearts and minds to the idea of igniting your own lives. We welcome you to share your story and become a new author in one of our upcoming books. Your message and your *Ignite Moment* may be exactly what someone else needs to read. Readers become authors, and we want that for you.

Thank you for being a part of the magical journey of IGNITE!

A deep appreciation also goes to each and every author who made *Ignite Your Faith* possible. It is their powerful and inspiring stories, along with their passion and desire to help others, that will *Ignite Faith* within each and every one of us.

Please know that every word written in this book and every letter on the pages has been meticulously crafted with fondness, encouragement, and clarity to not just inspire you, but to transform you. Many individuals in this book stepped up to share their stories for the very first time. They courageously revealed the many layers of themselves and exposed their weaknesses as few individual leaders do. Additionally, they spoke authentically from the heart and wrote what was true for them. We could have taken their stories and made them perfect, following every editing rule, but we chose instead to leave their unique and honest voices intact. We overlooked exactness to foster individual expression. These are their words, their sentiments, and their explanations. We let their personalities shine in their writing so you would get a true sense of who each one of them is. That's what makes IGNITE so unique. Authors serving others. Stories igniting humanity. No filters.

A tremendous thank you goes to all those on the IGNITE team who have been working tirelessly in the background, teaching, editing, supporting, and encouraging the authors to reach the finish line. These individuals are some of the most genuine and heart-centered people I know. Their dedication to the vision of IGNITE, along with their integrity and the message they convey, is of the highest caliber possible. They each want you to find inspiration and use the many IGNITE Moments in this book to rise and flourish. They all believe in you, and that's what makes them so outstanding. Their dream is for all of your dreams to come true.

Production Team: JB Owen, Peter Giesin, Katie Smetherman, Liana Khabibullina, Jana Rade, and Sinisa Poznanovic.

Editing Team: JB Owen, Alex Blake, Michiko Couchman, Mimi Safiyah, AnaMaria R. Navarrete, and Zoe Wong.

Project Leaders: Steph Elliott, Jameece Pinckney, and Ash Bhadani.

A special thanks and gratitude to the entire team for their support behind the scenes and for going 'above and beyond' to make this a wonderful experience. Their dedication made sure that everything ran smoothly and with elegance.

FIND OUT MORE ABOUT WHAT WE DO AT IGNITE

WRITE YOUR STORY
IN AN IGN🧬TE BOOK!!

THE ROAD TO SHARING YOUR MESSAGE AND BECOMING A BEST-SELLING AUTHOR BEGINS RIGHT HERE.

We make YOU a best-selling author in just four months!

If you have a story of perseverance, determination, growth, awakening, and change... and you've felt the power of your Ignite Moment, we'd love to hear from you.

We are always looking for motivating stories that will make a difference in someone's life. Our fun, enjoyable, four-month writing process is like no other—and the best thing about IGNITE is the community of outstanding, like-minded individuals dedicated to helping others.

With over 700 amazing individuals to date writing their stories and sharing their Ignite Moments, we are positively impacting the planet and raising the vibration of HUMANITY. Our stories inspire and empower others and we want to add your story to one of our upcoming books!

Go to our website, click How To Get Started, and share a bit of your Ignite transformation.

JOIN US TO IGNITE A BILLION LIVES WITH A BILLION WORDS.

Apply at: www.igniteyou.life/apply   Find out more at: www.igniteyou.life

Inquire at: info@igniteyou.life